NEW FLAVOURS *of the*
LEBANESE
TABLE

NADA SALEH

EBURY
PRESS

All recipes serve 4 people unless stated otherwise.

1 3 5 7 9 10 8 6 4 2

Published in 2007 by Ebury Press, an imprint of Ebury Publishing

Ebury Publishing is a division of the Random House Group

The Random House Group Limited Reg. No. 954009

Addresses for companies within the Random House Group
can be found at www.randomhouse.co.uk

A CIP catalogue record for this book is available from the British Library

Design: Estuary English and seagulls.net
Copy editor: Tessa Clark

Printed and bound in Great Britain by
Mackays of Chatham plc, Chatham, Kent

ISBN 9780091917241

Contents

Foreword

THE IDEA of writing about the Lebanese kitchen makes the blood rush to my brain and palpitates my heart.

I remember the delectable food, the garden, the picnics and my uncle climbing the fig tree as the beams of sunlight were just breaking through. I close my eyes and sense the deliciously sweet red-fleshed figs oozing their honey. But this time my memory is shrouded in a sombre melancholy. Every time I take up my pen I sink into deep thoughts of previous wars, stirred up by the last war of 12 July 2006 which saddened and brought distress to the Lebanese, and more waste to the beautiful country of the cedars.

It was Wednesday morning in Beirut, and I was sitting at home sipping coffee. Suddenly, I heard a rain of bullets which seemed to be coming from everywhere. Alarmed, I didn't leave the house. A day later, we heard a loud explosion; the airport had been hit. After a time of anxiety and unrest we saw on television that two more ships were evacuating those who wished to leave. Hesitant, yet desiring to escape, we finally made our decision after my daughter Nour had telephoned the British Embassy. We had two hours to reach the given destination in Beirut.

We left all our belongings behind except for our passports, money and a small bottle of water. The road was empty and seemed unending. My nerves were frayed by the booming music on the taxi's radio and by the driver who, when we were gripped by fear of rockets and the jets flying overhead, bombarded us with questions, turning towards us instead of looking at the road ahead. Grateful to have arrived safely at our destination, and after a long hour's wait, we boarded a warship and were greeted by officers and Royal Marines who were reassuring and most welcoming, greatly helping families with children. Suddenly I overheard the woman checking my daughter's passport saying: 'You're Nour, I'm glad you made it. I'm the one who spoke to you on the phone.' Her friendly tone put a smile back on my face.

We arrived in our cabin, which was tiny and below sea level, eager to leave Lebanese waters without incident; and our unease and tiredness faded, thanks to the wonderful, friendly marines and to the other evacuees with whom we shared our experiences. A happier feeling started to develop and a bond grew between us. We reminisced about the Lebanon we once knew, and talk of food kept panic at bay for most of us. At the army base at Larnaca we queued up for a hearty British breakfast, and it made me realize (when East meets West) how important food is in bringing people together no matter what their culture or religion. Two days later our plane landed at Gatwick airport, but it took quite a while for me to settle down; so many years of unhappy memories flooded into my brain, echoing as far back as 1958.

Cooking acted as a healer during this time. Smelling the irresistible scents of food escaping pans and wafting through the house stimulated my dormant senses, seducing me into feeling more hopeful. As I admired vegetables of rainbow colours, my thoughts and outlook became more positive; I went back to the pans and wooden spoons in my kitchen, cooking the comforting food of my childhood.

The small, beautiful country of Lebanon lies at the eastern end of the Mediterranean. Facing towards the west, it is bordered by Israel in the south and Syria in the east and the north, and is shielded by majestic mountains and valleys. It was brought to the forefront of history at an early period. Tyre, one of Lebanon's antique cities, resisted Alexander the Great who, to conquer it, built a causeway linking the island to the inland (no wonder Chateaubriand said: *'Je passai une partie de la nuit à*

contempler cette mer de Tyr, que l'Ecriture appelle le grand Mer'). Coastal
Lebanon was inhabited by fearless Phoenician sailors and merchants who
founded colonies such as Carthage (800 BC), which became a worldwide
power in the second century BC, and trading posts all around the
Mediterranean. Famed for its remarkable scenery, Mount Lebanon
provided the Bible's holy writers with many beautiful similes and
prompted them to mention its cool waters (Jeremiah 18:14) and famous
wine (Hosea 1:7). It intrigued many travellers, such as the French poet and
statesman Lamartine, and its cedars breathed lines into the poems of
Byron and Wordsworth. Beirut, the hub of Lebanon's economy, acquired
commercial importance and grew from a small walled town surrounded
with *tout* (mulberries) and *sobair* (prickly pears) to a thriving centre of
trade, and exported silk to Damascus, Venice and Lyon.

In modern times Lebanese cuisine has gained great favour in the Arab
world and has gradually been adopted by the West. It is the Lebanese
diaspora that helped to create this interest in the country's food. During
the 1975–90 war many cooks left Lebanon for the Gulf States and other
countries. They worked in hotels and wealthy households, and brought
Lebanese food with them. Restaurants, cafeterias and fast-food outlets
were opened in Europe, the United States, Australia and many other
parts of the world. They are popular mainly because of the *mezzé*, which
encourages people to share food and brings them together.

The expansion of Islam in the seventh to the twelfth centuries, the
golden age, made travel possible and merchants and pilgrims were able
to journey thousands of kilometres for business and religious reasons.
Chinese, Byzantines, Westerners, Christians and Jews came to Islamic
countries after obtaining an *aman* (passport) and, although there were
numerous means of transportation, they often spent weeks, sometimes
months if not years, in one place before moving to another. An example
is the travel writer Ibn Battuta, who left Tangier and spent many years

on the road with the ultimate aim of performing the hajj (pilgrimage). Another instance is the story of Ziryab, a singer who won royal acclaim when he performed before the caliph Haroun al-Rashid. He had to flee Baghdad, fearing the wrath of his master singer, and ended up in the emirate of Cordoba in Andalusia (AD 822). He had many talents and taught the provincial inhabitants of Cordoba to sing, more particularly about preparing food, how to eat and drink, how to dress the table – and how to dress themselves according to the season. Ziryab created imaginative recipes unknown in Spain until then, which eventually had an impact on Moroccan food.

So the Middle East and North Africa were influenced by the movement of people and influenced them in return. Lebanon's kitchen is no different, with the exception of the food of the Lebanese mountains, which is very specific. In general, mountain people had to eat what they cultivated and they were able, with the produce of their terraces, to give us simple yet interesting dishes, nutritious and economical. There were some foreign influences on the cuisine of the cities by the sea, but these were interpreted to suit the local (lemony) taste.

Through the centuries Lebanon has never ceased to be an important thoroughfare for travellers and a place of repose for invaders. I'll mention the Egyptians, the Persians, the Romans, the Byzantines, the Arabs, the Crusaders, the Ottomans and the French. All have left their mark. However, the Ottomans were the most influential as they ruled the country for over four hundred years until 1918. I believe they gave a lot but have also gained. In the early 1960s Mount Lebanon was granted quasi-independence from the Ottomans years before any other country.

Lebanon's food is on the world map and is much appreciated by many people – yet its array of numerous regional and home-cooked dishes still has to be discovered.

Introduction

BEIRUT, the mid-1960s ...

'Fish, fresh fish.' I woke up to the repeated calls, knowing it was Wednesday and seven o'clock in the morning. This was the day and time when the fisherman, not any intermediary, would stand beneath the balcony of my father's house and shout the praises of his fish to make my mother aware of his presence. Summoned by her nod through the window to come up to the first floor, he would place a large and shallow wicker basket full of various Mediterranean fish on the outside landing of our typical nineteenth-century house and prepare himself for some hard bargaining.

It was my grandmother, not my mother, who would challenge his asking price, no matter what that price was. The session of fierce bargaining would invariably end with my grandmother's seeming victory. 'These are the freshest fishes you can ever get; see you next Wednesday,' he would say before departing, adding some reassurance about the state of his supplies.

We were a large family and the entire contents of the fisherman's basket would habitually be prepared by my mother for our Wednesday lunch. I used to watch her calmly presiding over her kitchen, declining any help with this familiar but important ceremonial.

On Fridays we ate *mjaddara* (purée of lentils and rice) and *fattouche* (mixed salad with purslane and toasted bread). We knew, before any health pundits said so, that *mjaddara* was nourishing; my grandmother called it 'knees' nails' (*massamir al-rukab*). We know now that lentils are high in protein and fibre, rich in B vitamins and low in fat.

Whether at home in Beirut or in the countryside, *kibbeh* was our Sunday meal. *Kibbeh* is a traditional dish made of crushed wheat, meat and onions pounded together in a huge stone mortar. *Hummous* may be claimed by several Mediterranean countries, vegetables stuffed with meat and rice may be arrogated in turn by Persian, Turkish or Byzantine cuisine, but *kibbeh* and *tabbouleh* are part of Lebanon's cooking heritage and folklore.

Weather permitting, by the early beams of sunlight on a Sunday we would drive in the direction of the Shouf Mountains. As we reached the outskirts of our native town, Mukhtara, we would be struck by the deep silence; all that could be heard was the regular sound of water dripping on the rocks on its way to the valley in a thin and shiny meandering string. We could hear the leaves of the swaying poplars whispering, and we would breathe in the soothing scents of wood, earth and leaves. Calm and charm enveloped every soul.

The houses, which are scattered in no apparent order, seemed uninhabited until a vague silhouette emerged through the door to roam silently in the small adjacent kitchen garden, where parsley, mint, tomatoes, basil and lavender grew next to flowers and fruit trees.

As we followed the curved path up the hill, we would pass two churches, one for the Maronites and the other for the Melkites. From afar we could see a man in black with a white turban walking next to a slowly trotting donkey. His costume and headdress were typical of a Druse *sheikh* (holy man). In answer to my father's greetings he would invariably respond: '*Sabahnakom bi-Kheir* (May this day be of goodness to you all).'

In Mukhtara, we would feel eyes watching us from behind the drawn flimsy curtains. People of the mountains are cautious: they observe until they recognize you.

We would pick up my uncle and other relatives and head straight for Ain Murshid, the picnic spot. This was a large wooded site where poplars had pride of place, an indication that water was plentiful. The site gradually narrowed, leading us to the source of the water, which springs beneath a huge curved rock and immediately drops down in a precipitous fall. We used to sit in the cool next to the *nabaa* (spring) and in no time the *mezzé* was spread out. *Mezzé* – Lebanese appetizers – mainly comprised *hummous, tabbouleh, labneh*, olives, lots of bread, an accompaniment to every meal, and freshly cut or picked vegetables. These were followed by *kibbeh* as well as *meshwe* (grilled meat), one of the many culinary legacies left by the Ottomans, or possibly before them by the Crusaders.

After that locally grown fresh fruits in season were served; sometimes along with *muhallabiyah* or *baluza*. The former is a kind of pudding attributed to a seventh-century emir, Muhlab Ibn Safra, and the latter is a Persian recipe comprising wheat, water and honey, or, more often, molasses mixed with sesame cream or fig jam. Turkish coffee was abundantly provided in an attractive traditional coffee pot, and afterwards the grounds in the cup had to be read. Few of our company drank alcohol; when they did it was *arak* (anisette). Most of us were content to quench our thirst from the spring, using an earthenware jug with a narrow neck, handle and spout, probably handed down to us from antiquity.

Sites such as Ain Murshid made one realize that food at its best combines a way of life with nature. Nature has not been very generous to the inhabitants of Lebanon. Soil suitable for agriculture is limited. Nevertheless, the Lebanese have traditionally managed to use basic and sometimes dull ingredients to make noble food. *Kibbeh* is in reality a clever way of making poor quality meat deliciously edible. Grains, beans and pulses are prepared with imagination but in such a way that they

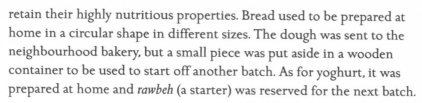

retain their highly nutritious properties. Bread used to be prepared at home in a circular shape in different sizes. The dough was sent to the neighbourhood bakery, but a small piece was put aside in a wooden container to be used to start off another batch. As for yoghurt, it was prepared at home and *rawbeh* (a starter) was reserved for the next batch.

Some dishes that were to be served cold were dressed with olive oil only. These were called *tabikh bil-zeit*. The traditional way of cooking was with *samneh* (sheep fat); more recently, vegetable oils other than olive oil have been used. These were wrongly assumed to be healthier than olive oil, but recent studies show that olive oil is to be preferred as it is monounsaturated and, unlike other vegetable oils, does not oxidize in a matter of seconds. In any case, olive oil is used extensively in Lebanon in places where olive trees grow. Not only is the olive tree deemed sacred – a belief derived from interpretations of the Bible, the Gospels and the Quran – but it is also valued for its yield of olives, oil, soap and wood.

This book is an attempt to present the food of my parents and what I have learned by experimenting in my kitchen. Some people think Middle Eastern meals are too rich and heavy. In most dishes I have tried to meet the challenge of showing how they can be made lighter and healthier while keeping their traditional flavour.

Besides enjoyment, food must supply our bodies with a variety of nutrients as providers of energy, cell renewal and hence longevity. A deficiency – as well as an excess – can disrupt the metabolism and be detrimental to health and well-being.

Some dishes are healthy and simple, and others can be made more so quite easily and without the need to become obsessive about health. Fortunately Middle Eastern dishes, specifically the Lebanese ones, lend themselves very readily to these possibilities.

Salads, Vegetables and Grains

IN ANCIENT TIMES the recurring wonder of spring was attributed to the gods by men who lived close to nature and lived off the produce of the earth. Sumer, Babylon and Assyria worshipped Thammuz, who died every year and rose again in spring (they sat 'weeping for Thammuz', Ezekiel, 8:14). The legend travelled west, and the Greeks named the god Adonis.

Thammuz, or Adonis, was revered in a temple (its ruins still stand) in the heights above Byblos, now in Lebanon. It was destroyed at Constantine's order when he became weary of the pagan ceremonies held there and the licentiousness that accompanied them every spring.

The history of certain places seems to emanate from them and sharpen the senses. Sitting on one of the fallen columns of the temple, I did not need any great effort of imagination to 'see' the legend of Adonis enacted in front of me. I could visualize Aphrodite rushing to help the fallen Adonis, gored to death by a wild boar while hunting; I could see her being pricked by a thorn and her blood dyeing the white anemone red, while Adonis's blood 'ran purple to the sea', forming what is now the Adonis River.

In the Lebanon we sow corn grains in small pots filled with earth just in time for them to sprout at Easter. The sprouting grains are not to be eaten, but are a symbol of rebirth, celebrating the emergence of the new crops.

Another tribute is paid to the ancient gods, albeit unwittingly, for we call fruits and vegetables that are not watered during the dry season *baal*, the ancient local name of the god of rain and fertility.

Grains, pulses and vegetables form the basis of the daily diet of the Lebanese, whether they live in the mountains or a city. In September, when this produce is abundant and cheap, every family joins in the ritual of amassing the *munee* (provisions) that give people a sense of security. The *munee* consists of sackfuls of *burghol* (cracked wheat), lentils, beans and chick-peas, less perishable products such as onions and garlic braided into long ropes, tough-skinned potatoes, olives (styled as *sultan al-sofra* – sultan of the table), olive oil, *kishk* (a combination of *burghol* and milk), *labneh* (cream cheese made from yoghurt), spices, *debs* (molasses, made either from carob or from grapes), jam preserves (apples, apricots, figs ...), as well as sun-dried vegetables and herbs, such as green beans, okra, courgettes and tomatoes (the last two are sliced and slightly salted), mint and thyme. Tomatoes are also prepared as a condensed purée to be used in *yakhne* (stew).

Vegetables such as cucumbers or *mikti* (wild cucumber), turnips, beetroots, cauliflowers, green and chilli peppers, carrots, okra, baby aubergines, fresh thyme and vine leaves are pickled in glass jars, either in vinegar or in slightly salted boiled water, topped with a fine layer of olive oil to keep out the air and prevent spoilage. An expensive delicacy is baby aubergines, stuffed with garlic, walnuts and almonds, and preserved in oil. Throughout the country these provisions are saved for the 'dead' seasons, and also for the hard times that have regularly afflicted Lebanon.

The stored grains and pulses are matched and mixed in an imaginative way with the vegetables, transforming a humble peasant diet into delicious and healthy meals, glorious in their simplicity and goodness. They are variously combined and prepared with olive oil and lemon juice, then presented as salads, stews, fried or boiled dishes such as the irresistible *tabbouleh*, the sublime *fattouche*, the delicious *mjaddara*, the satisfying potato salad, or the tasty and simply cooked *bamia bi-zeit*. This diet is substantially the food eaten daily by Lebanese throughout the country for their lunch or dinner, for parties or for *mezzé* (appetizers).

The Lebanese are vegetable-lovers. I still have vivid memories of the southern coastal strip, with its rich soil, where all types of citrus fruits and bananas grow, as well as lettuces, spring onions, radishes, parsley and mint. Fifteen years of war, from 1975 to 1990, brought suffering and misery, and once the conflict was over the Lebanese were able to rediscover their country, taking joy in the food of their parents and ancestors, and the tastes and sights of different regions.

People in the West have become increasingly aware of health, in particular of the need to include more vegetables, grains and pulses in their daily diet; consequently their attention has been drawn to the Lebanese culinary regimen. Nutritionists list it as one of the healthiest in the world and it is suitable for everyone, including vegetarians. The plant foods that are so central to the Lebanese diet supply a wealth of nutritional needs, being remarkably rich in roughage, vitamin C, protein, complex carbohydrates, B complex vitamins, iron and trace minerals.

'Let food be your medicine and medicine your food.'

Hippocrates

Cracked Wheat Salad
Tabbouleh

THIS IS AN EXOTIC and mouth-watering salad in which the dominant ingredient is parsley, a herb rich in antioxidants, vitamins A and C (important for good skin, collagen and cell renewal). Parsley is said to have been used by the ancient Greeks for medicinal purposes and it is mentioned in Homer's *Odyssey*. According to the eleventh-century Arab Christian physician Ibn Butlan it also helps combat constipation.

Tabbouleh has such pride of place in Lebanese cuisine that an early twentieth-century purchaser of some houses in the district of Mar Maroun, then outside Beirut's walls (where the nineteenth-century French poet Alphonse de Lamartine lived), converted them into a restaurant which he named Le Jardin de Tabbouleh. Isn't that romantic?

Tabbouleh is said to have originated in the random pickings of whatever the kitchen garden offered. In mountain villages, when a guest arrives parsley and mint are quickly gathered to prepare this soothing salad, which is served with tender vine leaves also picked freshly from the garden. For a long time the dominant component was *burghol* (cracked wheat) and there was barely any parsley. This version should thus be called *burghol* salad.

Nowadays Europe, in general, has reverted to the traditional way of making the Lebanese *tabbouleh*. Today Western supermarkets sell, and restaurants serve, it or give its name to their own version of this salad.

In Lebanon *tabbouleh* figures with the numerous dishes of *mezzé* (appetizers) and has long been a favourite for Sunday picnic lunches. Whenever you're in Lebanon go to the Shouf mountains, south-east of Beirut, pay a visit to the historical Amir Amin (Prince Amin) palace and enjoy a *tabbouleh*, overlooking a most picturesque valley. My family, like most Lebanese, spend summer vacations in the mountain. I remember that we ate *tabbouleh* almost every day.

A good one needs to be juicy. In Lebanon parsley, mint and tomatoes are incredibly flavourful, but in other countries such tasty ingredients may not be readily available. When this is the case, you can give the flavour a lift by tossing the ingredients with the juice of sour pomegranates. This also works with either home-made pomegranate syrup or the juice of a small orange diluted with a little lemon juice. Another tip is to dilute a heaped teaspoon of good quality or home-made tomato purée with lemon juice and a tablespoon of drinking water. Add a good pinch of *sumac* if it is available. You can also try shredding two tomatoes. When choosing flat-leaf parsley make sure to buy bunches that have small tender leaves; the curly version is also fine to use. Friends and those who attend my classes ask me about the ratio of parsley to mint. Well, with five bunches of parsley my mother used one bunch of mint. I always have followed this ratio accordingly.

150 g (5 oz) parsley

1 tablespoon vinegar

20–30 g (¾–1 oz) mint leaves, finely chopped

90–120 g (3–4 oz) fine *burghol*

500 g (1 lb 1 oz) red tomatoes

1¼ teaspoons salt or to taste

1 medium onion, finely chopped and/or 2 medium spring onions, finely chopped

Pinch of freshly ground black pepper

Pinch of *sumac* (optional)

3–4 tablespoons lemon juice or to taste

4 tablespoons extra virgin olive oil to taste

- Gather the parsley stems into small bundles so that the leaves are packed together at the same level and tie each bundle with a tender parsley stem. Place a bundle on a wooden chopping surface, grip the upper part firmly with one hand and with the other, using a sharp knife or scissors, slice or cut off the stalks, leaving about 3 cm (1½ in). Repeat with the remaining bundles and immerse the leaves in a basin of water to which the vinegar has been added. Leave for less than a minute, remove and gently squeeze out excess water. Repeat as needed but without the vinegar, until any grit has been removed and drain. Place the mint and *burghol* in a mixing bowl. Finely chop half the tomatoes and shred the remaining ones. Sprinkle all over with the salt and add to the bowl. Add the onion or spring onions, or both, and sprinkle with the pepper and the *sumac*, if using. Add the lemon juice and oil. Add the parsley to the ingredients in the bowl. Toss, taste and adjust the seasonings.

- Serve with lettuce, the tender leaves of a cabbage or tender vine leaves if available.

✾ ✾ ✾

Bread Salad
Fattouche

FATTOUCHE is a substantial salad that combines many herbs and vegetables found in Lebanese markets, grocer shops and gardens. It comes second in popularity to *tabbouleh* and appears at all times in a *mezzé*. Purslane distinguishes the salad from any other. A very healthy herb, excellent for pregnant women and diabetics, in Crete it is fed to chickens, which as a result lay large, nutrient-rich eggs. It comes in bunches, has a pale matt-green colour and is a medium-thick pear shape with smooth, slippery leaves. Its flavour is mildly peppery yet earthy and unique. The purslane season starts in spring and ends in mid-November and you can find it in Lebanese, Greek, Iranian and Turkish shops. *Fattouche* provides a wealth of nutrients and powerful antioxidants that increase vitality and protect the body from illness and premature ageing by neutralizing bad free radicals.

Preparation takes a little time, and when purslane is out of season I tend to add rocket leaves to give the salad a special deep taste and cut florets of cauliflower into chick-pea sizes. This is not authentic, but both are delicious in the salad. One especially amazing herb is Lebanese fresh thyme. If you can get hold of it, it is an absolute must because it gives *fattouche* an even more heavenly succulence.

1 garlic clove
1½ teaspoons salt or to taste
3–4 tablespoons lemon juice
4–5 tablespoons extra virgin olive oil
Juice of 1 pomegranate or ½ tablespoon pomegranate syrup (preferably home-made), optional
3 medium tomatoes, cut into 1.5 cm (½ in) cubes
1 bunch purslane, leaves and tender stems only
Handful of rocket leaves, thinly sliced
1 medium-size onion, thinly sliced
2–3 spring onions, sliced
1 baby cucumber, thinly sliced
3–4 radishes, sliced
2 large handfuls of whole or coarsely chopped parsley leaves
A few cos lettuce leaves, cut into thin slices (optional)
Large handful of chopped mint leaves

2 cauliflower florets, cut into chick–pea size
1–2 medium-size Lebanese breads, split and toasted
1 tablespoon *sumac* (see Glossary page 302)
Pinch of freshly ground black pepper

- Place the garlic and salt in a salad bowl and pound with a pestle until smooth. Stir in the lemon juice, 1 tablespoon of the oil and the pomegranate juice or syrup, if using. Add the tomatoes, purslane, rocket, onion, spring onions, cucumber, radishes, parsley, lettuce if using, mint and cauliflower. Break the bread into 2.5 cm (1 in) pieces and toss with the remaining oil. Add to the bowl, and sprinkle with the *sumac* and pepper. Toss well and adjust the seasoning if necessary.

Cabbage Salad
Salatet Malfouf

THERE IS NO DOUBT that cabbage salad is highly favoured by the Lebanese. Normally it accompanies *mjaddara* (Cream of Lentils, see page 58) and the national dish, baked *kibbeh* (see page 153), and some Lebanese fish *kibbeh* (see page 110). Lebanese cabbage has moisture and the leaves are more tender than those grown in Europe. It is therefore more suited for salads and for eating with *tabbouleh* (Cracked Wheat Salad, see page 4). Cabbage is an excellent source of the antioxidant vitamin C and scientists in various countries have been engaged in research into its curative properties. There is today, more than ever, strong evidence that it stimulates the immune system, and can lower the risk of many cancers and kill bacteria and viruses. It is said that the Romans, who incidentally introduced cabbage to Britain, regarded it as a panacea against the discomforts of high living as well as a neutralizer of the effects of alcohol. The Roman statesman Marcus Cato strongly advised the inclusion of raw cabbage in the diet as a prophylactic.

When *abou-sfayr* (Seville) oranges are available, use their juice and your salad will be outstanding. However, in their absence follow my way. It is delicious. Use the juice of clementines or other oranges, or both, and add this to the lemon and oil dressing. What could be a lovelier way to enrich your antioxidant vitamin C, giving a glow to your skin?

1 garlic clove
1 teaspoon salt or to taste
2 tablespoons extra virgin olive oil
2 tablespoons lemon juice
Juice of 1 clementine or orange
1 teaspoon cider vinegar
2 medium-size red tomatoes, peeled and cut into 2.5 cm (1 in) cubes
225 g (8 oz) cabbage, very thinly sliced
Handful of fresh mint, finely chopped, or 1 teaspoon dried mint

- Place the garlic and salt in a bowl and pound with a pestle until creamy. Stir in the oil, lemon and clementine juices and the vinegar. Add the tomatoes, give them a good stir, then add the cabbage and mint. Toss, coating the ingredients thoroughly with the dressing. Taste and adjust the seasoning.

Purslane Salad
Salatet al bakleh

PURSLANE HAS GROWN for centuries in the Middle East and is a valuable herb as it contains a high concentration of omega 3 and has natural diuretic properties. It blends very well with other herbs too. In Lebanese villages it is used as a filling, as in spinach *fatayer* (Spinach Triangles, see page 78). Its leaves are smooth to the touch and have a lovely peppery earthy flavour.

This exceptionally refreshing and soothing salad goes well with grain dishes such as *mdardara* (Lentils and Rice, see page 57) and is good in sandwiches with lamb or *kafta* (Fried Meat Patties, see page 180) and *mtabbal al-batinjan* (Aubergine Dip, see page 36). Alternatively, crumble some feta cheese over the salad, add a few green or black olives and have it as a main dish.

I garlic clove
I teaspoon salt or to taste
1½ tablespoons extra virgin olive oil
2 tablespoons lemon juice
I small onion, sliced (optional)
2 medium-size juicy tomatoes, peeled and cut into
    bite-size pieces
I teaspoon *sumac* (optional)
Pinch of freshly ground black pepper
1–2 bunches purslane, leaves and tender stems only

- Place the garlic and salt in a salad bowl and pound with a pestle until creamy. Stir in the oil and lemon juice and add the onion, if using. Mix the tomatoes into the sauce in the bowl. Sprinkle with the *sumac*, if using, and the pepper. Add the purslane and toss.

- Serve as an accompaniment to fish, chicken or pulse dishes.

Thyme Salad
Salatet al-zaatar l'akhdar

THIS INVIGORATING and aromatic salad is very simple to prepare. Thyme, fresh or dried, is loved by the Lebanese, and is a culinary legacy from the Greeks. One variety – *zaatar* – is picked, dried, crushed and stored in an airtight container after being mixed with *sumac*, toasted sesame seeds and a little salt, to be used for *mankoushi* (Thyme Bread, see page 75) or mixed with olive oil and eaten with Lebanese bread as a sandwich. Fresh thyme is also pickled. In the south of the country, another type of thyme is mixed into goat's cheese and prepared as in spinach *fatayer* (Spinach Triangles, see page 78).

This recipe uses a variety of thyme that is different in looks and taste from the British one, and is normally served as a part of the *mezzé*. When in season, starting in May, you can buy bunches of the thyme from Lebanese or Greek grocers. If you like, mix pitted green olives into the salad, along with 1–2 thin slices of lemon, peeled and quartered.

1 garlic clove
¾ teaspoon salt or to taste
2 tablespoons extra virgin olive oil
2–3 tablespoons lemon juice
1 medium-size onion, sliced or finely chopped
1 bunch thyme, leaves and tender stems only

- In a bowl, crush the garlic with the salt until smooth. Add the oil and lemon juice, and stir vigorously to combine well. Add the onion and the thyme and toss well.
- Serve with Lebanese bread and a side dish of green olives.

❀ ❀ ❀

Tomato and Onion Salad
Salatet banadoura bi-bassal

IF THE FRIDGE is empty of greens, this is the salad to prepare. Onions connect perfectly with tomatoes. In Lebanon tomatoes are not watered during the dry season, so they are called *baal*, the Phoenician name for the god of fertility. Another name derived from Baal is Baalbeck; in the second century AD an impressive Roman temple was built on the site of a Phoenician one dedicated to the god.

Tomatoes, called 'love apples', are highly valued for their antioxidant vitamins A and C, and onions, a natural antibiotic, were used by the Greeks for their curative powers. You can add a little dried or fresh mint to this recipe, along with diced radishes, sliced cucumber and cos lettuce to make another refreshing salad, *salata arabieh* (Oriental Salad).

I garlic clove
1¼ teaspoons salt or to taste
3 tablespoons extra virgin olive oil
1½ tablespoons lemon juice
550 g (1¼ lb) tomatoes, peeled and cut into 2 cm (¾ in) pieces
1 medium-size onion, finely chopped

- Place the garlic and a quarter of the salt in a salad bowl and pound with a pestle until smooth. Stir in the oil and lemon juice. Add the tomatoes and sprinkle with the remaining salt. Finally add the onions and toss well with the dressing.
- Serve with grilled *kafta* (see page 180) and Lebanese bread.

Special Christmas Salad
Salatet id al-milad

THIS COLOURFUL salad brings life to the table. It is a speciality of my mother's and I believe it should be called Munira's Christmas Salad, since she prepared it only at this special festive time, when it was greedily relished by all. It is packed with healthy fruits and vegetables that boost energy and give a glow to the skin. Home-toasted peanuts are thrown over it, but remember to check with friends and family members that they're not allergic to them.

4–5 small beetroots
5 tablespoons lemon juice
2½–3 tablespoons extra virgin olive oil
3–4 large navel oranges, sliced
2 Braeburn apples, sliced
¾ teaspoon salt or to taste
6 leaves of cos lettuce, cut into medium-thin ribbons
4–5 tablespoons red wine
Good pinch of freshly ground black pepper
Handful of watercress leaves with tender stalks
Handful of toasted organic peanuts

- Place the beetroots in a steaming basket and set into a pan over 2.5 cm (1 in) of boiling water. Cover and steam for 30 minutes or until tender. Remove and leave to cool.

- Meanwhile, put the lemon juice and oil in a mixing bowl. Add the oranges and squeeze any juice from the orange peel. Add the apples. Sprinkle with the salt, then add the lettuce leaves.

- Peel the beetroots, cut them into 2.5 cm (1 in) slices and place them over the lettuce in the bowl. Add the wine and sprinkle with the pepper. Toss well. Taste and adjust the flavourings if necessary. Spread the watercress over the salad and top with the peanuts. Serve.

Artichoke Salad
Salatet ardi-chowki

THE GLOBE ARTICHOKE IS native to the Mediterranean. Its Arabic name, *al-kharshuf*, is the origin of its Italian name, *carciofo*, and its Spanish name, *al cachofa*. Artichokes have a subtle, sweet taste and are an excellent source of fibre and vitamin C. In this salad the artichokes are steamed to retain their valuable nutrients. The fleshy ends of the leaves are excellent for dieters or those who need to de-stress.

4 globe artichokes
1 garlic clove
1 teaspoon salt or to taste
2–3 tablespoons lemon juice
2 tablespoons extra virgin olive oil
2 heaped tablespoons parsley leaves, finely chopped

- Trim the tops of the artichokes with a sharp knife or scissors, and remove and discard the stalks close to their bases. Place the artichokes in a steaming basket large enough to hold them and set into a pan over 2.5 cm (1 in) of boiling water. Cover and steam for 40 minutes.

- Meanwhile, place the garlic and salt in a salad bowl and pound with a pestle until smooth. Stir in the lemon juice, olive oil and parsley.

- When steaming time is up, remove the artichokes and allow them to cool. Then remove all the outer leaves of each artichoke (the fleshy ends can be eaten separately as an appetizer) until you reach the choke in the middle. With a spoon or a sharp knife, gently remove the choke and discard it. Cut each heart crosswise to make four equal pieces. Add the artichoke pieces to the bowl, toss and adjust the seasonings.

- Serve as an accompaniment to Chicken Kebab (see page 130).

Monk's Salad
Batinjan l'raheb

THIS SUPERB SALAD is attributed to a head monk (*raheb*), who was hugely fond of aubergine dishes, especially this one. It is said that he gave orders to the monastery's cook to prepare it whenever aubergines were in season (in summer). Another account tells us that the salad is called *al-raheb* because it is meatless and eaten by monks during Lent.

In Lebanon aubergines come in various sizes and shapes. For a special occasion, or just whenever you find them in the market, prepare medium- or small-size aubergines as below. And when pomegranates are in season benefit also from the hidden goodness of their seeds and juice. If the pomegranates are sweet combine them with a splash of lemon juice.

3 medium-size aubergines
I small garlic clove
I teaspoon salt or to taste
2 tablespoons extra virgin olive oil
2 tablespoons lemon juice
I small red or green pepper, cored, deseeded and diced
I medium-size tomato, peeled and diced
2–3 large spring onions, thinly sliced
Handful of parsley leaves, chopped
2 radishes, thinly sliced (optional)
Handful of semi-sour or sweet pomegranate seeds and
   juice (in season)

- Prick each aubergine in two places. Place them on the hob and turn until they have blackened on all sides, then remove. Place them upright and wait a few seconds before handling them. Peel off and discard the skin. Rinse the aubergines under running water to make sure there is no black skin on their flesh. Gently press them between the palms of your hands to remove excess water. Using your fingers or a knife divide each one lengthwise into four or five pieces.

- Now, in a serving dish pound the garlic and salt with a pestle until creamy, then add the oil and stir in the lemon juice. Place the aubergine pieces over the dressing and stir them gently to coat well. Decorate with the pepper, tomato, spring onions, parsley, radishes, and the pomegranate seeds and juice, if available. Taste and adjust the seasoning.

Green Bean Salad
Salatet loubieh

GREEN BEANS have been known as French beans since they were taken from France to England in 1594. Lebanese villagers used to pick the *loubieh* (beans) in September, spread them over straw trays to dry and store them as a supply for winter. This easy salad makes an excellent accompaniment to barbecued food.

> 225 g (8 oz) green beans, topped, tailed and strings
>   removed
> 150 g (5 oz) baby carrots
> 1 small garlic clove
> 1 teaspoon salt or to taste
> 1½–2 tablespoons lemon juice
> 3 tablespoons clementine juice
> 1½–2 tablespoons extra virgin olive oil
> 1 small onion, sliced
> Pinch of freshly ground black pepper

- Cut the beans diagonally into 1.5 cm (½ in) slices. Arrange the beans and carrots in a steaming basket and set into a pan over 2.5 cm (1 in) of boiling water. Cover tightly and cook until tender (about 10 to 12 minutes). Meanwhile, in a salad bowl pound the garlic and salt with a pestle. Stir in the lemon and clementine juices and oil, and then the onion.

- Remove the beans and carrots from the steamer and add to the bowl. Toss well with the dressing and onion and sprinkle with the pepper.

- Serve warm or cold with fish, meat or Chicken Kebab (see page 130).

NOTE: Another delicious way to prepare the beans and carrots is to place them in a wide pan with 120 ml (4 fl oz) water. Bring to the boil, reduce heat to low, cover and simmer for 15–20 minutes (check the water level halfway through). Add the vegetables, with their juices, to the dressing and toss.

Potato Salad with Cream of Sesame
Salatet al-batata bi-thini

THIS SALAD IS excellent for a variety of occasions. An interesting combination of flavours helps to produce a nutritious and filling dish. I'm very fond of the *tahini* sauce and often replace the lemon juice with the juice of Seville oranges. When these are not available, I combine orange and clementine juices and stir them well into the sauce. It's fab.

> **450 g (1 lb) potatoes, unpeeled, washed, scrubbed and cut into 1.5 cm (½ in) cubes**
>
> *For the tahini sauce:*
> **1 garlic clove**
> **Pinch of salt or to taste**
> **4 tablespoons *tahini***
> **4 tablespoons lemon juice**
> **½ teaspoon paprika or a pinch of cayenne pepper (optional)**
> **1 heaped tablespoon finely chopped parsley**

- Place the potatoes in a steaming basket and set into a pan over 2.5 cm (1 in) of boiling water. Cover and steam for about 10 minutes or until tender. Remove and leave to cool a little.

- Meanwhile, prepare the sauce. In a serving bowl, pound the garlic and salt with a pestle until smooth. Add the *tahini* and lemon juice and whisk gently. Add 4 tablespoons of water while gradually whisking slowly, clockwise and back. Eventually the sauce will become cream-like. Gently fold the potatoes into the *tahini* sauce; sprinkle with the paprika or cayenne, if using, and the chopped parsley.

VARIATION: Omit the sesame cream. Mix together 1 tablespoon lemon juice and 1½ tablespoons of olive oil. Stir in ¼ teaspoon cinnamon and some black pepper. Toss with the potatoes and sprinkle over the paprika or cayenne and watercress instead of chopped parsley.

❋ ❀ ❋

Chick-pea Salad
Balila

THIS CLASSIC CHICK-PEA salad originated in western Asia. Chick-peas are among the most nutritious beans, rich in protein, good fats, carbohydrates, fibre and valuable vitamins and minerals; they are also free of gluten, of which some people are intolerant. *Balila* is usually served with wholemeal bread as part of a *mezzé*.

225 g (8 oz) chick-peas, soaked overnight, drained and rinsed
1 garlic clove, crushed

1 teaspoon salt or to taste
½ tablespoon *tahini* (optional)
½–1 tablespoon lemon juice
3–4 tablespoons extra virgin olive oil or to taste
1 teaspoon ground cumin

- Place the chick-peas in a medium pan and cover with 2.5 cm (1 in) water. Bring to the boil over medium-high, skimming the foam from the surface of the water. Reduce the heat to low, cover and simmer until the chick-peas are very soft, about 2 hours. Check the water level at intervals, taste a chick-pea and if necessary add hot water. Alternatively, cook in a pressure cooker for about 40 minutes, following the maker's instructions. Drain the chick-peas, reserving a few tablespoons of the cooking liquid.

- Meanwhile, in a serving bowl pound the garlic and salt with a pestle until creamy. Add the *tahini*, if using, and the lemon juice. Stir in the reduced cooking liquid and the chick-peas, crushing some of them lightly. Drizzle the oil all over and toss. Season with the cumin.

- Serve with Lebanese bread, spring onions and watercress.

Field or Brown Bean Salad
Foul mdammas

FOUL MDAMMAS is the staple food of the poor, but it occupies an honoured place in Lebanese cuisine. Traditionally it is eaten either at breakfast, washed down with cups of Lebanese coffee, or is part of the *mezzé. Foul mdammas* recalls the old days of enchanting Beirut when the Lebanese made their way after partying to have their breakfast at Ajami, one of the city's most renowned and magnetic restaurants. There was a narrow street next to it where tables were placed. The street led to an amazing fountain surrounded with all kinds of fruits and *jallab* (a drink made from raisins) and liquorice drinks. This was demolished during the war and the restructuring of Beirut.

The humble brown bean (*foul*), is thought to have garnished the pharaoh's table in Egypt, where it originated. I like to use the smaller brown beans; the flesh is meatier as they soften and they have a lovely succulence, *Foul* can be purchased nowadays from health shops. In the Lebanon some villages put dried pomegranate skins and bay leaves along with the beans or pulses when they are packed. This is said to make them keep longer.

200 g (7 oz) brown beans (*foul*), soaked overnight, drained, rinsed and drained again
1 teaspoon salt
5 tablespoons extra virgin olive oil
1 garlic clove
3–4 tablespoons lemon juice
Juice of 1 small orange or 2–3 Seville oranges (in season)
3 tablespoons chopped parsley or coriander
½ teaspoon paprika (optional)

• Place the beans in a pan with 600 ml (1 pint) water. Add ¾ teaspoon of the salt and ½ tablespoon of the oil and bring to the boil over high heat. Reduce the heat to low, cover and simmer for about 40–45 minutes or until the beans are very tender.

• Meanwhile, in a bowl pound the garlic and the remaining salt with a pestle until smooth. Add the beans, with the reduced liquid, and stir well, mashing some of the beans lightly to coat them with the garlic.

Add the lemon and orange juices, stir and top with the remaining oil. Sprinkle with the parsley or coriander and the paprika, if using.

• Serve hot with Lebanese bread, onions, tomatoes and radishes.

VARIATION: To make *Foul moutamam* (*foul* complete) prepare half the amount of Chick-pea Salad (see page 18) and place on top of the brown bean salad.

Butter Bean Salad
Salatet al-fassoulia l'baida

BUTTER BEANS have a distinctive flavour and are nourishing while being low in fat and high in fibre. Eat with warm wholemeal Lebanese bread to provide a balance of nutrients and satisfy the appetite. In Mount Lebanon sacks of beans and pulses are stacked as *munee* (provisions for the year. When the sun appears the beans are exposed to remove humidity and keep them longer. Some people put dried herbs and spices with them – it is believed the strong smell of these keeps parasites away. The juice of Seville oranges can be used instead of lemon.

> **225 g (8 oz) butter beans, soaked 6–8 hours, drained and rinsed**
> **I carrot, peeled and cut diagonally into thin strips**
> **I garlic clove**
> **Good pinch of salt or to taste**
> **3 tablespoons lemon juice**
> **2 tablespoons extra virgin olive oil**

1 teaspoon cider vinegar
Handful of parsley leaves, chopped

- Place the beans in a medium pan with 600–900 ml (1–1½ pints) water and bring to the boil over medium heat, skimming the foam from the surface of the water. Reduce the heat to low, cover and simmer until the beans are soft but not disintegrating, about 40–60 minutes. Check the water level and if necessary add a little hot water. Add the carrots 8 minutes before the end of the cooking time.

- Meanwhile, in a salad bowl pound the garlic and salt with a pestle, then add the lemon juice, oil, vinegar and parsley. Add the beans and carrots and the very reduced stock. Toss gently with the dressing.

- Serve with Lebanese bread and spring onions.

Lentil Salad
Salatet al-adas

ARCHAEOLOGICAL FINDS indicate that lentils were widespread from China to Europe in ancient times. Lentils come in various colours: green, brown and orange-red when split. This salad calls for brown ones. It is succulent and requires few ingredients, so whenever the cupboard begins to look bare and I am too lazy to go shopping, lentil salad comes first to my mind.

200 g (7 oz) lentils, picked over and rinsed
1 teaspoon salt or to taste
1 garlic clove

2–3 tablespoons lemon juice
3–4 tablespoons extra virgin olive oil
½ teaspoon cumin or to taste
Handful of finely chopped parsley, to garnish (optional)

- Place the lentils in a pan with 650–700 ml (23–25 fl oz) water, add ½ teaspoon of the salt and bring to the boil over high heat. Reduce to medium-low heat, cover and simmer the lentils for about 35–45 minutes (the time varies with their origin). Check the water level at intervals and if necessary add a little hot water.

- Meanwhile, in a salad bowl pound the garlic and the remaining salt with a pestle. Add the lentils, with their reduced liquid, and stir well, mashing some of them lightly. Add the lemon juice and oil and stir again. Sprinkle with the cumin, and sprinkle with parsley if you wish.

- Serve hot or warm with wholemeal bread and lots of spring onions.

Fried Cauliflower
Arnabeet mikli

A TASTY WAY to prepare cauliflower. If you wish to follow the traditional manner, you need to boil the florets until soft and then deep-fry them until they are brown and crisp. However, the demand for healthier eating is on the increase, therefore steaming is a good option. There is no doubt about the fondness of the Lebanese for crisp florets, especially when presented with a bowl of *Tahini* Sauce (see page 300).

1.25 kg (2½ lb) cauliflower, cut into florets
½–1 tablespoon salt
Groundnut or olive oil, for deep-frying

- Bring a pan of water to the boil, then add the salt. Plunge the cauliflower florets into the water and allow them to boil for 3–5 minutes. Remove the florets gently with a slotted spoon, drain and leave to cool.

- Meanwhile, half-fill a medium pan with the oil and place over medium heat. When the oil is hot but not smoking add as many florets as it can take. After a few minutes shake the pan and leave the cauliflower to cook until golden brown and crisp. The florets will shrink so add more. Remove the florets as they brown, and drain on kitchen paper. Arrange them on a serving dish and serve with Lebanese bread and *Tahini* Sauce.

Fried Potatoes
Batata mikli

FRIED POTATOES are comforting, irresistible and loved by old and young alike. In Lebanon they come on request or as an accompaniment to *shawarma* (lamb or chicken kebab, see pages 184 and 130). Because they have a high fat content I decided to try the oven. The potatoes are left unpeeled and cut as if they were to be fried, then they are combined with a small amount of olive oil. My daughter Nour and her friends assure me that this way of preparing the potatoes is still loved by them.

1 kg (2¼ lb) potatoes, unpeeled, washed and scrubbed
2–3 tablespoons extra virgin olive oil
Salt to taste (optional)

• Preheat the oven to 200°C/400°F/Gas Mark 6. Cut the potatoes
lengthwise into 1.5 cm (½ in) slices, then cut each slice, as best you can,
into uniform sticks. Put the oil in a bowl, then add the potatoes and
coat them all over with the oil. Arrange evenly on a baking sheet and
cook for 40–50 minutes or until the potatoes are golden and crunchy.
Serve hot, sprinkled with salt if using.

❀ ❀ ❀

Green Beans in Oil
Loubieh bi-zeit

LOUBIEH BI-ZEIT is popular all over the Lebanon. In general the
loubieh (green beans) used for it are the flat ones, but you can use what's
available. The dish is simple to make and can be prepared ahead of time,
since its taste becomes even better the following day.

2–3 tablespoons extra virgin olive oil
200 g (7 oz) onions, thinly sliced into half-moon shapes
7 garlic cloves, cut into thick slivers
450 g (1 lb) green beans, topped, tailed and strings
    removed and cut at an angle
1¼ teaspoons salt or to taste
¼ teaspoon freshly ground black pepper
¼ teaspoon ground cinnamon
Pinch of allspice

**450 g (1 lb) ripe tomatoes, peeled (optional) and
   thickly sliced**
1–2 slices of green pepper (optional)

- Heat the oil in a pan. When it is hot but not smoking, add the onions
  and garlic and cook over moderately high heat for about 2–3 minutes
  or until golden in colour. Add the beans and sprinkle with the salt,
  pepper, cinnamon and allspice. Reduce the heat to moderately low.
  Cover and let the beans sweat for about 10–15 minutes. Stir them
  once or twice without disturbing the onions, or shake the pan. Gently
  stir in the tomatoes and pepper, if using, cover and simmer over
  moderately low heat for about 20–25 minutes, allowing the beans to
  cook in the juice of the tomatoes.
- Serve warm, or at room temperature, with bread.

Wild Chicory in Oil
Hindbeh bi-zeit

THIS IS A PEASANT DISH loved by almost everyone in Lebanon.
Wild chicory has a dark green colour, elongated leaves with curly edges
and a bitter taste that is reduced by boiling. One of the oldest vegetables,
it is believed to have medicinal properties. In fact it is rich in iron and
folic acid, is an excellent detoxifier and stimulates the liver. Here it is
not boiled as customary, but instead is simmered in its juices to retain
most nutrients. Bunches of wild chicory are sold by Lebanese and
Cypriot grocers and the season starts in early autumn.

Hindbeh bi-zeit requires the onions to brown and I like to scatter a good
pinch of sugar over the onions to caramelize them; the sweetness

counterbalances the bitterness of the chicory. Also, when pomegranates are in season I use their fabulously delicious juice adding a little lemon juice, and their ruby red seeds, as the dish benefits from the flavour and the fruit's health-giving properties.

4 bunches wild chicory, roots removed
90 ml (3 fl oz) extra virgin olive oil, plus 1 tablespoon
4–5 tablespoons lemon juice or 290 ml (10 fl oz) of sour or
**   semi-sour pomegranate juice**
Handful of pomegranate seeds
½ teaspoon salt
3–4 medium-size onions, thinly sliced
Good pinch of sugar

- Wash the wild chicory but do not leave it to soak as nutrients will be lost. Drain and slice into thin ribbons. Place a large pan over heat and add the wild chicory in batches. As these reduce in size add more. Cover and simmer the chicory in its own juices for 3–5 minutes. Remove, place over a sieve to drain and leave to cool slightly.

- Meanwhile, in a salad bowl place the 1 tablespoon oil and the lemon or pomegranate juice. Lightly squeeze excess water from the chicory. Add the chicory to the dressing and scatter with the pomegranate seeds. Sprinkle with the salt and gently toss. Heat the remaining oil in a medium-size non-stick frying pan and when it is hot add the onions. Sauté, stirring occasionally, until they reach a beautiful deep golden colour. Halfway through sprinkle with the sugar and finish the cooking. Remove and drain on kitchen paper. When the onions are cool distribute them over the wild chicory.

Broad Beans in Oil
Foul bi-zeit

THIS IS HEAVENLY because it is so effortless to make. *Foul bi-zeit* can
be served as a starter or as part of a buffet, and makes a good companion
to grilled sausages, lamb cutlets, chicken and fish. It can be eaten hot,
with a little yoghurt spooned over, or on its own with bread. I have used
frozen broad beans here, but when fresh beans are in season make use
of them. The cooking time will depend on the beans' tenderness. The
addition of sugar is optional. It acts as a preservative and it is said that it
helps to retain the beans' lovely colour.

> 3–4 tablespoon extra virgin olive oil
> I large onion, finely chopped
> I kg (2 lb 2 oz) frozen broad beans
> Good pinch of sugar (optional)
> 3–4 tablespoons hot water
> ½–I bunch coriander, leaves and tender stems only,
>   finely chopped
> Juice of I lemon or to taste

- Warm the oil in a large frying pan, add the onions and sauté them,
  stirring occasionally, until they are transparent and yellowish in colour.
  At this point stir in the beans, sprinkle with the sugar, if using, and
  cook for 3–4 minutes. From time to time give them a stir. Then add
  3–4 tablespoons hot water, stir and simmer covered for a further
  2–4 minutes. Uncover, add the coriander and simmer for a further few
  minutes or until the beans are soft. Stir in the lemon juice and serve.

Okra (Lady's Fingers) in Oil
Bamieh bi-zeit

OKRA IS NATIVE TO AFRICA. Vegetable dishes cooked in olive oil play an important role in the Lebanese kitchen and *bamieh bi-zeit* is one of them. In Lebanon the baby okra are so beautiful it's impossible not to buy them. In this dish the okra simmer gently with sun-ripened tomatoes and aromatic herbs and spices, releasing a glutinous substance that thickens the sauce. When the cooking is over they are left to reach room temperature. This preparation is simple and is served as an everyday meal or to adorn a buffet table at parties. Oily dishes come into favour during Christian Lent, and during the holy month of Ramadan.

To be authentic the okra should be fried, but they can be grilled for a few minutes, as here, or even used without precooking. When sour pomegranates are in season add a little of their juice. It imparts a special deep tangy flavour.

> 500 g (I lb I oz) okra
> 2 tablespoons extra virgin olive oil
> 225 g (8 oz) onions, thinly sliced, or 10 baby onions
> 8 garlic cloves, halved
> 500 g (I lb I oz) tomatoes, quartered
> 2 large handfuls of finely chopped coriander leaves
> 1½ teaspoons salt or to taste
> Good pinch of ground cinnamon (optional)
> Pinch of allspice (optional)
> ¼ teaspoon freshly ground black pepper
> 5–6 tablespoons hot water
> 3–4 tablespoons lemon juice

- Thinly peel the pointed tops of the okra making sure they keep their shape; don't cut them off. Grill the okra for about 2 minutes under a medium grill. Heat the oil in a medium-size pan and when it is hot but not smoking add the onions and sauté for a minute, then stir in the garlic and sauté until both are golden in colour. Add half the tomatoes and the coriander and okra. Add the salt, cinnamon and allspice, if using both, pepper, water and the remaining tomatoes. Shake the pan or stir gently to help release the liquid. Cover and cook over medium-low or low heat for 30 minutes.
  A minute or two before the end of cooking add the lemon juice.
- Serve at room temperature with home-baked Lebanese bread.

❀ ❀ ❀

Aubergine Moussakaa
Batinjan mtabbak bi-zeit

THIS LEBANESE PREPARATION is inspired by an Ottoman recipe and is unlike the Greek one, despite the similarity of their names. We know that the sultan used to send his cooks to their provinces to come back with original dishes or ideas to use for their famed banquets. We also know that cultural changes and movements between villages and provinces flowed. In this lovely Lebanese *moussakaa*, the aubergines, onions, garlic and chick-peas are sautéed in a generous amount of olive oil, then simmered with fresh, ripe tomatoes and the taste is heightened by spices. Sometimes a little of the fragrant pomegranate syrup is added. Here small aubergines are used; however, if they are not available cut large ones into chunks, then follow the instructions overleaf. Sometimes, when preparing for a big party, I halve the baby ones and they look very attractive.

12 baby aubergines
4 tablespoons olive oil
2 onions, thinly sliced
10–12 small garlic cloves, whole or cut into thick slivers
Handful of chick-peas, soaked overnight, drained, rinsed
    and precooked until tender
1 tablespoon pomegranate syrup or to taste (optional)
450 g (1 lb) tomatoes, quartered
1½ teaspoons salt or to taste
½ teaspoon ground cinnamon (optional)
Pinch of allspice
¼ teaspoon freshly ground black pepper
150 ml (¼ pint) hot water

- Trim the green tops of the aubergines, leaving one half of the stem intact if possible; peel, leaving lengthwise stripes about 1.5 cm (½ in) wide, as prepared traditionally. Heat 3 tablespoons of the oil in a pan over medium-high heat and sauté the aubergines for about a minute or until golden in colour. Now and then shake the pan. With a slotted spoon remove the aubergines to a side dish and reserve.

- Add the remaining oil to the pan and sauté the onions and garlic, reducing the heat to medium and stirring constantly until they are pale golden in colour and soft (about 2–3 minutes), adding more oil if necessary. Add the chick-peas and stir for a few minutes longer, then the pomegranate syrup, if using. Return the reserved aubergines to the pan. Add the tomatoes, sprinkle with the salt, cinnamon, if using, allspice and pepper and add the water. Bring to the boil and quickly reduce the heat to moderately low. Cover and simmer for 30–40 minutes.

- Serve warm or at room temperature. Eat with wholemeal bread as a starter or as part of a large buffet.

Whole Broad Beans in Oil
Foul akhdar bi-zeit

BROAD BEANS, also known as fava beans, are popular in the
Mediterranean where they originated. This aromatic dish is easy to
prepare and much appreciated by the Lebanese as an accompaniment to
other dishes. Lebanese food varies in certain villages in the north of the
country where cinnamon is not used in oily dishes.

> 2 tablespoons extra virgin olive oil
> 2 medium-size onions, finely chopped
> 500 g (I lb I oz) broad beans, topped, tailed, strings
>   removed, and cut into 2.5 cm (I in) long pieces
> 3–4 large garlic cloves, crushed
> ½ bunch coriander, leaves and tender stems only, chopped
> I teaspoon plain flour
> I teaspoon salt or to taste
> ¼ teaspoon ground cinnamon (optional)
> ¼ teaspoon freshly ground black pepper
> Pinch of allspice
> 170 ml (a little under ⅓ pint) hot water
> 2 tablespoons lemon juice or to taste

- Heat the oil in a medium-size pan over moderately high heat, add the
  onions and sauté until pale and transparent, stirring all the time (about
  I minute). Add the beans, cover, reduce the heat to medium and let
  them sweat in their own juices for 8 minutes. Uncover the pan, add the
  garlic, coriander and flour, and stir them with the beans for a few
  seconds. Season with the salt, cinnamon, if using, pepper and allspice.

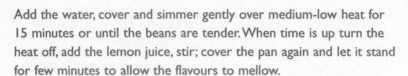

Add the water, cover and simmer gently over medium-low heat for
15 minutes or until the beans are tender. When time is up turn the
heat off, add the lemon juice, stir; cover the pan again and let it stand
for few minutes to allow the flavours to mellow.

• Serve warm or at room temperature with wholemeal bread and a bowl
of yoghurt.

Chick-pea Dip
Hummous

HUMMOUS is extremely popular in the Middle East and, nowadays,
known and loved all over the world. A *mezzé* table cannot be considered
complete without it. Ajami, a famous restaurant in downtown Beirut,
used to prepare it before the war in Lebanon. Finely chopped parsley,
minced garlic and chopped chillies were mixed with whole cooked
chick-peas. This preparation was topped with *foul mdammas* (Field or
Brown Bean Salad, see page 20). It tasted great and nutritionally was
considered a complete meal, more so when eaten with bread. Nowadays
some Lebanese restaurants in London serve *hummous Beiruty*, made by
mixing garlic, parsley and hot pepper into the *hummous* dip. The chick-
peas are combined with *tahini* paste, which is readily available in
supermarkets. When Seville oranges are in season use their juice and
you will have an outstandingly flavoursome *hummous*. To have the juice
when the oranges are out of season, I freeze it in ice-cube trays and
store the cubes in freezer bags. *Hummous* is simple to prepare, freezes
well without the garlic and is rich in B vitamins and minerals.

**200 g (7 oz) chick-peas, soaked overnight, drained and
  rinsed**
1 clove garlic
6–7 tablespoons *tahini*
3 tablespoons lemon juice
Juice of 1 clementine or ½ orange
1½ teaspoons salt or to taste
¼ teaspoon cayenne pepper (optional)
Extra virgin olive oil to taste

- Place the chick-peas in a pan with 450–600 ml (¾–1 pint) water and
  bring to the boil, skimming the foam from the surface of the water.
  Reduce to very low heat, cover and simmer until the chick-peas are
  very soft, about 2–2½ hours. Reserve a few tablespoons of the cooking
  liquid, and a small handful of whole chick-peas to place over the
  puréed *hummous*.

- Place the chick-peas, while hot, in a blender with the reserved liquid
  and the garlic and blend until smooth. Add the *tahini*, lemon and
  clementine or orange juices, salt and a seville orange ice cube if
  necessary. Purée until smooth, taste and adjust the seasonings.
  Spread the *hummous* over a plate and top with the whole chick-peas.
  Sprinkle with the cayenne, if using, and drizzle with oil.

- Serve with Lebanese bread or cos lettuce and strips of orange pepper.

NOTE: A pressure cooker will shorten the cooking time, use less water
and reduce the loss of nutrients. If you are using one always follow the
maker's instructions.

Aubergine Dip
Mtabbal al-batinjan

A POPULAR LEBANESE CLASSIC, *mtabbal al-batinjan* is served cold as part of a *mezzé*. Aubergines can be grilled, baked, charred over an open fire or even steamed and they will retain their distinctive taste. This dish has a good combination of textures and a lovely smoky flavour. *Tahini* is added to the puréed flesh along with lemon juice, enhancing the taste of the dish and topping up the minerals. If you are counting the calories, replace half the *tahini* with thick, low-fat yoghurt or *labneh* (concentrated yoghurt) and make sure you combine them thoroughly.

> **675 g (1½ lb) aubergines**
> **1 small garlic clove (optional)**
> **Good pinch of salt or to taste**
> **2–2½ tablespoons *tahini***
> **3–4 tablespoons lemon juice**
> **Large handful of pomegranate seeds (in season)**
> **1–1½ tablespoons extra virgin olive oil (optional)**

- Slit the skin of each aubergine once or twice. Put them on a baking sheet and place under a preheated grill 10 cm (4 in) away from the heat. Grill the aubergines for 20 minutes, or until the skins have blackened and blistered, and the pulp is soft, turning them once halfway through. A quicker way is to place them on a griddle over the hob for 3–4 minutes, turning them over to blacken. Leave the aubergines to cool slightly.

- Meanwhile, in a glass bowl pound the garlic, if using, and the salt with a pestle. Scrape the pulp from the aubergine skins, place it in a blender and purée for a few seconds only to get a medium-smooth texture, unless you prefer your dip very smooth. Remove from the blender and put in the bowl with the garlic, if using. Add the *tahini*, stir, and finally add the lemon juice. Mix well, taste and adjust the seasonings. Place in a serving dish and scatter with the pomegranate seeds. Drizzle with the oil, if using.

• Serve with wholemeal bread or romaine lettuce leaves.

Pumpkin Dip
Laktin m'tabal bi-thini

PUMPKIN IS LOW IN FAT and an excellent source of the potent antioxidant beta-carotene, which protects the body from cancer. This dip is unusual, inexpensive and healthy. The amount of *tahini*, a sesame cream, can be halved and replaced with concentrated yoghurt.

675 g (1½ lb) pumpkin, peeled, deseeded and cut into
**   2.5 cm (1 in) pieces**
1 garlic clove
1 teaspoon salt or to taste
3 tablespoons *tahini*
3 tablespoons lemon juice
Handful of finely chopped parsley or watercress leaves,
**   to garnish**

• Place the pumpkin pieces in a steaming basket and set into a pan over 2.5 cm (1 in) of boiling water, cover and cook over moderate heat for 10 minutes or until tender. Meanwhile, in a serving bowl pound the garlic and the salt with a pestle until creamy.

- Remove the pumpkin pieces, drain, squeeze out some of their excess water and purée them in a blender or use a vegetable mill. Add to the garlic in the bowl. Add the *tahini* and lemon juice, mix well, taste and adjust the seasonings. Garnish with the parsley or, better still, watercress.

- Serve with cos lettuce, endive or a mixture of orange, red and yellow pepper slices.

Cracked Wheat with Tomatoes
Burghol bi-banadoura

Cracked wheat or *burghol* is a staple in the Lebanese kitchen and was known in the Middle East for centuries before Christ. Long ago *burghol* was more commonly used in cooking. Today, rice has become the star and is favoured in certain dishes. Nevertheless, *burghol* is still largely in use and very much liked – more so in Lebanese villages where it is added to beans or lentils and used with herbs and spices to stuff courgettes and other vegetables.

Burghol bi-banadoura has an exquisite, clean flavour. It can be a side or main dish. I often prepare it for my lunch, especially in winter. Long ago, a tablespoon of Kawarma (see Glossary page 302) was added while the ingredients were simmering to add more substance and flavour. Here the dish uses fresh tomatoes. If these are not very tasty add a little tomato purée.

I tablespoon extra virgin olive oil
I medium-size onion, chopped
225 g (8 oz) tomatoes, peeled and chopped

200 g (7 oz) coarse *burghol*
I teaspoon salt or to taste
½ teaspoon ground cinnamon

- Heat the oil in a medium-size pan and sauté the onion until it is a deep golden colour. Stir in the tomatoes, cover and simmer over very low heat for 5 minutes. Uncover, add 300 ml (½ pint) water, stir in the *burghol*, and season with the salt and cinnamon. Bring to the boil. Reduce the heat to very low, cover and simmer until the water is absorbed, about 8–10 minutes.

- Serve hot on its own or with yoghurt.

❀ ❀ ❀

Courgettes with Cracked Wheat
Koussa bi-bourghol

SEVERAL LEBANESE DISHES are made with courgettes. Here they are combined with coarse *burghol*. This humble and savoury dish is an indication of how housewives with large families create a welcoming meal from basic ingredients. The onions are sautéed in olive oil then the cubed courgettes are gradually stirred into them – as they become coated with oil they glisten and turn into the beautiful yellowish colour of the moon. You can enrich the dish by adding scented mint, which works wonderfully with courgettes. But try it first without, as mint is very aromatic and may overpower the flavours of the other ingredients.

2 tablespoons extra virgin olive oil
I medium onion, finely chopped

1 teaspoon salt or to taste
500 g (1 lb 1 oz) courgettes, cut into 1 cm (½ in) cubes
450 ml (¾ pint) hot water
225 g (8 oz) coarse *burghol*

- Heat the oil in a medium-size pan and stir in the onion. Sprinkle with ¼ teaspoon of salt. Sauté over medium-high heat for 1 minute, stirring occasionally. Reduce the heat and cook until the onion is golden in colour. Add a handful of the courgettes and stir.

- Repeat until all the courgettes are in the pan. This will take about 5–7 minutes. The courgettes will reduce in size and become a lovely yellowish colour. Add the water and the remaining salt, reduce the heat to low and simmer for about 25 minutes. Stir in the *burghol*, cover and simmer again over low heat for about 6–8 minutes or until the water is absorbed. Taste one *burghol*. If it isn't tender add very little hot water and finish the cooking.

- Serve on its own or with Cucumber and Yoghurt Salad (see page 229).

Flamed Green Wheat with Vegetables
Freekeh bil-khodar

FREEKEH BIL-KHODAR is simple to prepare and has a warm, welcoming flavour. Here, for it to be authentic it is essential to cook the *freekeh* and vegetables separately. Some village women told me that they even soak the *freekeh* in hot water before cooking. This is not followed in this recipe but the *freekeh* and the flavourful vegetables are combined to simmer together for few minutes, and as a final touch they're spiced with cumin. If you cannot find *freekeh*, use coarse cracked wheat (*burghol*) or rice instead. They don't need to be cooked separately from the vegetables, which is a plus, although they will not replicate the *freekeh*'s amazing smoky taste.

   3–4 tablespoons extra virgin olive oil
   3–4 onions, finely chopped
   2 large garlic cloves, pounded until creamy
   3 medium-size tomatoes, peeled and finely chopped
   I heaped tablespoon double concentrated tomato purée
   500 g (I lb I oz) aubergines, cut into 1.5 cm (½ in) cubes
   450g (I lb) courgettes, cut into 1.5 cm (½ in) cubes
   Pinch of ground cinnamon
   Pinch of allspice
   Pinch of freshly ground black pepper
   1¼ teaspoons salt to taste
   250 ml (8 fl oz) hot water
   275 g (10 oz) *freekeh*, rinsed once and drained
   Good pinch of cumin or to taste (optional)

• Heat 2 tablespoons of the oil in a large non-stick pan. Add half the onions. Stir for a few minutes over medium-high heat, then add the garlic and reduce the heat to medium-low. Stir now and then until the onions are a yellowish golden colour. Add the tomatoes, stir and cook over low heat for about 5–7 minutes. Stir in the tomato purée then, after a few more minutes, add the aubergines. Every 2 minutes give them a good stir. After about 5–6 minutes add the courgettes and stir them every 2 minutes. The whole process should take about 15–20 minutes or until the vegetable juices coat the pan. At this point stir in the cinnamon, allspice, pepper and half the salt and add the hot water.

Bring to the boil, cover and simmer over low heat for about 8–10 minutes or until the courgettes are tender.

- Meanwhile, heat the remaining oil in a medium-size pan. Add the remaining onions and sauté until they are a yellowish golden colour. Add the *freekeh*, the remaining salt and 600 ml (1 pint) water. Bring to the boil, cover and simmer over low heat for about 8–10 minutes or until the water is absorbed. When time is up add the *freekeh* to the vegetables in the other pan. Allow to simmer for about 5 minutes. Sprinkle with cumin, if using, taste, adjust the seasonings and serve.

Potato Kibbeh Patties
Akrass kibbeh al-batata

WHO IS NOT FOND of potatoes?! This enjoyable dish relies on the pure flavour of fresh local produce. The mashed potatoes are kneaded with *burghol*, onions, spices and coriander to produce a delectable dough. It is baked as in *kibbeh al-samak* (Fish Kibbeh, see page 110) or fried. Another good option is to grill it, as in this recipe. The patties make an interesting starter or can sandwich a cabbage salad, which marries wonderfully with them. You can also spread the dough over a serving plate without frying it. Scatter with sliced spring onions, mint, parsley, chillies, drizzle with extra virgin olive oil and serve.

500 g (1 lb 1 oz) potatoes, unpeeled and halved
1 small onion
½ bunch coriander, leaves and tender stems only
¼ teaspoon freshly ground black pepper
Pinch of ground cinnamon

½ **teaspoon ground coriander**
I **teaspoon salt or to taste**
150 g (5 oz) **fine white** *burghol* **(do not rinse)**
I **tablespoon unbleached white flour (optional)**
Olive oil, for brushing

- Place the potatoes in a steaming basket and set into a pan over 2.5 cm (I in) of boiling water. Cover and steam for about 20 minutes or until soft. Leave the potatoes to cool a little.

- Meanwhile, place the onion, fresh coriander, pepper, cinnamon, ground coriander and salt in a blender and blend until smooth.

- Peel the potatoes and mash until smooth. Add to the coriander and onion mixture, and add the *burghol* and flour, if using. Mix thoroughly to form a medium-soft dough. Then make the potato patties. Take small portions at a time and, with oil-moistened hands, shape each portion into 4 cm (1½ in) patties. Preheat the grill. Heat a baking sheet, brush it with olive oil, arrange the patties on it and cook them 10 cm (4 in) from the heat for 5–7 minutes or until lightly browned on both sides.

- Serve hot or cold with Bread Salad (see page 6) or Cabbage Salad (see page 8).

VARIATION: Sauté pine nuts in olive oil until golden and remove them to a side dish. Thinly slice 2–3 medium-size onions, add more oil to the pan and sauté the onions until they are a golden colour. Return the pine nuts and sprinkle with salt. Place in a baking dish and cover with the dough. Drizzle with olive oil, cut into squares and bake as *kibbeh al-samak* (see page 110). Walnuts can be used instead of pine nuts.

Pumpkin Kibbeh
Kibbeh lakteen

PUMPKIN *KIBBEH* is the vegetarian version of the traditional meat *kibbeh* (see page 153) and is specifically prepared in villages in the Shouf mountains and where pumpkins grow. This type of *kibbeh* has increased in popularity among Lebanese who have become more aware of how healthy mountain food is.

The dough combines *burghol* (cracked wheat) with orange-coloured pumpkin, which is rich in the highly powerful antioxidant, beta-carotene. When pomegranates are in season I add a handful of seeds to the filling. A delicate dough with various spices is fabricated and flour cements it.

Making pumpkin *kibbeh* shells calls for a little patience. A quicker method is to sandwich the filling between two layers of dough as below. Or you can make patties, grill them and top each one with some filling.

500 g (1lb 1oz) pumpkin, peeled and cut into thick slices
175g (6 oz) fine *burghol*, preferably white (do not rinse)
1 small onion, grated
1 teaspoon salt
½ teaspoon ground cinnamon
Pinch of allspice
¼ teaspoon freshly ground black pepper
45 g (1½ oz) unbleached white flour (or as necessary)

For the filling:
50 g (2 oz) chick-peas, soaked overnight, drained and rinsed (optional)

**90 ml (3 fl oz) extra virgin olive oil, plus 1 tablespoon and
  extra for brushing**
1 medium-size onion, chopped
75 g (2½ oz) walnuts, coarsely chopped
1 tablespoon pomegranate syrup
½ tablespoon lemon juice
½ teaspoon salt or to taste
½ teaspoon ground cinnamon
1 medium-size aubergine, cut into cubes and fried

- Prepare the chick-peas for the filling, if using. Place in a pan, cover with 5 cm (2 in) water and bring to the boil, skimming the foam from the surface of the water. Cover and simmer over low heat for 2 hours or until tender. Remove and split chick-peas.

- Meanwhile, place the pumpkin pieces in a steamer basket and set into a pan over 2.5 cm (1 in) boiling water. Cover and cook for about 8–10 minutes or until just soft. Remove and drain the pumpkin and squeeze out excess water using the back of a jug.

- In a bowl, place the *burghol*, onion, salt, cinnamon, allspice, pepper and pumpkin and knead to form a slightly moist dough. Add the flour and mix well. Cover and leave to stand in the fridge for 30 minutes.

- In the meantime, prepare the filling. Heat 1 tablespoon of olive oil in a pan and sauté the onions until lightly golden. Stir in the chick-peas, if using, and the walnuts, pomegranate syrup, lemon juice, salt, cinnamon and aubergine. Give the mixture a good stir and remove from heat.

- Preheat the oven to 180°C/350°F/Gas Mark 4. Brush a 21 cm (8½ in) diameter round baking tin with a little olive oil. Take just under half the dough and spread evenly over the base of the tin. Cover with the filling.

Then take small portions of the remaining dough and flatten between the palms of your hands, moistening your hands as necessary. Spread the pieces of dough out over the top, then smooth and drizzle over the 90 ml (3 fl oz) of olive oil. Run a sharp knife around the edge of the baking tin and cut into squares. Bake for 30–40 minutes or until browned. Serve warm or at room temperature.

Split Broad Beans and Coarse Burghol
Baklet foul

THIS LOVELY RECIPE will surprise you. The ingredients, though basic, produce a comforting and very tasty dish that is appreciated by everyone, even young children. A plus is that the split broad beans do not require any soaking. (Nevertheless, I like to soak them for 10–15 minutes with water, just enough to cover them.) The combination of the *burghol* and the beans creates a flavour that is earthy and nutty, yet subtle, leaving you with a happy feeling, a clean aftertaste and a rich pocket.

I believe one should not be tempted to add any other ingredients for more flavour or to lift *baklet foul*'s lovely yellowish colour. It has a distinctive taste and look, and it would be a pity for it to lose its character. On the other hand, to enjoy it further it must be eaten with *salatet banadoura bi-bassal* (Tomato and Onion Salad, see page 12).

> **225 g (8 oz) split broad beans**
> **3–4 tablespoons extra virgin olive oil**
> **2 medium-size onions, very finely chopped**

I teaspoon salt
About 145 g (4½ oz) coarse *burghol*

- Place the beans in a medium-size pan with 1 litre (1¾ pints) water and bring to the boil, skimming the foam from the surface of the water. Reduce the heat to low, cover and simmer for about 20–25 minutes or until the beans are very soft.

- Meanwhile, heat 2 tablespoons of the oil in a small non-stick frying pan, add the onions, and sprinkle with half the salt. Stir constantly until the onions are a deep yellowish to golden colour, about 5–6 minutes. When the beans in the pan have softened add the onions and the *burghol*. Sprinkle with the ramining salt and bring to the boil. Cover and simmer over low heat for about 10 minutes or until the water is absorbed, but the mixture is still moist. Turn the heat off and quickly stir in the remaining olive oil. Cover and leave for few minutes.

- Serve with Tomato and Onion Salad (see page 12)

Mixed Grains and Beans
Makhlouta

A FEAST and a real peasant dish, *makhlouta* is prepared during winter in Lebanese villages, as it provides energy and natural heating, and is most effective in preventing colds. Traditionally, mountain people add about two heaped tablespoons of *kawarma* (see Glossary page 302) to give the dish extra flavour and substance. Departing from the traditional recipe, the onions in this one are not fried. *Makhlouta* keeps well in the fridge for up to 3–4 days. And it is delicious without any additions.

120 g (4 oz) kidney beans, soaked overnight, rinsed and
drained
120 g (4 oz) large white beans, soaked overnight, rinsed
and drained
85 g (3 oz) chick-peas, soaked overnight, rinsed and
drained
120 g (4 oz) brown lentils, picked over and rinsed
½ tablespoon extra virgin olive oil
1 large onion, finely chopped
120 g (4 oz) coarse *burghol*, rinsed and drained
1½ teaspoons salt or to taste
1½ teaspoons cumin or to taste
¼ teaspoon ground black pepper
¼ teaspoon white pepper

- Place the kidney beans, white beans and chick-peas in a medium-size
pan with 1.5–1.75 litres (2½–3 pints) water and bring to the boil over
high heat, skimming off the foam from the surface of the water. Cover
and simmer for at least 5 minutes, then reduce the heat to low and
cook until tender (about 60 minutes). Add the lentils, oil and onion,
bring to the boil, cover and simmer over medium-low heat for 30
minutes. Then add the *burghol*, salt, cumin and black and white peppers.
Stir, cover and simmer for a further 10–15 minutes or until the beans,
chick-peas and lentils are tender and the water has been absorbed.
Taste and adjust the seasonings.

- Serve with tender cabbage leaves, or grilled aubergines or courgettes.

❊ ❊ ❊

Falafel

AN EGYPTIAN SPECIALITY known as *taamia, falafel* are very popular in the Middle East and are much enjoyed by the Lebanese in the form of takeaway sandwiches. Food vendors gathered along the side streets of Beirut, close to the universities and nightclubs, provide a satisfying, hearty quick fix. Traffic jams are often caused by crowds hanging out at the vendors or at open-air cafés. In the West *falafel* are served in restaurants.

The gloriously rich, fragrant *falafel* is a combination of puréed chick-peas and broad (fava) beans complemented by a powerful mixture of fresh spices and herbs and made into small round patties; a little raising agent is added to puff up the patties and they are then fried until brown and crisp. *Falafel* are ideal as a starter and make an excellent meal for vegetarians. For canapés make small versions. Here green peppers and fresh herbs are included to make them even more healthy and tasty. For further additions, a little fresh fennel or dill would add stronger flavours.

> **175 g (6 oz) chick-peas, soaked overnight, drained and rinsed**
> **85 g (3 oz) dried, skinned broad (fava) beans, soaked overnight and drained**
> **2 large sprigs of coriander, leaves only**
> **Large handful of parsley leaves**
> **¼ medium onion**
> **1 large spring onion**
> **4 garlic cloves**
> **1 small green pepper, cored, deseeded and quartered**
> **1 small red pepper, cored, deseeded and quartered**

1 red chilli, deseeded
1 ½ teaspoons salt or to taste
2–3 teaspoons ground cumin
2–2½ teaspoons ground coriander
¼ teaspoon freshly ground black pepper
¼ teaspoon cayenne pepper or to taste
4–5 tablespoons sesame seeds
¼–½ teaspoon baking soda
Groundnut oil, for deep-frying

- Place the chick-peas and broad beans in a blender with the coriander leaves, parsley, onion, garlic, green and red peppers, and chilli. Season with the salt and add the cumin, ground coriander, and black and cayenne peppers. Purée until smooth. Place the moist dough in a bowl and mix with the sesame seeds. Cover with a cloth and leave to rest for 30 minutes.

- Just before frying thoroughly incorporate the baking soda. Heat the oil in a small pan. While it is heating up, make the *falafel* patties. For each one, take a small piece of dough and press it lightly between the palms of your hands to form a patty 2.5 cm (1 in) in diameter. Gently drop as many patties as the pan can hold into the hot oil and leave them to fry undisturbed until they float to surface. At this point, turn them and fry them until they are golden brown. Remove with a slotted spoon and drain on kitchen paper.

- Serve with *Tahini* Sauce (see page 300), Lebanese bread and a mixture of finely chopped spring onions, chopped tomatoes and sliced radishes, and, if desired, a dish of diced Pickled Cucumber (see page 295).

Artichokes, Broad Beans and Swiss Chard
Ardichowki-bil foul wa-silk

THIS WHOLESOME and filling dish combines varied textures and flavours. It is highly nutritious and rich in B vitamins, iron and fibre. It can be prepared ahead of time; in fact it tastes even better the following day. Like most Lebanese dishes, if well stored, it will keep for about 3–4 days.

Ardichowki bil-foul wa-silk is frequently made in Lebanon when artichokes are in season. Fresh produce tastes better but takes longer to prepare. Frozen artichokes and broad beans are a good alternative. This dish can be served as a starter, or as a main dish with Lebanese bread and cheese such as feta or *kashkaval*.

I tablespoon extra virgin olive oil
I medium-size onion, finely chopped
4 garlic cloves, crushed
4 sprigs of coriander, leaves and tender stems only
675 g (1½ lb) broad (fava) beans, podded
3½ tablespoons lemon juice
Pinch of sugar (optional)
250 g (9 oz) Swiss chard, tough stems removed, leaves
    sliced into 1.5 cm (½ in) ribbons
4 artichoke hearts, each cut crosswise into 4 pieces
¼ teaspoon white pepper
Pinch of ground cinnamon (optional)
Pinch of allspice
¾ teaspoon salt or to taste
200 ml (7 fl oz) boiling water

- Heat the oil in a pan, add the onions and cook over high heat for 30 seconds, stirring frequently. Reduce the heat to medium and sauté until golden in colour; add the garlic, coriander and broad beans. Cook for a minute then add 1 tablespoon of the lemon juice and the sugar, if using, and stir. Add the Swiss chard, cover and let the mixture sweat for about 4–5 minutes over medium-low heat. Add the artichokes and sprinkle with the white pepper, cinnamon, if using, allspice and salt. Add the boiling water and cook for 15–20 minutes over medium-low heat. Add the remaining lemon juice 1 minute before the end of cooking.

- Serve warm or at room temperature.

NOTE: To give the dish an oily flavour add ½–1 tablespoon extra virgin olive oil as you turn the heat off, shake the pan and leave covered for a few minutes before serving.

Black-eyed Beans and Swiss Chard
Fassoulia bi-silk

THIS IS ANOTHER of the Lebanon's oily dishes. Prepared with black-eyed beans, it is highly nutritious, low in fat and simple to make. The beans simmer gently until soft and are then combined with Swiss chard, one of the oldest vegetables the world has known, which is also called silver beet. Their flavour is greatly enhanced by the use of aromatic herbs and spices, while olive oil acts as a medium to bring everything together, giving the dish its distinctive flavour and aroma. *Fassoulia bi-silk* is ideal for vegetarians and people with diabetes.

200 g (7 oz) black-eyed beans, soaked for 6–7 hours,
    drained, rinsed and drained again
1 large onion, finely chopped, and 2 medium-size onions,
    thinly sliced
3–4 tablespoons extra virgin olive oil (or as necessary)
3–4 garlic cloves, pounded until creamy
1 bunch coriander, leaves and tender stems only, finely
    chopped
1 bunch Swiss chard, tough stems removed, leaves sliced
    into 1.5 cm (½ in) ribbons
Good pinch of salt
Pinch of freshly ground black pepper
Juice of ½ lemon or to taste
Juice of 1 sour pomegranate (in season)
Large handful of pomegranate seeds
Good pinch of sugar

- Place the beans in a pan with 600 ml (1 pint) water and bring to the boil, skimming the foam from the surface of the water. Cover, reduce the heat to medium-low, and simmer for about an hour or until the beans are tender. Taste one to check whether they are soft.

- Meanwhile, heat 2 tablespoons of the oil in a large deep frying pan and sauté the chopped onions until golden brown in colour. Add the garlic and coriander, and sauté with the onions for about 30 seconds or until their lovely aromas are released. At this point add the Swiss chard in batches, stirring until each batch reduces in size. Stir in the softened beans and their reduced liquid. Sprinkle with the salt and pepper and simmer for a few minutes to allow the flavours to blend together. Add the lemon and pomegranate juices. If pomegranates are not in season you may need to add more lemon juice, so taste for sharpness. Give all the ingredients a good stir and turn the heat off after a few seconds. Place on a serving dish and scatter with the pomegranate seeds.

- Now heat the remaining oil in a frying pan. When it is hot but not smoking, sauté the sliced onions, stirring occasionally. Halfway through, sprinkle with sugar and continue sautéing until the onions are a deep golden colour. Remove and drain on kitchen paper. Gently separate the onions – sugar caramelizes and they may stick together – and spread them over the beans and Swiss chard.

- Serve warm or at room temperature.

Vermicelli Rice
Ruz bi-shaiirya

THE ARABS INTRODUCED RICE into Europe through Spain and in the Middle East it has almost the character of a sacrament and is served practically every day. Nowadays it provides the basis of the Lebanese cuisine and symbolizes good fortune; for that reason a bride is showered with it for good luck. The same is done at funerals, especially when the deceased is young.

I love rice and it revives memories of my childhood, when after school I hurried to the kitchen to eat it straight from the pot. At that time I knew only white rice. Afterwards, when I settled in England, I discovered the qualities of the brown version, which is a good source of fibre and energy. In general, I especially like the aromatic white basmati rice. Brown rice takes longer to cook, and therefore needs more water. This recipe can also be made with coarse *burghol* and is especially tasty. For plain rice omit the vermicelli and oil if desired.

½–1 tablespoon extra virgin olive oil
1–2 vermicelli nests, broken by hand into small pieces
200 g (7 oz) white rice, preferably basmati
1 teaspoon salt

- Heat the oil in a small pan over medium-high heat. Do not allow it to smoke. Add the vermicelli, and sauté it stirring constantly until it is golden in colour (do not burn). Add the rice and stir with the vermicelli, then add 450 ml (¾ pint) water, season with the salt and bring to the boil. Cover and simmer over low heat for 7 minutes or until the rice is tender and the water has been absorbed. Keep the pan covered and undisturbed for 1 minute.

- Serve hot on its own, or with yoghurt or Lebanese stews.

NOTE: If you use brown rice you will need 500 ml (17 fl oz) water and a cooking time of 30–35 minutes over low heat. However, the time will depend on the kind of brown rice you are using.

Rice with Markouk Bread
Ruz bil markouk

THIS IS ONE of the most delicious ways to eat rice. It's quick to prepare and takes rice to another lovely dimension. I like to mix some *miskee* (see Glossary page 302) into the rice, which gives the dish a very distinctive aroma and a lovely exotic feel. *Markouk* is a paper-thin flat round loaf about 50 cm (20 in) in diameter. If it is difficult to obtain use the large thin Lebanese bread that's nowadays on sale in most supermarkets.

225 g (8 oz) long grain white rice, preferably basmati
Good pinch of salt
¼ teaspoon *miskee*
Small pinch of sugar
30 g (I oz) unsalted butter
½–I tablespoon extra virgin olive oil
I *markouk* loaf, thick edges removed

- Place the rice and salt in a small pan with 600 ml (I pint) water and bring to the boil over medium-high heat. Continue boiling for 4 minutes or at the most 5 minutes. Remove and drain the rice, rinse lightly under cold running water and drain again.

- While the rice is cooking, gently pound the *miskee* pieces with a little sugar until it is powdery. Mix this thoroughly into the drained rice. Now heat half the butter and the oil in a wide, preferably non-stick pan. When they are just hot put the bread in the pan and quickly spread the rice over it. Dot the remaining butter all over the rice. Fold in the overlapping bread – gently so that its edges don't break – to make a round pie shape. Cook over medium-low heat until the bread is browned but not burned, about 3–5 minutes. When time is up, place a plate over the top of the bread and rice and turn the pan upside down. Now place the pan over the uncooked side of the bread, turn it upside down and gently remove the plate. Allow about 4–5 minutes for the uncooked side of the bread to brown, then place a serving dish over the bread and turn the pan upside down again. Serve.

Lentils and Rice
Mdardara

THIS IS A MOST loved dish in Mount Lebanon and Beirut. *Mdardara* is traditionally prepared with white rice or, as long ago in mountain Lebanon, coarse *burghol* (cracked wheat). Here I use brown rice, which marries wonderfully with the lentils in texture and flavour; in addition it makes a healthy meal that is rich in essential amino acids. It would be good served with a vitamin C-rich vegetable salad, like Purslane Salad (see page 10), as vitamin C aids the absorption of iron. Traditionally, this enticing dish is embellished with glistening browned onions. To give a sweeter taste to the onions, and one that becomes them, I like to sprinkle sugar over them. They caramelize and it's impressive how this finishing touch can make the dish more special.

> 5½–7 tablespoons extra virgin olive oil
> I large onion, chopped, and 2–3 medium onions, thinly
>   sliced
> 200 g (7 oz) brown lentils, picked over and rinsed
> 120 g (4 oz) brown rice, rinsed once
> I teaspoon salt or to taste
> Pinch of freshly ground black pepper
> Pinch of ground cinnamon (optional)

- Heat 2 tablespoons of the oil in a pan over medium-high heat. When it is hot but not smoking, add the chopped onions and sauté them, stirring frequently, until golden brown, about 3 minutes. Add the lentils, brown rice, 900 ml–1 litre (1½–1¾ pints) water and the salt. Bring to the boil, reduce the heat to medium-low, cover and simmer for 30–40 minutes.

Halfway through cooking season with the pepper and the cinnamon, if using. When cooking time is up, transfer the *mdardara* to a serving plate.

- To prepare the browned onions, heat the remaining oil in a frying pan and add the sliced onions. Sauté over medium-high heat for few minutes, then reduce the heat and continue to cook until the onions are a golden brown colour, about 10–15 minutes. Halfway through cooking sprinkle them with sugar. When time is up drain them on kitchen paper. Gently separate the onions – sugar caramelizes and they may stick together – and spread them over the *mdardara*.

- Serve warm or at room temperature with Bread Salad (see page 6) or Tomato and Onion Salad (see page 12).

Cream of Lentils
Mjaddara

THIS IS ONE of my favourite dishes. It evokes those happy childhood days when I watched my brother Riaya smothering the plate of *mjaddara* with red wine vinegar – not to everyone's taste. *Mjaddara* was prepared every Friday and we ate it along with *salatet malfouf* (Cabbage Salad, see page 8) that swam in an ample amount of *assir abou sfayr* (Seville orange juice). This humble dish is found on the dining tables of Lebanese Christian communities during Lent. In the days when my mother prepared it she never measured the oil; she poured it into the pan and added more onions as they browned. The lot would join the lentils to enhance the flavour. In the recipe below a small amount of oil and two kinds of lentils are used. I find that in combination with the brown lentils, green ones give a richness and smoothness to the velvety purée. However, you may use either one or the other as you wish.

3 medium-size onions
175 g (6 oz) green lentils, picked over and rinsed
120 g (4 oz) brown lentils, picked over and rinsed
1¼ teaspoons salt
1½–2 tablespoons extra virgin olive oil
60 g (2 oz) white rice

- Cut 2 of the onions into 6 pieces each and place them in a pan with the lentils and 1.3 litres (2¼ pints) water. Add the salt and bring to the boil. Reduce the heat to medium-low, cover and simmer for 30–40 minutes or until lentils are tender.

- Meanwhile, chop the third onion. Heat 1 tablespoon of the oil in a small non-stick small frying pan and add the chopped onion. Sauté gently until the onion is deeply browned but not burned, stirring occasionally. Add the onion to the lentils a few minutes before the end of their cooking time. Pass the lot through a vegetable mill. Alternatively, drain the lentils, reserving the liquid, and place them in a blender. Blend until creamy, adding, if necessary, very little of their cooking liquid, then return the lentils to their liquid. Whichever method you use, return the lentils to the pan they were cooked in. Add the rice and stir until it comes to the boil. Reduce the heat and cook for 8 minutes or until the rice is tender and the lentils are smooth and slightly thick. Add the remaining oil towards the end of the cooking, mix well and then pour the mixture over individual plates or a large serving dish. The purée will set within moments.

- Serve warm or at room temperature, with Lebanese bread, Cabbage Salad (see page 8) or Purslane Salad (see page 10).

Spinach with Rice
Sabanekh bi-roz

ANOTHER HEARTY and appetizing dish made of a mixture of fresh ingredients, aromatic herbs and spices. Nourishing, inexpensive and remarkably light to digest, it is one of the finest and simplest of meals. In addition, the dish is prepared with very little oil.

1 tablespoon extra virgin olive oil
1 large onion, finely chopped
6 sprigs of coriander, leaves and tender stems only, chopped
675 g (1½ lb) spinach, tough stems removed, chopped
200 g (7 oz) long grain white rice, preferably basmati
½ teaspoon ground cinnamon
¼ teaspoon freshly ground black pepper
½ teaspoon allspice
1¼ teaspoons salt or to taste

- Heat the oil in a medium-size, thick-bottomed pan over medium-high heat. Add the onions and cook until soft (about 2–3 minutes), stirring constantly. Add the coriander, reduce the heat to medium and sauté it, stirring, for a few seconds. Add the spinach in batches. As it reduces in size, add the rice, stir gently and season with the cinnamon, pepper and allspice. Stir, then add 200–250 ml (7–8 fl oz) water and the salt. Bring to the boil, reduce the heat to low, cover and simmer for 10 minutes or until the rice is soft. Turn the heat off and leave the pan covered for 2 minutes before serving.

- Serve on its own or with yoghurt.

Potatoes and Rice
Batata bi-roz

THIS IS ANOTHER simple and highly nourishing dish. Mount Lebanon has an amazing array of potato dishes that are warming, comforting and provide energy for athletes and active people. *Batata bi-roz* has a pleasant flavour. Here, instead of using white rice as tradition dictates, I am taking advantage of wholesome brown rice. However, if you choose to use white rice, which is quicker, then I favour basmati rice. Remember to add it 10 minutes before the end of cooking and to cut the water down to ¾ pint (15 fl oz).

As an accompaniment a watercress or Purslane Salad (see page 10) marries extremely well with *batata bi-roz* and adds highly valuable nutrients. Sometimes I spoil my family and prepare Aubergines in Yoghurt (see page 231), a delicacy that fits perfectly with this dish.

> **200 g (7 oz) long grain brown rice, preferably basmati**
> **2 tablespoons extra virgin olive oil**
> **I large onion, finely chopped**
> **500 g (I lb I oz) potatoes, cut into 2 cm (¾ in) cubes**
> **1½ teaspoons salt or to taste**
> **½ teaspoon allspice**
> **½ teaspoon ground cinnamon**
> **¼ teaspoon freshly ground black pepper**
> **2 tablespoons double concentrated tomato purée**

- Place the rice in a medium-size pan with 600–750 ml (1–1¼ pints) water and bring to the boil. Cover and simmer over low heat for about 20 minutes.

- Meanwhile, heat the oil in a medium-size non-stick frying pan and add the onion. Sauté the onion and as it reduces in size add the potatoes and sprinkle with the salt. Cook, shaking the pan or stirring occasionally. Cover with a lid and leave for a minute or two, uncover and stir. Both will take a golden colour. This operation takes about 10 minutes or a little less. However, keep an eye on the heat and reduce or put it up when necessary.

- Towards the end of cooking, add the allspice, cinnamon and pepper. Stir in the tomato purée, then give the mixture a good stir and add the lot to the rice in the pan. Check the water level and if necessary add hot water. Bring to the boil, cover and continue to simmer over medium-low heat for a further 15–20 minutes or until the rice and potatoes are soft and the liquid has been absorbed. Turn the heat off and allow a few minutes for the flavours to blend.

- Serve with fried or grilled aubergine slices or as recommended in the introduction to the recipe.

Rice and Chick-peas
Roz bedfine

THIS WHOLESOME and inexpensive mixture of chick-peas speaks for itself. From time out of mind *roz bedfine* has enriched the Lebanese menu – mainly in the mountains where the staple *burghol* (cracked wheat) was used instead of rice. It was one of the dishes that gave villagers the energy to work in the fields. People knew by instinct what science has now confirmed, that whole grains are an excellent source of complex carbohydrates, protein and fibre. To add an interesting and attractive note to this humble peasant dish, scatter a handful of watercress over it. The

Persian philosopher Ibn er Rumi (d. 1273) used the preparation of the dish as a metaphor to convey his senses and what surrounded him:

> *A chick-pea leaps almost over the rim of the pot where it is being boiled*
> *The cook knocks him (the chick-pea) down with the ladle*
> *Don't you try to jump out*
> *I'm giving you flavour*
> *So you can mix with spices and rice*
> *And be the lovely vitality of human being.*

120 g (4 oz) chick-peas, soaked overnight, drained, rinsed and precooked for 1½ hours
1½–2 tablespoons extra virgin olive oil
2 medium-size onions, roughly sliced
½ teaspoon ground cinnamon
¼ teaspoon allspice
¼ teaspoon white pepper
900 ml (1½ pints) hot water
200 g (7 oz) long grain brown rice, preferably basmati
1–1½ teaspoons ground caraway
1¼ teaspoons salt or to taste

• Drain the chick-peas. Heat the oil in a pan, add the onions and sauté until soft, about 2–3 minutes, stirring constantly. Reduce the heat to medium, and add the chick-peas. Cook for few minutes longer, stirring occasionally. Stir in the cinnamon, allspice and pepper, and add the rice and water. Bring to the boil, cover and simmer over low heat for 40 minutes or until the rice and chick-peas are tender. Season with the caraway and salt 5 minutes before the end of the cooking time, then stir and cover for a couple of minutes before serving.

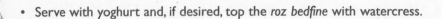

- Serve with yoghurt and, if desired, top the *roz bedfine* with watercress.

NOTE: If you use white rice add it to the chick-peas 10 minutes before end of cooking and use less water. Start with 600 ml (1 pint) and add more if necessary.

Green Beans Buried in Rice and Olive Oil
Madfounet al loubieh wa roz bi-zeit

THIS SAVOURY DISH belongs to southern Lebanon and is much loved and popular among Shiite Muslims. It is simple to prepare and fulfilling. In general it is made with coarse *burghol* (cracked wheat) or rice. Either grain produces a delicious dish. For this recipe I use basmati rice, which is a favourite, and the dish is spiced with chillies. Cumin, which is not included here, can be added. For a change from green beans try making this dish with fried or grilled okra (see Okra in Oil, page 30).

> 250 g (9 oz) green beans, topped, tailed and strings removed
> 1½–2 tablespoons extra virgin olive oil
> 2–3 small onions, thinly sliced
> 1 teaspoon salt
> 3 medium-size tomatoes, thickly sliced
> 1 green chilli, deseeded and thickly sliced
> 300–450 ml (½–¾ pint) hot water
> 140 g (4½ oz) white rice, preferably basmati

- Cut the beans diagonally into 2.5 cm (1 in) lengths and set aside. Heat the oil in a medium-size pan, add the onions and sprinkle with ¼ teaspoon of the salt. Stir to coat the onions with oil, then cover the pan and cook the onions over medium heat for 1 minute. Uncover and stir the onions again, repeating the process until the onions have softened and are a yellowish colour. This will take about 5 minutes. At this point add the tomatoes, sprinkle with the remaining salt and add the beans. Cover and leave the beans to sweat for about 10–15 minutes. Uncover, add the chilli and hot water and bring to the boil. Reduce the heat to medium-low. Cover and simmer for 15–20 minutes or until the beans are tender; check the water level and add hot water if necessary. Add the rice and shake pan to distribute it. Cover and simmer for a further 10 minutes or until the rice is tender. Keep covered for about 5 minutes before serving.

Stuffed Swiss Chard
Silk bi-zeit

THIS TRADITIONAL DISH is one of the most favoured among the Lebanese. Preparing it requires a little patience, especially when a huge quantity is to be made. This recipe differs from the traditional one by using brown instead of white rice. It is a good way to accustom a wary family to the brown variety because its presence is not conspicuous. *Silk bi-zeit* is ideal for a buffet on warm days or can be eaten as a main dish any day with yoghurt. For a meal that is richer in nutrients, it would be good to add a raw vegetable salad and some white cheese. If you are short of time, simply sandwich the filling between several Swiss chard leaves rather than rolling into cigar shapes. Cook in the same way and finish in the oven.

4½ tablespoons extra virgin olive oil

I large potato, unpeeled, scrubbed and sliced thickly

45 g (1½ oz) chick-peas, soaked overnight, drained, rinsed
and cooked for I hour

120 g (4 oz) long grain brown rice, preferably basmati,
rinsed once and drained

3–4 medium-size ripe tomatoes, finely chopped, and1 large
tomato, cut into 1.5 cm (½ in) slices

I small bunch parsley, leaves only, chopped

Large handful of mint leaves, chopped

I medium-size onion, grated

4½ tablespoons lemon juice

½ teaspoon allspice

½ teaspoon ground cinnamon

¼ teaspoon ground black pepper

2 teaspoons salt or to taste

I kg (2lb 2oz) Swiss chard leaves, white ribs cut off and
reserved

- Put I tablespoon of the oil on the bottom of a medium-sized thick-bottomed pan and cover with the potato slices.

- To make the filling drain the chick-peas and place them in a mixing bowl with the rice, chopped tomatoes, parsley, mint, onion and lemon juice. Add the allspice, cinnamon, pepper and I teaspoon of the salt. Add 2½ tablespoons of the oil and mix thoroughly. Bring salted water to the boil in a pan and add the Swiss chard, in batches; leave each batch for less than a minute or until it is soft and pliable. Remove and drain in a colander.

- Place one leaf on a working surface with the raised rib facing up. Slice the rib to make it level with leaf, or smooth it by pressing it down with your thumb. Place I tablespoon of the filling at the rib end, and roll the

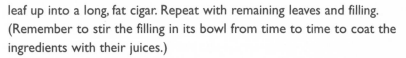
leaf up into a long, fat cigar. Repeat with remaining leaves and filling. (Remember to stir the filling in its bowl from time to time to coat the ingredients with their juices.)

- Place 3–4 reserved white ribs over the potato slices in the pan to make a level layer. Arrange the stuffed Swiss chard 'cigars' seam sides down and top with the sliced tomato. Add the remaining oil and sieve over what's left of the filling juices into the pan. Season with the remaining salt and barely cover with boiling water (about 150 ml/¼ pint). Place over high heat and bring to the boil, then cover and simmer over medium-low or low heat for 1 hour.

- Leave to cool for at least 2 hours before serving. Turn the 'cigars' upside down on to a dish, with their reduced liquid which contains many of their vitamins.

- Serve with bread and, if desired, yoghurt.

NOTE: Boil the remaining Swiss chard ribs with water to cover until tender, then stir into *Tahini* Sauce (see page 300).

❀ ✿ ❀

Potatoes with Fragrant Spices and Walnuts
Batata bil kammouneh

THIS TRADITIONAL SPECIALITY belongs to the Shiite Muslims of south Lebanon. *Kammouneh* comes from *kammoun* (cumin) and designates the most pronounced flavour of this unusual and interesting combination. It includes several fresh herbs and perfumed spices concocted by southern Lebanese from the pickings of their gardens

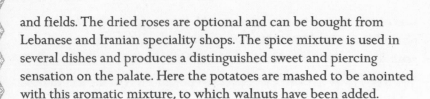

and fields. The dried roses are optional and can be bought from Lebanese and Iranian speciality shops. The spice mixture is used in several dishes and produces a distinguished sweet and piercing sensation on the palate. Here the potatoes are mashed to be anointed with this aromatic mixture, to which walnuts have been added.

3–4 medium-size potatoes, unpeeled
Freshly ground black pepper
Extra virgin olive oil

For the **kammouneh:**
1 small onion
60 g (2 oz) shelled walnuts
1 red chilli, deseeded and roughly chopped
1–2 spring onions
1 teaspoon salt or to taste
8–10 fresh basil leaves or 1 teaspoon dried basil
8 mint leaves
1 teaspoon marjoram or to taste
2 teaspoons ground cumin seeds
2 dried roses
2 tablespoons fine *burghol* (optional)

- Place the potatoes in a steaming basket and set into a pan over 2.5 cm (1 in) of boiling water. Cover and steam for about 20–30 minutes or until tender.

- Meanwhile, prepare the *kammouneh*. Place the onion, walnuts, chilli, spring onions and salt in blender and blend until quite fine. Add the basil, mint, marjoram, cumin and roses and blend for a few seconds.

- Peel and finely mash the potatoes while they are still relatively hot and knead with the *burghol*, if using. Leave to cool. Dip small pieces of the mashed potato into the *kammouneh* and arrange them on a serving plate. (It may be easier to flatten the potato piece on the plate and gently press small spoonfuls of the *kammouneh* over its surface; use a moistened spoon.) Sprinkle with pepper and drizzle with a little oil.

- Serve with a bowl of green olives.

Walnuts with Cayenne
Mhammara

THIS POWERFUL AND TASTY dip is one of my favourites. *Mhammara* comes traditionally from the south of Lebanon – its preparation varies, depending on individual taste. It is also enjoyed in Turkey and in Aleppo in northern Syria. In autumn look out for the wet walnuts and use them to make this addictive dip – it can also be served as a starter. When fresh pomegranates are in season combine some of their juice with the syrup. For a smoother taste I add a teaspoon of yoghurt or *labneh* (concentrated yoghurt); this is not authentic but give it a try some time. You could even add cream or mascarpone, both of which add flavour and smoothness.

I medium Lebanese loaf
½ teaspoon cayenne pepper or to taste
90 ml (3 fl oz) hot water
I red pepper (optional)
½–I tablespoon extra virgin olive oil
I red chilli, deseeded and roughly chopped
225 g (8 oz) shelled walnuts
I–2 tablespoons pomegranate syrup

1 tablespoon lemon juice
2 teaspoons ground cumin
¾ teaspoon salt or to taste
Pinch of white pepper
Pinch of freshly ground black pepper
1 tablespoon *labneh* (concentrated yoghurt) or yoghurt (optional)
4 tablespoons pine nuts, soaked for 30 minutes in water to cover

- Place the loaf in the oven at 200°C/400°F/Gas Mark 6 and toast until deep golden in colour and crisp. Turn the oven off and leave to cool. Remove and blend to a powder. Measure 3 tablespoons of the powder and place in a mixing bowl. Sprinkle with the cayenne and stir in the water. Place the red pepper, if using, under a preheated grill or over the hob. When it is charred peel, deseed and slice it. Put the slices in a blender, add the chilli, walnuts, powdered bread, pomegranate syrup, lemon juice, salt, black and white peppers, and blend until fine. Taste and adjust the seasonings. Stir in the yoghurt, if using. Drain the pine nuts and sprinkle them over the *mhammara*.

❉ ✿ ❉

Butter Beans in Tomato Sauce
Fassoulia baida bi-salset al banadoura

BUTTER BEANS have a distinctive flavour and, like other beans, provide a lot of nourishment. In this simple dish, the onions and garlic are not sautéed in oil as is traditional. Instead, oil is added towards the end of cooking to round up the flavour. Eating this dish with brown rice makes the meal more complete in protein. Just remember, the cooking time of beans varies with brands; for example, organic ones sometimes take longer and you may need to add more hot water. Traditionally, lamb meat and the bones from a leg of lamb are used, but this meatless version makes it a more economical dish that is still rich in nutrients.

250 g (9 oz) organic butter beans, soaked for 6–8 hours
1 medium-sized onion, finely chopped
6 garlic cloves, crushed
1 medium-size tomato, peeled and finely chopped
2–3 tablespoons double concentrated tomato purée
1½ teaspoons salt or to taste
½ teaspoon ground cinnamon
¼ teaspoon freshly ground black pepper
Handful of coriander leaves with only tender stems,
**   coarsely chopped**
½ tablespoon extra virgin olive oil (optional)

- Drain the beans, rinse under cold running water, drain again and place in a medium-large pan. Cover with 900 ml (2 pints) water and bring to the boil, skimming the foam from the surface of the water. Cover and simmer over medium-low heat for 50 minutes, or until the beans are tender. When the cooking time is up add the onion, garlic, tomato and tomato purée. Bring to the boil, then reduce the heat and simmer for 20–30 minutes. About 5 minutes before the end of the cooking time sprinkle with the salt, cinnamon, pepper and coriander and oil, if using.

- Serve hot with Vermicelli Rice (see page 54).

NOTE: Kidney beans can be prepared in the same way (omit the coriander). Wild rice marries wonderfully with beans.

Bread

No fork, no spoon and also no fingers, but a sensual way of eating.
Traditionally, a piece of bread is used to scoop food from the plate and
convey it to the mouth. Bread is not just an accompaniment, but is an
essential part of any Lebanese meal. It is hard to imagine eating a plate
of *hummous* or *foul mdammas* without it. It adds to the enjoyment of the
great Lebanese stews and of *shawarma* (Spiced Meat, see page 184), *falafel*,
meat *kebab* and chicken with their outstanding garlicky sauces. To make
a most enjoyable sandwich, spread a bread with *baba ghanouj*, top it with
kafta kebab (Fried Meat Patties, see page 180), then fold.

The consumption of bread in Lebanon may date back as far as the time
of the pharaohs. In the millennia before Christ the country was under
their influence and they made use of its timbers and quarries, if not of
its soil, when fighting the people of Mesopotamia. It is likely that wheat,
of which bread is made, was part of the exchange between the Egyptians
and the Phoenicians. During Roman times the Bekaa Valley, located
between Mount Lebanon and Anti-Lebanon, was an important granary
for the empire. Bread was, and for many still is, treated with respect,
since it is regarded as a gift from God. When a piece falls on the floor it
is picked up, kissed and put on the forehead. A menstruating woman
should not knead dough, which is also protected from *saybit al ain* (the
evil eye). During Epiphany, which falls on 6 January, a small portion of
unleavened dough is hung on, or placed next to, a fig or mulberry tree
so that it will be blessed as Christ passes, and will perpetuate. The
dough ferments and at dawn it is used to make bread.

During the First World War, a time of famine, the Sunni Muslims of
Beirut prepared a dough and rolled it out to a thickness of about ½ cm

('/4 in). It was sliced into finger-like shapes, dusted with flour and added to a pan of salted water into which a knob of *samneh* (fat or butter) had already been put. This preparation, known as *markoun*, was given to people, especially the old and children, at breakfast time to sustain them.

Two kinds of bread are prepared in Lebanon and both are much favoured: round flat loaves that vary in size, and mountain bread, *markouk*, which is paper thin and very large – approximately 50 cm (20 in) in diameter. It is most delicious, specially when drizzled with olive oil and *zaatar* (a dried blend of thyme and spices), or when spread with *labneh* (concentrated yoghurt) and olive oil and dotted with olives and mint. Another tasty filling is thin slices of *halloumi* cheese, cucumber and few leaves of fresh mint.

Markouk is artistically prepared by women who sit on low wooden chairs to be at the right level for the *saj* – a large, black iron dome, which is directly heated from below. A piece of dough is tapped down, and is then skilfully shifted from one hand to another, and from one arm to another, until the desired thickness and roundness are reached. The dough is flipped on to a round cushion and then turned over on to the hot *saj*. It browns within seconds. Nowadays, in some Lebanese restaurants you can see women preparing fresh *markouk* from start to finish; a most beautiful sight to watch.

Another great feature of the Lebanon is its many bakeries. Early in the morning, as soon as the sun spreads its rays, it is magical to see a baker throwing roughly circular bread doughs close to the powerful flames of his oven. He takes them out, puffed up and beautifully browned. The aroma of the baking bread wafts through the air and it is impossible not to be tempted. *Kaak bi simsom* are also made from bread dough. They are sold by street vendors who carry them over their heads on rectangular wooden trays. Long ago, we waited eagerly for the vendor, who used to pass by at four o'clock, to eat *kaak* as a snack.

Lebanese breads and *markouk* are both tasty and, surprisingly, they won't make you feel bloated. The breads are on sale in supermarkets while *markouk* is available from Lebanese shops. However, you can always experiment and bake your own bread at home.

Bread
Khoubz

FLAT LEBANESE LOAVES are nowadays readily available in many parts of the Western world. As this was not the case a few years ago, I used to bring breads back with me from Lebanon when I returned from visits home, not simply as a treat but because some of our dishes – *shawarma* (Spiced Meat, see page 184), *mjaddara* (Cream of Lentils, see page 58), *falafel* and *kafta* (Fried Meat Patties, see page 180), for instance – taste better with them.

Bread bought in Britain is perfectly acceptable, but if you have the time to experiment and make your own it will have a better flavour. Here dried yeast is used, but feel free to replace it with fresh or easy-blend; the only difference to the traditional recipe is that honey is included for flavour and colour.

> I heaped teaspoon honey or sugar
> 3 tablespoons lukewarm water, plus 250 ml (8 fl oz) or as necessary
> 2 teaspoons dried yeast
> 450 g (I lb) wholemeal flour, plus extra for dusting
> I ¼ teaspoons salt

- Dissolve the honey or sugar in the 3 tablespoons water, and stir in the yeast. Cover with cling film and leave to stand in a warm place for 10 minutes or until froth appears on the surface. Combine the flour and salt in a bowl, then add the yeasty water and the remaining lukewarm water, and gradually mix into the flour until firm. Turn the dough on to a lightly floured working surface and knead for 10 minutes or until the dough is smooth and elastic. Oil your hands and smooth all over the dough. Place in a bowl, cover with cling film and a tea towel and leave to rise in a warm, draught-free place for up to 2 hours.

- Preheat the oven to 230°C/450°F/Gas Mark 8 and preheat a baking tray. When the dough has doubled in size, punch it down in the centre to release the air, knead lightly and form into 6 balls. Place the balls onto a floured tray 5 cm (2 in) apart, cover and leave in a warm place to rest for 20 minutes. Remove, place each on a lightly floured surface and, with a floured rolling pin, roll them into circles 3 mm (⅛ in) thick and 13 cm (5 in) in diameter. Dust with a little flour, cover with a clean cloth and leave to rest in a warm place for another 30 minutes.

- Gently transfer the bread circles to the baking tray and bake until they have puffed up, about 8–10 minutes. Cool and store in polythene bags in the fridge. Reheat before using.

Thyme Bread
Mankoushi bi–zaatar

MANHOUSHI IS A MUCH-LOVED BREAKFAST. The Lebanese eat it anywhere, in their homes, on foot and while driving. If you stroll through the streets of Beirut early in the morning you will be inebriated by the smell of *mankoushi* coming from wood-fire ovens. To appease my homesickness I have to make my own. Prepare *bouchees manakish* for serving with cocktails.

270 g (9½ oz) plain white flour, plus extra for dusting
¾ teaspoon salt
I teaspoon easy-blend or quick-action dried yeast
I tablespoon extra virgin olive oil, plus extra for greasing
½ teaspoon honey or a good pinch of sugar (optional)
150 ml (¼ pint) lukewarm water

For the topping:
5 tablespoons *zaatar*
6 tablespoons extra virgin olive oil
I small onion, finely chopped (optional)

- Sift the flour and salt into a large bowl. Add the yeast then rub the oil well into the flour. Dissolve the honey or sugar, if using, in the lukewarm water and add gradually to the flour to form a sticky dough. Turn on to a lightly floured working surface and knead until the dough is smooth, shiny and elastic, for about 8 minutes. Form into a ball and place in a lightly floured bowl, cover with cling film and leave to rise in a warm, draught-free place for about 2 hours.

- Remove from the bowl and place on a lightly floured surface. Knead briefly, caressing the dough and rotating it under the palms of the hands. Stretch with the heel of the hand and bring back the dough towards you. Divide into 6–8 equal balls and leave to rest for about 5–8 minutes. Roll each ball lightly in flour, coating all sides to prevent sticking. With your hand flatten each ball, then roll it out with a rolling pin into a circle 3 mm (⅛ in) thick and 13 cm (5 in) in diameter. Repeat with the remaining dough balls. Cover with a clean cloth and leave to rest in a warm, draught-free place for a further 5 minutes.

- Meanwhile, make the topping. Mix the *zaatar* with the oil, and the onion if using (it gives a good flavour).

- Heat a lightly oiled heavy-bottomed non-stick pan over medium heat. Using your fingers, pinch all around each dough circle to form a rim 5 mm (¼ in) high, and place it in the pan. Spread about 1 tablespoon of *zaatar* mixture on the surface. To make the traditional patterns, bring your little fingers together to form an upside down V, and press over the surface of the circles, starting in the centre and finishing at the edges, to prevent the dough puffing up (you could also make indents with the your index finger). Wipe the *zaatar* from your hands and repeat with the other circles. Place one or two circles inside the pan. Leave to cook undisturbed for 1–2 minutes or until the base is golden brown and the edges are relatively dry. Check by lifting the side of the dough circle; if the base is golden and dry remove with a spatula and place on a baking tray. Every time you finish one or two circles, grease the pan with an oil-damped piece of cotton wool.

- Preheat the grill. Cook the circles until the tops are golden, about 1–2 minutes.

- Serve sandwiched with lots of fresh mint and spring onions.

VARIATION: A speciality of the shouf mountain region, particularly the Druse, the topping is generally made with onions, *kishk* and oil. My mother added lemon juice and ketchup to lift the taste. Mix together 2 grated onions, 4 tablesppons *kishk*, 1 teaspoon paprika, 5 tablespoons ketchup, a larger handful each of crushed walnuts ad sesame seeds, 1 tablespoon pomegranate syrup, 4 tablespoons lemon juise, ¼ teaspoon cayenne pepper and 6 tablespoons olive oil (or half oil, half water). Follow the recipe as above, but spread 3 tablespoons of this mixture on each dough circle.

Spinach Triangles
Fatayer bi-sabanekh

THIS NUTRITIOUS Lebanese speciality is made with a dough that is kneaded with olive oil, producing a lovely pastry to encase a tasty blend of spinach, onions, pine nuts and pomegranate seeds combined with exotic and aromatic spices. In Mount Lebanon they are filled with sorrel, purslane, the leaves of Swiss chard, wild chicory or with any wild herb according to season or to what grows in the region.

The triangles are an attractive accompaniment to practically any meal. They are handy when unexpected guests appear or for parties; so bake a large amount and then freeze them. Reheat as necessary.

Makes 30–32 triangles
250 g (9 oz) wholemeal or unbleached white flour, plus extra for dusting
½ teaspoon salt
2–3 tablespoons extra virgin olive oil, plus extra for greasing and brushing
100–125 ml (4–5 fl oz) lukewarm water (in winter) or as necessary

For the filling:
225 g (8 oz) spinach leaves
1¼ teaspoons salt or to taste
75 g (2½ oz) onion, finely chopped
¼ teaspoon freshly ground black pepper
3 tablespoons pomegranate seeds (in season)
½ teaspoon pomegranata syrup (optional)

2½ tablespoons pine nuts
3 tablespoons lemon juice
3 tablespoons extra virgin olive oil
¼ teaspoon cayenne pepper
1 teaspoon *sumac* (optional)

- Place the flour and salt in a large bowl, add the oil and rub into the flour. Gradually add the water. Work the dough until it is firm, then transfer to a clean surface and knead for 5–7 minutes or until smooth and elastic. Form the dough into a ball, put in a bowl, cover with a clean cloth and leave to rest for 30 minutes.

- Meanwhile, remove the tough stems from spinach leaves. Sprinkle 1 teaspoon of the salt all over them and rub until the spinach reduces in size. Squeeze out excess water, chop the leaves finely and place in a bowl. Lightly rub the onion with the remaining salt and the pepper and combine with the spinach. Add the pomegranate seeds and syrup, if using, and the pine nuts, lemon juice, oil, cayenne and *sumac*. Mix thoroughly.

- Preheat the oven to 200°C/400°F/Gas Mark 6. Remove the dough from the bowl, knead for 1 minute and divide into two equal parts. Taking one part at a time, place on a lightly floured surface and roll out the dough until it is medium-thin. Cut out circles with a 4 cm (1½ in) pastry cutter. Spoon about 1 tablespoon of the spinach mixture on to the centre of each circle. Bring up three sides of the pastry to the centre, at the same time pinching the edges firmly to seal in the filling, and form a triangle with three pronounced edges. Place the circles on a greased baking tray, brush generously with oil and bake for 15–20 minutes or until golden and crisp.

- Serve warm or at room temperature.

Fish in Pastry with Vegetables and Parsley
Fatayer bil samak

THIS ATTRACTIVE and enticing dish is simply prepared using leftover fish to which parsley, lemon juice and spices are added. However, you can add vegetables or herbs such as *habak* (basil) or *mardakouche* (marjoram). Sometimes my mother added cooked potatoes and instead of pastry used a bread dough that included some butter. Here I use ready-prepared puff pastry – organic versions without additives are available nowdays. *Fatayer bil samak* is greatly satisfying, can be prepared in any size and shape you choose and freezes well. I use turbot in this recipe, but any white fish will do. Salmon is an excellent substitute and a good way to feed omega 3 oils to children.

> 225 g (8 oz) turbot, or other white fish, or salmon
> 1¼ teaspoon salt or to taste
> Good pinch of freshly ground black pepper
> 1 tablespoon extra virgin olive oil
> 1 medium-size onion, finely chopped
> 1 carrot, about 115 g (4 oz) shredded
> 6–8 heaped tablespoons finely chopped parsley
> 60 g (2 oz) chopped mushrooms (optional)
> Knob of butter
> 2–3 tablespoons lemon juice or to taste
> Flour, for sprinkling
> 410 g (14½ oz) puff pastry sheets

• Preheat the oven to 200°C/400°F/Gas Mark 6. Sprinkle the turbot with half the salt and the pepper. Place in a steaming basket and set into a pan over 2.5 cm (1 in) of boiling water. Cover and steam for about 4 minutes. Remove and flake, and set aside. Discard the skin.

- Heat the oil in a frying pan, add the onion and sauté until transparent and lightly golden, about 1–2 minutes. Add the carrot, parsley, flaked fish, mushrooms, if using, butter and the remaining salt. Stir in the lemon juice and turn the heat off.

- Sprinkle a little flour over the puff pastry sheet then roll the pastry out as thinly as you can without tearing it. Cut out rectangles 13 cm (5 in) long and 5 cm (2in) wide, and turn them upside down so that the unfloured surface is facing you (makes about 40 pieces). Place 1 tablespoon of the fish mixturein the centre of each rectangle, fold the pastry over and pinch it with your fingers to seal. Place on a baking tray and bake until puffed up and nicely browned, about 20 minutes but follow the instructions on the puff pastry packet. Serve, or freeze and reheat when necessary.

VARIATION: If you wish, instead of pastry use the dough for the Turnovers Filled with Meat (see below), or use filo pastry and seal with tahini instead of egg yolk.

Turnovers Filled with Meat
Sambousek bi-lahm

CRISP TURNOVERS filled with delightful mixtures to suit everyone's taste. In Mount Lebanon, in coastal towns and in Beirut they are often part of a *mezzé* or a large buffet.

A poem recited at the courts of the Abbassid caliphs reflects the origins of *sambousek*; more ingredients were used then compared with today, including moist green cabbage, fresh coriander, ground cloves, cumin and ginger (I use fresh).

Makes 24–28 sambousek
250 g (9 oz) unbleached white flour, plus extra for dusting
½ teaspoon salt
30 g (1 oz) softened butter
1–2 tablespoons extra virgin olive oil
120 ml (4 fl oz) lukewarm water
Groundnut oil, for frying

For the filling:
½–1 tablespoon extra virgin olive oil
30 g (1 oz) pine nuts
1 small medium onion, finely chopped
200 g (7 oz) lean mince (preferably lamb)
Pinch of allspice
½ teaspoon ground cinnamon
¼ teaspoon freshly ground black pepper
½ teaspoon salt or to taste
1 teaspoon *sumac* (optional)
2 handfuls of parsley leaves, finely chopped

- Sift the flour and salt into a bowl, add the butter and oil and work them into the flour with your fingertips. Add the lukewarm water gradually; when the dough is firm enough, transfer to a clean, lightly floured surface and knead for 6–8 minutes. Form into a ball, place in a polythene bag and refrigerate for 30 minutes to 1 hour.

- Meanwhile, prepare the filling. Heat the oil in a heavy-based frying pan over medium-high heat and when it is hot but not smoking sauté the pine nuts until golden in colour. Remove to a side dish with a slotted spoon, allowing the oil to drip back into the pan, and set aside.

• Add the onion and mince to the pan and sauté until lightly browned, about 3–4 minutes. Stir and break any lumps with the back or side of a wooden spoon. Season with the allspice if using, cinnamon, pepper and salt. Stir well and turn off the heat. Add the *sumac*, if using, and parsley, and stir in the pine nuts. Set aside.

• Divide the dough into two equal parts. Take one part and with a rolling pin roll out over a lightly floured surface into a circle 3 mm (⅛ in) thick. Cut out circles with a 6 cm (2½ in) pastry cutter, and place 1 heaped teaspoonful of the filling in the centre of each circle, then fold the pastry over the filling to form a half-moon shape. Pinch the edges to seal. Place the *sambousek* on the extremity of your open hand and with your thumb and knuckle make a notch, knocking the pastry edge inwards to form a pleat. A simpler method is to fold the pastry over the filling and press around the edge with a fork.

• Heat the oil in a pan over medium heat and deep-fry the *sambousek* until golden brown and crisp.

• Serve with aubergine dip or hummous.

NOTE: To moisten the meat filling, stir into it 1–2 teaspoons of *labneh* (see page 224).

VARIATION: You can, if you wish, replace the meat filling with a cheese one. Mash 200 g (7 oz) white cheese (preferably a mixture of *halloumi* and goat's cheese or feta) with a large handful of chopped parsley, mint leaves or wild thyme and a pinch of white pepper and prepare as above.

Pastry with Meat and Sumac
Sfiha bi-lahmeh

Sfiha bi-lahmeh is much liked by Lebanese and the way it is prepared in south Lebanon and Baalbeck is famous. However, every region has its own version and shape, and the filling is different from one household to another. *Sumac* or pomegranate syrup may be added. The same goes for pine nuts. I like to add pomegranate seeds when the fruit is in season. The dough is lovely and can be used as a base for any other filling, and even to make Lebanese breads (pittas).

Makes 8–10
225 g (8 oz) organic all-purpose white flour, plus extra for
    dusting
Good pinch of salt
I teaspoon sugar
I teaspoon easy-blend yeast
150 ml (¼ pint) warm water or as necessary
½ tablespoon extra virgin olive oil
I teaspoon butter

For the filling:
225–250 g (8–9 oz) lamb mince
I medium-size onion
I teaspoon salt
2 small-medium tomatoes, peeled, deseeded and finely
    chopped
Pinch of ground cinnamon
Pinch of allspice

Good pinch of freshly ground black pepper
½–1 tablespoon *sumac*
30 g (1 oz) pine nuts

- Sift the flour into a mixing bowl and sprinkle with the salt, sugar and yeast. Gradually add the warm water. A sticky dough will form at first. Turn it onto a lightly floured working surface. Knead for about 4 minutes, add the oil and keep kneading, adding more water if the dough is stiff, for about 10 minutes. Form the dough into a ball. Oil your hands and coat the ball all over. Place in a deep bowl, cover with a clean cloth and leave for 2 hours to rise in a warm draught-free place.

- Meanwhile, place the mince in a bowl, grate the onion over it and sprinkle with the salt. Mix in the salt and add the tomatoes, cinnamon, allspice, pepper, *sumac* and pine nuts. Mix thoroughly and refrigerate for just under 2 hours, then remove the meat from the fridge.

- Preheat the oven to 200°C/400°F/Gas Mark 6 and grease a baking tray with clarified butter. Punch down the dough and roll it under the palm of your hand to make it into a ball. Oil your hands again and divide the dough into 8–10 equal portions. Roll the portions into small balls and place them on the baking tray. Spread them out with your fingers to form rounded-rectangular shapes and spread with equal amounts of the meat mixture. Again with your fingers, press and spread out the meat and dough.

- Bake for about 15–20 minutes or until browned. If you wish to brown the meat further, place under a hot grill for 1–2 minutes. Be careful it doesn't burn.

Soups

COULD YOU IMAGINE going through winter without a hot bowl of soup? More reason, then, to look out for recipes that today are quick to prepare. The Lebanese repertoire provides a variety of soups, from the mother of them all, wholesome chicken soup known for its medicinal properties, to the more simple, hearty and velvety lentil soup.

Lebanese soups are appreciated equally as a first or main course. Served in elegant bowls and embellished with a sprinkling of fresh herbs, they are seductive and inviting, besides being wholesome and filling. They are a wonder for the calorie-conscious and the elderly, since many of them are prepared using very little olive oil, if any. Moreover, they are not just served at ordinary meals. Soups, especially *adas bi-hamud* (Lemony Lentil Soup, see page 89), are relished and adorn the table during the holy month of Ramadan, while the meatless ones feature during the Christian Lent. During the *nafèss* (postpartum period) soups, specifically chicken soup, were given to mothers to nourish them and their babies. It is also worth mentioning that a simple chicken soup can be ceremonial. Some Christians serve it at Christmas, believing that its pronounced parsley flavour gives it a mystical dimension.

Soups are enjoyed all over the Lebanon and every region has its own speciality and style. They can be prepared ahead of time and reheated when needed. With leftover turkey and some herbs you can produce a complete nutritional one-dish meal. Soups are kind to the system, economical and bestow gastronomic gratification. How cosy and pleasing it feels after a long day's work to curl up on the sofa with a warm bowl of a soup and home-baked bread.

Soups promote mental stamina, which encourages a feeling of well-being, and in addition they supply a handful of nourishing vitamins and minerals. Working on this chapter jogged my memory of a story about a miser who had a severe chest cough and a cold. The people around him all had their opinions about what he should eat or which medication he should take. One told him to have a kind of sugary dessert (*sukkar nabat*), another mentioned a soup made with cornflour, sugar and almond oil. The miser expressed his feelings about the soup and said it was heavy on the pocket. After five days, he recounted that the sky opened up and sent him a person who recommended drinking quite hot bran water. 'So I drank it. It's so delicious and filling that I wasn't hungry any more, to the extent that I didn't need to eat before the midday prayer. By the time of lunching and washing my hands the afternoon prayer arrived. Since dinner was close to lunch I forgot the dinner. So I told the woman, "Why don't you prepare every morning the bran for the family? Its water is excellent for the chest and on the other hand it is nourishing. Besides, after its water is drunk you leave the bran to dry and come back to how it was, then you can sell it. We would have gained in that way." She replied by saying: "I hope that God gathered with your cough many benefits. It has allowed you to know the bran which benefited your body and also your purse!"'

'You are right,' said his friends, 'That sort of reasoning could only come from a divine inspiration!'

Though the miser's soup was heavy on the pocket, I can assure you that most of these soups are quite economical.

Chicken Soup with Rice and Parsley

Shorba djaj bi-roz wa bakdouness

A soothing version of chicken soup, flavoured with fresh parsley which imparts a refreshing taste. It is pleasantly satisfying, nutritious and low in fat, making it perfect as part of a healthy calorie-controlled diet. Frankly you do not need to use a whole chicken as in the recipe. Nowadays chicken pieces are readily available from supermarkets and butchers, which is useful for working and single people.

I kg (2 lb 2 oz) chicken, cleaned (see page 122) and cut
  into 4–6 pieces
I small onion, studded with I clove
I bouquet garni (2 bay leaves, 4 cardamoms, 5 black
  peppercorns, I large cinnamon stick)
80 g (3 oz) brown or white rice, preferably basmati
30 g (I oz) parsley, finely chopped
1½ teaspoons salt or to taste
Lemon wedges, to serve

• Place the chicken pieces in a large pan with 1.4 litres (2½ pints) water to cover and bring to the boil, skimming the foam from the surface of the water. Add the onion and bouquet garni, reduce the heat to medium, cover and simmer for 30 minutes. Add the brown rice and cook for a further 20–30 minutes or until the chicken and rice are tender (if using white rice add it 10 minutes before the end of cooking). A few minutes before the end of the cooking time, add the parsley, season with the salt, and taste and adjust the seasonings. Cover and finish cooking.

- Serve with lemon wedges – a few drops of lemon juice will give the soup a delicious taste.

NOTE: Before you add the parsley you can remove the chicken from broth, debone it and carve it into bite-size pieces. Discard the bones. Return chicken pieces to the pan, add the parsley and the salt and finish cooking. This makes it easier to serve and eat the soup.

❀ ❀ ❀

Lemony Lentil Soup
Adas bi-hamud

A HEARTY and substantial soup that sparkles with healthful ingredients, rich in B vitamins, minerals and fibre. Traditionally the onions are browned in olive oil and added to the lentils with the oil towards the end of cooking, as are the garlic and coriander. Omitting frying whenever possible without substantially changing the flavour is a wise healthy option. *Adas bi-hamud* has a special and regular place on most tables during the holy month of Ramadan, and Christians include it in their meals during Lent. It is also enjoyed as an everyday starter or main course.

225 g (8 oz) green lentils, picked over and rinsed
1 large onion, finely chopped
2 medium-size potatoes, unpeeled, scrubbed and cut into
   2.5 cm (1 in) cubes
5–6 Swiss chard leaves, sliced into ribbons
Sprigs of coriander, leaves and tender stems only, finely
   chopped
4 garlic cloves, crushed

1¼ teaspoons salt or to taste
¼ teaspoon freshly ground black pepper
1 tablespoon extra virgin olive oil
4 tablespoons lemon juice

- Place the lentils in a medium-size pan with 1.2–1.5 litres (2–2½ pints) water and bring to the boil over high heat. Add the onion, potatoes and Swiss chard, and bring to the boil again. Reduce the heat to medium, cover and simmer for 10–15 minutes. Add the coriander and garlic, season with the salt and pepper, stir, cover and simmer over medium-low heat for 15–20 minutes or until the lentils are soft. Add the oil towards the end of the cooking time. Remove from the heat and stir in the lemon juice.

- Serve with crunchy bread.

Creamy Lentil Soup
Crema shorba al-adas

A COMFORTING SOUP that is so quick to make. Eat with wholemeal bread and cheese to obtain a good balance of nutrients, and include foods rich in vitamin C, such as tomatoes and peppers, to enhance your body's ability to absorb the iron in the lentils. I hated this soup when I was young but my mother went out of her way to feed it to me when I had chickenpox. Bless her soul. Nowadays I love it.

225 g (8 oz) brown lentils, picked over and rinsed
1 small onion, roughly chopped
1 carrot

1 medium potato, peeled
2 Lebanese wholemeal breads, cut into 2.5 cm (1 in)
    squares
¼ teaspoon ground cinnamon
Pinch of freshly ground black pepper
1 teaspoon salt or to taste
2 tablespoons extra virgin olive oil (optional)
Large handful of parsley, finely chopped, to garnish

- Preheat the oven. Place the lentils in a pan with 1.2 litres (2 pints) water and bring to the boil over high heat. Add the onion, carrot and potato. Reduce the heat to medium-low, cover and simmer for 25–30 minutes or until the lentils are soft.

- Meanwhile, spread the bread squares out on a baking tray and bake in the oven until they are golden and crunchy. Turn the heat off and leave the bread in the oven for 10 minutes or more before removing them.

- Place the lentils and their liquid in a blender and blend until creamy. Return them to the same pan, and add the cinnamon, pepper and salt. Stir well, cover and simmer for 5 minutes.

- Serve hot garnished with parsley, with the bread squares placed over the soup. If desired, toss the squares in 2 tablespoons extra virgin olive oil just before serving.

Soup with Meat
Shorba al-ima

THIS RICH, VERY FLAVOURFUL and unusual soup is healthy and satisfying. Traditionally the cubed lamb, mini-meatballs and onions are fried in butter before being simmered in the liquid. Here I leave out this practice to avoid too much saturated fat. The liquid is enriched by the meat, which produces a delicious stock. The soup requires little preparation and is worth trying.

As leaves abandon their trees and clouds crowd the sky, *shorba al-ima* will make up for the lack of sun and give you the warmth you may need.

> *Je vis de bonne soupe et non de beau langage.*
> *Vaugelas n'apprend point à bien faire un potage;*
> *Et Malherbe et Balzac; si savants en beaux mots,*
> *En cuisine, peut-être, auraient été des sots.*
>
> Molière, *Les Femmes Savantes*

225 g (8 oz) meat from the leg of lamb, cut into 2.5 cm
    (1 in) pieces
1 bouquet garni (1 bay leaf, 1 cinnamon stick,
    4 cardamoms, 5 black peppercorns)
1 small onion, finely chopped
2 teaspoons salt or to taste
1–1½ teaspoons double concentrated tomato purée
225 g (8 oz) lean mince, preferably lamb
¼ teaspoon ground cinnamon
¼ teaspoon freshly ground black pepper
¼ teaspoon allspice
2 medium-size tomatoes, peeled and finely chopped
50 g (2 oz) short grain white rice, rinsed once and drained
50 g (2 oz) parsley, finely chopped
Lemon wedges, to serve

- Trim any extra fat from the lamb pieces and place them in a large pan with 1.5 litres (2½ pints) water. Bring to the boil over high heat, skimming the foam from the surface of the water. Add the bouquet garni and onion, bring to the boil again and reduce the heat to medium. Season with half the salt and add the tomato purée. Cover and simmer until the meat is nearly tender, about 40 minutes.

- Meanwhile, combine the mince with the cinnamon, pepper, allspice and ½ teaspoon of the remaining salt. Divide the mixture into 36 portions and roll each one with your fingers to form a cherry-size mini-meatball. Preheat the grill. Place the meatballs on an ungreased, hot baking tray and place under the grill for 5 minutes or until they are nicely browned (no need to turn them, they will cook on all sides). Add the meatballs to the lamb when its cooking time is up. Add the tomatoes and rice and bring to the boil. Reduce the heat, cover and simmer over medium heat for a further 15 minutes or until the rice and meat are soft. A few minutes before the end of cooking add the parsley to the stock and check the seasonings; if necessary, add the remaining salt.

- Serve in a large soup bowl with a dish of lemon wedges. A few drops of lemon juice enhance the flavour greatly.

Dried Pea Soup
Shorba al-bazela

SOUPS ARE THE ANSWER for anyone who is on a low budget. This very tasty thick one is a beautiful, attractive, bright green colour and it is rich in B vitamins, iron and fibre. Its velvety appearance makes it perfect to serve as a first course at dinner, accompanied by home-baked bread. Fromage frais is not a traditional addition, but I recommend it to enrich the taste. Otherwise use a little cream, excellent for flavour and for beautifying the skin. A little goes a long way.

200 g (7 oz) dried split peas, rinsed and drained
I medium-size onion, chopped
I leek, sliced
1¼ teaspoons salt or to taste
3 tablespoons fromage frais or I tablespoon cream (optional)
I tablespoon parsley, finely chopped (optional)

- Place the peas, onion, leek and salt in a large pan with 1.2 litres (2 pints) water and bring to the boil. Cover and simmer over medium heat for 40–50 minutes. Remove from the heat and gently pour into a blender. Blend until the pea mixture is smooth and creamy. Return to the same pan, and bring to the boil over medium-low heat. Add the fromage frais or cream, if using, swirl the pan, and heat gently for 1–2 minutes but do not let the soup boil again. Remove from heat and sprinkle with the parsley, if using.
- Serve with toasted wholemeal bread tossed in extra virgin olive oil.

Thick Red Lentil Soup
Shorba al-adas al ahmar

THIS SOUP IS HEALTHY and utterly satisfying. Traditionally, it uses short grain white rice and in some villages coarse *burghol* (cracked wheat) is still used. To provide more nourishment and a stronger flavour

I have used brown rice, which marries well with lentils. Because it takes longer to cook than white rice it is precooked. A good quantity of onions is sautéd in olive oil until golden brown, which contributes beautifully to the soup's flavour. For a quicker version use white basmati rice which has a delicate taste and is delicious. This does not need precooking and is added directly to the lentils in the pan.

225 g (8 oz) split red lentils, picked over and rinsed
1 teaspoon salt or to taste
85 g (3 oz) brown rice, cooked in 200 ml (7 fl oz) water
   over low heat until soft
2–3 tablespoons extra virgin olive oil
1 medium-size onion, thinly sliced in half-moon shapes
½–1 teaspoon sugar
1 teaspoon ground cumin

- Place the lentils in a large pan with 1.2 litres (2 pints) water and bring to the boil. Add the salt and simmer over medium heat for 5 minutes; partially cover the pan if the water seems a bit low. Add the rice and if necessary add more hot water (but remember this is a thick soup). Cover and simmer for 8 minutes.

- Meanwhile, heat the oil in a non-stick frying pan over medium-high heat. When it is hot but not smoking add the onions. Sauté for about 2–3 minutes, then reduce the heat and cook, stirring occasionally, until the onions are a nice golden brown colour (do not let them burn). Halfway through, sprinkle them with the sugar. Add the onions to the lentils and rice. After less than a minute, season the soup with the cumin.

- Serve immediately in separate bowls.

VARIATION: Sprinkle with cumin and spread over the onions. Sometimes I double the quantity of onions.

❈ ❁ ❈

Mung Bean Soup
Shorba al-mash

ONE OF THE HEARTIEST of soups, this is very popular in the Nabatieh village and its surroundings in south Lebanon. Mung beans grow only around this region – they are native to India and are cultivated there and in China. The beans are high in magnesium, iron and B vitamins such as niacin, thiamine and folate. Because the beans are left whole their skins float to the surface of the soup. Some people take them out but I don't. Besides I like to blend the soup while still keeping its gritty feel. I also add rice, to make sure there are enough body-building amino acids. If you fancy using brown rice remember to cook it beforehand and add it to the soup about 5–8 minutes before the end of the cooking time.

> 175 g (6 oz) mung beans, rinsed and drained
> 2–3 tablespoons extra virgin olive oil
> I large onion, finely chopped
> I teaspoon salt or to taste
> 30 g (I oz) white rice, preferably basmati
> Slices of lime or Seville oranges (optional)

- Place the beans in a medium-size pan with 1.2 litres (2 pints) water and bring to the boil. Cover and simmer over medium-low heat for about 25 minutes. Reduce the heat to low and continue simmering until the beans are soft. Meanwhile, heat 1½ tablespoons of the oil in a small, preferably non-stick, pan. Add the onion and sauté, stirring occasionally, until dark brown in colour.

- When the beans have been simmering for 30 minutes, measure about 5–8 tablespoons of the stock and stir this into the browned onions. Simmer the onions over very low heat until the liquid evaporates, then turn the heat off and add the remaining oil. Give the contents of the pan a good stir.

- Pour the beans and their liquid into a blender and blend the mixture to a medium-smooth texture. Return it to the same pan and bring to the boil. Add the salt and rice and cook until it is tender (about 6–7 minutes), stirring occasionally so that it does not stick to the pan. A minute before the end of cooking add the onions and oil, and stir. Serve hot with a crusty bread.

VARIATION: If desired, sauté some sliced onions in olive oil until they are deep golden in colour (see Cream of Lentils, page 58). This will embellish the soup and add extra flavour.

Fish

IN 1915 AMIN AL-RIHANI, a great Lebanese writer contemporary
with Kahlil Gibran, published *Zanbakat al-Ghor* (Lily of the Valley),
in which one of his characters said, 'Fish is the most digestible and
nutritious meal'. Long before that the Hebrews had attributed an
additional virtue to fish which they called *dag*, denoting fecundity.

During the early Christian era, especially during periods of persecution,
fish symbolized Christ, as is reflected by a mosaic depicting fish found
in a house at Pompeii. Fish has, too, a special status in the holy Quran,
the sacred book of Islam; while the destruction of all animals, except
noxious ones, is forbidden during the pilgrimage, fishing in the sea is
permitted (s. 5: 97).

Fish is highly valued all over the world, in particular for its delicate flesh
and adaptability to various ways of cooking. Still, not everyone thought
so, as suggested by an old French saying: '*La sauce fait manger le poisson*'
(Sauce helps the fish go down). It must have been some sort of an
eccentric who risked such an emphatic statement. In my experience, in
addition to their healthful qualities many fish – like sea bass, sea bream,
red mullet and numerous others – have a wonderful flavour when they
are just grilled, baked or fried. The different sauces in my recipes
complement the fish, to make the dishes more imaginative and satisfy
the Lebanese palate which likes variety.

The Lebanese are great lovers of fish – the sea stretches along Lebanon's
entire length, some 220 kilometres from Nahr al-Kabir in the north to
Ras Nakura in the south, overlooked by various-sized cliffs and hills,
and mountains that are crowned by snow for most of the year.

Historic towns are scattered along Lebanon's coast: Tripoli (site of a Crusaders' fortress and then a Mamluk stronghold), Byblos (the world's oldest town, still inhabited, where the alphabet was invented – and from where the cedars to build the sacred ship of Amon in Egypt were sent), Beirut (basically Ottoman, then a cosmopolitan city), Sidon (the oldest fishing settlement in history) and Tyre (famous for its desperate resistance to Alexander the Great). Phoenicians, Greeks, Romans, Byzantines, Crusaders, Arabs, Ottomans and French have in turn occupied these cities and left an imprint on Lebanon's culture and way of life, and definitely on its culinary traditions.

From ancient times to the present fishing methods have probably remained the same. Fishermen leave in their small boats in the middle of the night; the faint glow of their lanterns sprinkles light on the dark blue waters, seemingly rendering back the reflections of the stars in the clear sky. They silently await their catch, which will be sold to the many restaurant owners who wait to buy as their first choice the most favoured fish in Lebanon – the *sultan ibrahim* (red mullet) – and thus meet the demands of the innumerable customers who fill rustic and inexpensive restaurants as well as more elegant and expensive ones.

With today's growing awareness of health, the nutritional value of fish is increasingly recognized. It provides a good mixture of lightness, taste and nourishment, and is low in fat and high in the polyunsaturates that protect arteries from damage; it is an excellent source of protein and iodine, is easily digestible and contains a significant amount of essential amino acids.

In the Levant basin of the Mediterranean as many as 324 species of fish are listed, of which 177 are in the coastal waters of Lebanon. I will name those which are most commonly used in cooking.

Sultan ibrahim (red mullet) is the most expensive. The most sought-after one in Lebanon is small, and will be deep-fried until crisp and served hot. It has a distinctive and wonderful flavour, and looks marvellous when served in quantity on a large platter covered with fried bread and always accompanied by lots of lemon wedges and a bowl of *tahini*. In restaurants it is brought to the table after the *mezzé* and served as a main dish.

The *lukos* (sea bass) is also a delicacy with its firm flesh and subtle flavour. It is quite large and is served as a main dish. It can be either seasoned with herbs and baked, or served cold as *samakeh harra* (chilli fish), one of the many dishes for a buffet.

The *farride* (sea bream) can weigh as much as 3.5 kg (8 lb). It is tasty and costs less than sea bass, which it can replace in *samakeh harra*. Small specimens (about 14 cm/5½ inches long) are deep-fried and served as a main dish, accompanied by fried pitta bread and lemon wedges.

Next there are different kinds of tiny fish: *sultan ibrahim bizri* (red mullet babies) are golden red; *samak bizri* (whitebait), which are light silver grey; and garfish babies, similar to sardines but lighter in colour. All are served hot or warm, mostly as a starter, and washed down with *arak*, the favourite native alcoholic drink.

Tuna, called *balamida* is a silver-blue grey. Its flesh is firm, strong in flavour and dry. My mother used it in *tagen al-samak* (Fish with Tahini, see page 103) where its dryness was camouflaged by *tahini* and onions.

These are the fish that are most commonly seen on Lebanese tables. There are many more including *samakat al-hafsh* (sturgeon) which is considered inferior to sea bass. It has a meaty white flesh and can be used for *sayadieh* (fish with rice and cumin) or *samakeh harra*; stickleback, called *samakat al-shok* in Beirut and *ikais* in the north, has a dark silver-grey colour for the male and a light silver-grey for the female. It has to be handled carefully as its fins are slightly poisonous. Nonetheless it is a good fish for frying. Fishermen use a lilac leaf to attract the *samakat al-zalak* (rabbit fish or spine-foot). It is good grilled – juicy with a mild flavour. *Hankliss* (eel) is another tasty fish and is mostly fried. And then there are the sea animals and shellfish like *al-kalam* (calamari), *sabideg* (squid), *akhtabout* (octopus), *karakand* (lobster) and, lastly, shrimps. All these are scarce and are generally prepared following western recipes.

There was a time when the Lebanese could not imagine eating anything but fresh fish. Frozen ones were snubbed. Although hard times have changed this, whenever possible they still favour fresh fish recognizable by their bright, bulging eyes, reddish gills, firm flesh and unadulterated odour. Frozen fish should not be refrozen once it has thawed.

Never overcook fish as it will lose its moistness and flavour. Ask your fishmonger to scale the fish for you and cut its fins; this will save you some work. Otherwise grasp the tail firmly, and with a sharp knife remove the scales as well as the fins. Rub fish with a piece of lemon to remove any rank odour, then wash it in cold running water and keep it in the coolest place in your refrigerator until it is ready to be cooked. If it is very fresh it should keep for two days but it is best to cook fish on the day of purchase. Always bear in mind this Spanish proverb, which embodies popular wisdom: 'Guests and fish stink on the third day.'

The fish recipes chosen for this book taste delicious and are aesthetically attractive.

Fried Red Mullet
Sultan ibrahim mikli

SULTAN, A TITLE OF HONOUR, indicates the pre-eminence of red mullet among fish.

During a visit to Beirut I was taken for lunch to a restaurant located on the outskirts of the picturesque and historical town of Byblos. The unpretentious restaurant, Ain-Al-Tufaha (Apple's Source), which is built on rocks alongside the sea, turned out to serve good yet simple food. What I really wanted to do was chat to the owner who is a real fisherman. He was not very talkative and I could barely extract any information.

He advised my host to have the fresh yield of the day, which was red mullet and sea bream instead of sea bass. In a matter of seconds our table was laid with a *mezzé* consisting of nearly a dozen wonderfully tasty dishes, such as *hummous* (Chick-pea Dip, see page 34), *tabbouleh* (Cracked Wheat Salad, see page 4), fried aubergines and *fattouche* (Bread Salad, see page 6). This was followed by the most glorious platter of *sultan ibrahim* covered with golden-coloured Lebanese breads (they are cut into quarters before being fried in the oil in which the fish was cooked), accompanied by a dish of lemon wedges, a bowl of *tahini* and French fries. The meal deserved three Michelin stars.

4 small or medium-size red mullets, gutted and scaled
Plain flour, for dredging
3–4 tablespoons groundnut or olive oil, for frying
Salt
Freshly ground black pepper to taste (optional)

- Wash the fish in cold running water, pat dry with kitchen paper and score diagonal cuts on each side. Sprinkle inside and out with salt, and pepper, if using. Leave to stand for a few minutes then dredge in flour. Shake off excess.

- Heat the oil in a frying pan big enough to take the four mullets. When it is hot but not smoking add the fish and cook for about 3–4 minutes on each side. Shake the pan now and then.

- Serve with lemon wedges, fried Lebanese bread and a bowl of *Tahini* Sauce (see page 300).

Fish with Tahini
Tagen al-samak

THIS IS NOURISHING and heavenly – more so when it is eaten at room temperature, as it is in some fish restaurants in Beirut and in others along the coast, where it is served as part of a *mezzé*. *Tagen al-samak* consists of fish steaks, onions and *tahini* (sesame paste). In Lebanon thrifty housewives used the leftovers of any baked fish to make *tagen* and it is said the dish originated from this practice. The recipe does not bind you to one kind of fish. I find, for instance, that tuna blends well with *tahini*, which moistens its dryness. Sea bass is favoured traditionally; however, any other white fish will do. It appears that the ninth-century Arabic poet Ibn er Rumi had a desire and fondness for fish. In nine poems out of ten he urges a friend to keep his promise to supply fish regularly.

4 cod fillets, skinned
I teaspoon salt or to taste
¼ teaspoon freshly ground black pepper or to taste

Plain flour, for dredging
3–4 tablespoons extra virgin olive oil
170 g (6 oz) onions, thinly sliced into half-moon shapes
100 ml (4 fl oz) *tahini*
90–100 ml (3–4 fl oz) lemon juice or juice of 2 Seville
   oranges
Handful of finely chopped parsley

- Preheat the oven to 180°C/350°F/Gas Mark 4. Wash the cod in cold running water, pat dry with kitchen paper and sprinkle with the salt and pepper. Dredge in flour, shaking off excess. Leave the fish in a cool place to absorb the seasonings.

- Meanwhile heat 2 tablespoons of the oil in a medium-size, non-stick frying pan. Add the onions and sauté over moderately high heat, stirring frequently, for about 2 minutes. Reduce the heat to medium and cook until the onions are golden in colour. Remove the onions with a slotted spoon, allowing the oil to drip back into pan, and spread them evenly in a baking dish. Heat the remaining oil in the same pan over medium heat. Add the fish and sauté for about 2 minutes on each side. Remove gently with a spatula and place over the onions in the baking dish.

- Put the *tahini* in a bowl and gradually whisk in the lemon or orange juice and 150 ml (¼ pint) water. Continue to whisk until the sauce has the consistency of single cream.

- Pour the sauce over the fish and onions in the baking dish and sprinkle with the parsley. Bake in the oven for about 18–20 minutes or until the top is pale brown.

- Serve hot with Vermicelli Rice (see page 54) and an Oriental Salad (see page 12) or at room temperature with Lebanese bread. A plate of fresh radishes makes a pleasant and healthy accompaniment.

Fish with Rice and Cumin
Sayadieh

SAYADIEH comes from the word *sayad* (fisherman). It is said that this dish was originally created by *sayadine* (fishermen) and with time has become more sophisticated. It reflects the pleasure Lebanese take in cooking fish. Delicious and fragrant, *sayadieh* is favoured by the locals of Tripoli in the north of Lebanon and is also popular all along the coast. In some restaurants it is served as a *plat du jour*, normally on Fridays. In homes it crowns the table on special occasions or to honour guests. A hostess feels great pride when she serves it, since preparing this dish and achieving the right flavour requires delicacy. Don't we all think that getting the perfect texture of a fish can be tricky! *Sayadieh* may be elaborate – its preparation requires time and a little patience, especially the first time you make it – but once you get acquainted with the process and have tasted it you'll be hooked and find the results rewarding. For this dish I normally choose a sea bass. However, any fleshy white fish like cod (which needs to be dredged in flour and sautéd before it is served) will do, as long as you have a fish head and bones to add that essential flavour to the stock, an elementary part of a tasty dish.

To ease its preparation it is best to think of it in stages: poaching the fish, separating the stock, sautéing the onions and so on. For parties of ten or more it is easier to immerse fillets of sea bass in the aromatized, fresh-tasting home-made fish stock to simmer gently. One final touch: pine nuts and almonds. This enriches the presentation and tempts diners. I find that flaked almonds marry well with the delicate fish and pine nuts.

150 ml (¼ pint) extra virgin olive oil
Handful of pine nuts
3 medium onions, thinly sliced
I kg (2 lb 2 oz) sea bass with head, gutted, scaled and
    halved
3 teaspoons salt or to taste
I bouquet garni: I large cinnamon stick, 2 bay leaves,
    4 cardamoms, 6–8 black peppercorns, 2 parsley sprigs,
    I coriander sprig
275 g (10 oz) long grain white rice, preferably basmati
I–1¼ teaspoons ground cumin
¼–½ teaspoon ground cinnamon
Good pinch of white pepper

For the sauce:
I–2 teaspoons plain flour
Good pinch of ground cumin
Good pinch of ground cinnamon
3 tablespoons lemon juice or to taste

- Heat ½ tablespoon of the oil in a medium-size frying pan, add the pine nuts and sauté until golden. Remove to a side dish. Heat the remaining oil in the pan and sauté the onions until really dark brown, about 10–15 minutes, stirring occasionally.

- Meanwhile, rinse the sea bass under cold running water, dry with kitchen paper and sprinkle inside and out with 2 teaspoons of the salt. Leave to stand for a few minutes. Make a bed of the bouquet garni on the base of a medium-size pan and place the fish over it. Cover with 1.2 litres (2 pints) water and bring to the boil. Reduce the heat and simmer over medium-low heat for 5–6 minutes. Remove the fish and as soon as it is easy to handle, remove its flesh, cover with a little stock to keep moist, and set aside. Return only the head, bones and skin to the stock in the pan. Bring to the boil, cover and simmer over low heat for 15 minutes. Strain the stock into a bowl, and discard the head, bones, skin and bouquet garni. Return the stock to the same pan.

- Remove the dark brown onions from the frying pan with a slotted spoon and add to the fish stock (in Lebanon the oil is also added). Cook over low heat for 8–10 minutes to soften the onions and give a chestnut colour to the stock. Remove the browned onions and, with the back of a spoon, force them through a sieve set over a bowl, adding a little stock to ease them through. Scrape the onions on the back of the sieve into the bowl. Mix with the remaining stock and give it all a good stir. Place 300 ml (½ pint) of the stock in a pan with 150 ml (¼ pint) water and combine well. Add the rice and bring to the boil. Reduce the heat, cover and simmer over low heat for 8 minutes or until the stock has been absorbed. A few minutes before it dries out add the cumin, cinnamon and pepper. When time is up turn the heat off.

- Finally, prepare the sauce. Place the remaining stock in a pan, whisk in the flour making sure no lumps form, and bring to the boil. Allow to thicken and reach a velvety consistency, about 5 minutes at the most. Stir in the cumin, cinnamon and lemon juice. Turn the heat off. The flavour of the sauce should be sharp yet smooth and subtle.

- To assemble the dish, divide the fish into medium-size pieces. Place the rice on a warm serving dish and spread the fish over it. Sprinkle with the pine nuts and serve the sauce separately.

Chilli Fish
Samakeh harra

ANOTHER SIMPLE and highly nourishing fish dish. *Samakeh harra* is a favourite of the coastal people in Lebanon, especially the inhabitants of Tripoli in the north where it originated. It is also appreciated by my non-Lebanese friends.

Traditionally the fish, usually sea bass or *miskar* (dogfish), is baked and the bones are removed. The flesh is then artistically reconstituted and covered with a cream-like sauce with a tangy, nutty and spicy flavour. In this recipe the fish is grilled and the bones remain in situ.
I have used sea bass, but hake is more economical.

> 1 x 900 g (2 lb) sea bass, gutted and scaled
> 1¼ teaspoons salt or to taste
> ¼ teaspoon freshly ground black pepper
> ¼ teaspoon ground cinnamon or to taste
> 1 garlic clove, pounded until creamy
> 2 stems of coriander with leaves
> 1 thick slice of lemon (with rind), cut into 6 pieces
> 2 tablespoons extra virgin olive oil
>
> *For the sauce:*
> 5–6 tablespoons *tahini*
> 4–6 tablespoons lemon juice
> Juice of 1 orange or Seville orange (in season)
> 1½ tablespoons extra virgin olive oil
> 4–6 large cloves garlic, chopped
> 1 red chilli, deseeded and finely chopped

Handful of coriander leaves and tender stems, finely chopped
¼ teaspoon cayenne pepper
60 g (2 oz) pine nuts, finely chopped
80 g (3 oz) shelled walnuts, finely chopped
½ teaspoon salt

- Wash the sea bass in cold running water, pat dry with kitchen paper and score 3 diagonal cuts on each side. Sprinkle with the salt and pepper. Rub cavity with the cinnamon and garlic, then fill it with the coriander and lemon slices. Place in a baking dish and smear inside and out with the oil. Marinate in the fridge for 1 hour to allow the fish to absorb the seasonings. Remove from the fridge 5 minutes before cooking. Preheat the grill and cook the fish for about 7 minutes, then gently turn it over to grill the other side until the skin flakes. If you prefer, you can bake the fish (see page 112 for method).

- Meanwhile, make the sauce. Place the *tahini* in a bowl and gradually whisk in the lemon juice and the orange juice, if using. Add 6–7 tablespoons water and keep whisking until the liquid is smooth. Set aside. Heat the oil in a frying pan over medium-low heat, add the garlic and sauté it for a few seconds, but do not let it brown. Add the chilli, coriander, cayenne, pine nuts and walnuts. Give them a good stir and add the *tahini* mixture. Cook for about 1 minute, stirring frequently, and remove from heat before the sauce thickens.

- Remove the fish from the grill and leave for a few seconds as it will be hot, then carefully peel off the skin, leaving the head intact. Spread the sauce over all the fish except its head, or serve the sauce separately.

- Serve warm or at room temperature. During spring or summer accompany with *tabbouleh*.

Fish Kibbeh
Kibbeh al-samak

THIS EXCEPTIONAL RECIPE is another favourite of mine. It is said that *kibbeh al-samak* was originally prepared during Lent by the inhabitants of Lebanon's coastal towns, and was soon adopted enthusiastically by most Lebanese.

Traditionally sturgeon or sea bass, both white and meaty, are used for this dish. Here I have used cod, which is versatile and blends successfully with other ingredients. A good substitute is monkfish.

Kibbeh al-samak is ideal for parties and has the advantage that it can be prepared in advance. Its taste matures wonderfully by the following day.

120 ml (4 fl oz) extra virgin olive oil
500 g (1 lb 1 oz) onions, thinly sliced into half–moon shapes
½ teaspoon saffron threads
¼ teaspoon turmeric
¼ teaspoon white pepper
¼ teaspoon salt

For the dough:
1 onion (about 85 g/3 oz)
¼–½ teaspoon grated orange zest
¼ teaspoon freshly ground black pepper
¼ teaspoon ground cinnamon
½ teaspoon salt
175 g (6 oz) fine *burghol*
550 g (1¼ lb) cod fillets, skinned and cut into chunks
4 tablespoons plain flour

6–8 sprigs of coriander, leaves and tender stems only
75 ml (3½ fl oz) extra virgin olive oil

- Preheat the oven to 180°C/350°F/Gas Mark 4. Heat the oil in a frying pan and when it is hot but not smoking add the onions and sauté for 3 minutes. Reduce the heat to medium and continue cooking until the onions are golden in colour, stirring frequently. Add the saffron, turmeric, pepper and salt and stir well. Remove from the heat and spread evenly over the base of a baking dish.

- Make the dough. Grate the onion over a mixing bowl. Add the orange zest and sprinkle with the pepper, cinnamon and salt. Rinse the *burghol* and quickly squeeze out the excess water. Mix with the onions and spices in the bowl. Rub the fish chunks with the flour and shake off the excess.

- In a blender, alternately add the fish chunks and coriander, and blend to a uniform consistency. Gradually add the *burghol*. Blend for a few more seconds to combine well. Remove the resulting moist dough. Take a small portion of it, flatten it between your palms and place it over the onion mixture in the baking dish; dip your hands in flour as the dough may be sticky. Repeat until all the onions are covered.

- Smooth the surface, cover with the oil and quickly cut a criss-cross pattern into the dough, right down to the onions, allowing the oil to seep through. Bake for 30 minutes or until the top is nicely browned. Remove from the oven and leave to cool slightly.

- With a small palette knife, remove the lozenges of *kibbeh* following the criss-cross pattern. Place them in a serving dish with the onions facing upwards. You can adjust the onions if some portions have less than others.

- Serve warm or cold with Cabbage Salad (see page 8).

Baked Fish
Samak mishwi

IN LEBANON UNTIL the 1950s, before people had ovens in their homes and when each corner had its baker, fish was wrapped in newspaper and sent to the local bakery to be cooked. *Samak mishwi* is excellent to serve for buffets. Accompany with the classic *Tahini* Sauce (see page 300), which adds a succulent flavour to the dish, and a separate bowl of lemon wedges.

Here again I use sea bass, one of my favourite fish. However, hake or sea bream are also good choices. Sometimes when baking or grilling I don't scale the fish. However, I remove the skin before serving. If you like your fish with the skin it must be scaled.

1 x 900 g (2 lb) sea bass, gutted
1 teaspoon salt, or to taste
¼ teaspoon freshly ground black pepper or to taste
¼ teaspoon freshly grated nutmeg
¼ teaspoon ground cinnamon
2 slices of lemon (with peel), halved
1 small onion, sliced
2 stems of coriander or parsley with leaves
2–3 tablespoons extra virgin olive oil

• Preheat the oven to 180°C/350°F/Gas Mark 4. Rinse the fish under cold running water, pat dry with kitchen paper and score 2 diagonal cuts on each side. Sprinkle inside and out with the salt and pepper. Rub the cavity with the nutmeg and cinnamon and fill with the lemon and onion slices and the coriander or parsley. Place in a baking dish and smear inside and out with the oil. Allow a few minutes for the fish to absorb the seasonings, then bake for about 20 minutes. Do not overcook, as it will become dry and chewy. Remove from the oven, peel off the skin and place on a warm serving dish.

- Serve with lemon wedges and a bowl of *tarrator bi-bakdouness* (*tahini sauce with parsley*) or potato salad in a *tahini* sauce.

VARIATION: Combine finely chopped green pepper and finely chopped red chilli with 2 teaspoons *zaatar*, minced garlic, lemon juice and olive oil. Stuff some inside the cavity of the fish and spread the rest all over the fish (except the head). Bake as above or grill on a barbecue.

Fried Whitebait
Samak bizri makli

SOMAK, BIZRI, OR WHITEBAIT are traditionally fried in olive oil until crisp. They are served as an appetizer with lemon wedges and sometimes a bowl of *Tahini* Sauce (see page 300). For some people, sipping *arak* (a drink based on aniseed) with *samak bizri* is a must.

These tiny fish are not gutted and may taste bitter, but my mother gave me a tip to avoid this: soak the fish for half an hour in lemon juice or milk. I recommend the latter which, in my opinion, renders the fish more delicious.

Another tip was given to me by a woman fishmonger who presides over a stall in the amazing Marche Forville in Cannes in the south of France. Her advice was to soak the fish in beer for 15 minutes then fry them until crisp in hot oil. Indeed, it works wonderfully. However, mixing the

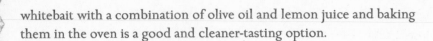

whitebait with a combination of olive oil and lemon juice and baking them in the oven is a good and cleaner-tasting option.

450 g (1 lb) whitebait
Milk
Plain flour
Olive oil, for frying
Salt to taste
Pinch of freshly ground black pepper
Lemon wedges

- Place the whitebait in a bowl with milk to cover and leave for about an hour in a cool place. Drain, pat dry, dredge in the flour and shake off any excess.

- Heat the oil in a frying pan until hot but not smoking. Add a few whitebait at a time and fry, shaking the pan gently to prevent the fish sticking. Cook until crispy and light gold in colour. Remove the fish from the pan, drain on kitchen paper and sprinkle with salt and black pepper.

- Arrange on a serving dish with lemon wedges. If desired, accompany with *Tahini* Sauce (see page 300) as a dip.

Fish with Rice
Samak bi-roz

TRADITIONALLY THIS SUCCULENT saffron-scented dish is prepared with sea bass or another meaty fish. My choice here is monkfish, which I came to like after I settled in England. It has a firm texture that holds well while cooking, and a delicious subtle taste. Because ground saffron loses its flavour, especially when stored for a long time, I favour the use of saffron threads. They release a wonderful aroma and a beautiful yellow-orange colour.

2 tablespoons extra virgin olive oil
Handful of pine nuts
I medium-size onion, thinly sliced into half-moon shapes
½ teaspoon saffron threads
½ teaspoon turmeric
675 g (I½ lb) monkfish, cut into about 16 equal pieces
225 g (8 oz) long grain white rice, preferably basmati
I½ teaspoons salt or to taste
¼ teaspoon white pepper

- Heat the oil in a pan, add the pine nuts and stir until golden in colour. Remove to a side dish. Add the onion to the same oil and sauté for 2–3 minutes, stirring frequently, until it loses its strong smell and becomes golden in colour. Stir in the saffron and turmeric and 450 ml (¾ pint) water and bring to the boil. Add fish pieces and rice, stir and return to the boil. Reduce the heat to medium-low and season with the salt and pepper. Cover and simmer for 8–10 minutes or until the water has been absorbed by the rice. Remove from the heat but keep the pan covered for a few minutes, to allow the flavours to blend.

- Spread over a warm serving dish and garnish with the pine nuts. Serve with Cabbage Salad (see page 8) or Bread Salad (see page 6).

❀ ❁ ❀

Prawns
Kraidis mikli

ALONG THE LEBANESE SHORES small prawns are found in limited quantities and for a short season (summer). Traditionally, they are not prepared elaborately but are simply boiled; their small size renders them unsuitable for grilling. Some years ago, under the combined influence of the East and the West, prawns started to be served either in curry or *à la provençale*.

This recipe was prepared in my kitchen with my friend Yankit So, the eminent writer of Chinese cookery books. The prawns were marinated in the Chinese style, then fried the Lebanese way in olive oil, garlic and a splash of lemon juice. The result was much more interesting than if they had been merely fried.

> **12 large raw prawns in their shells**
> **½ teaspoon salt**
> **1 teaspoon cornflour**
> **1 tablespoon egg white, beaten lightly**
> **3–4 tablespoons extra virgin olive oil**
> **1–2 large garlic cloves, pounded until creamy**
> **3 tablespoons lemon juice**
> **1 tablespoon chopped parsley**

- Shell the prawns: hold each one between your fingers and using a pointed knife make a slit along its back, removing and discarding the black vein, if any.

- To marinate the prawns, place them in a mixing bowl, add the salt and stir in one direction for about few seconds. Add the cornflour and egg white and stir again as before. Cover and refrigerate for 2–4 hours. This will make the prawns crisper in texture. Remove the prawns from fridge and just before frying separate them.

- Heat the oil in a frying pan and when it is really hot add the prawns. Sauté for about 20 seconds, then add the garlic, stirring all the time, and continue this operation for about 30 seconds or until the prawns become pinkish in colour, and curl up at the same time. At this point add the lemon juice, stir once and remove from heat.

- Serve with the juices from the frying pan.

❀ ❀ ❀

Fish with Almonds
Samak bi-loz

THIS PRACTICAL AND EASY recipe reflects a style of French cooking, and makes a luxury lunch or dinner – or even a treat for yourself.

Originally trout was used for *samak bi-loz*, even though it was never abundant in Lebanon's rivers until farming was introduced in the 1960s. Since then it has been served in restaurants near trout farms such as Sad al Karoun in the western Bekaa Valley, or in Chtoura, a town where shops, cafés and restaurants line both sides of the main road offering local produce on the road to Damascus. Here I have used Dover sole, which is as succulent as Lebanon's trout.

> 2 tablespoons extra virgin olive oil
> 4 tablespoons almond flakes
> 2 Dover soles, filleted into 8 fillets

15 g (½ oz) unsalted butter
¾ teaspoon salt or to taste
I tablespoon lemon juice

- Heat the oil in a large, non-stick frying pan, and when it is hot but not smoking add the almond flakes. Sauté until golden in colour. Remove with a slotted spoon and set aside, allowing the oil to drip back into the pan.

- Rinse the fillets under cold running water and pat dry with kitchen paper. Heat the butter with the oil in the pan, add the fish fillets and sauté for about 3 minutes over medium heat. Turn gently on to the other side and sauté. Sprinkle with the salt and almonds and leave on the heat for a few more seconds. Finally, splash all over with the lemon juice, if using. Remove the fillets and almonds and place on a warm serving dish or on separate plates.

- Serve immediately with Purslane Salad (see page 10) and fried or grilled aubergines.

❀ ❀ ❀

Chilli Fish with Pine Nuts
Samakeh harra bil-snoubar

AS A GENERAL RULE *Samakeh harra* is prepared with *lukoz ramli*, which is similar to sea bass. However, I decided to make it with halibut which has thick white meat. It is a coastal dish prepared in Tripoli, the historic city of north Lebanon where the Crusaders' fortress still stands. Its preparation and presentation differ slightly from house to house. For instance, some people make it with pine nuts, while others use walnuts.

500 g (1 lb 1 oz) halibut, cut into 4 pieces
1¼ teaspoons salt or to taste
Pinch of freshly ground black pepper
90 g (3 oz) pine nuts
3 tablespoons *tahini*
4–5 tablespoons lemon juice
Juice of 2 clementines
1 red chilli, deseeded
1¼ tablespoons extra virgin olive oil
175 g (6 oz) onions, thinly sliced
½ teaspoon ground coriander
1–2 large handfuls of fresh coriander leaves, chopped
Good pinch of cayenne pepper

- Sprinkle the fish with ¾ teaspoon of the salt and the pepper and set aside. Place the pine nuts, *tahini*, lemon and clementine juices and the chilli in a blender and blend until smooth.

- Heat the oil in a non-stick frying pan and add the onions and the remaining salt. As the onions become translucent and reduce in size, about 2 minutes, reduce the heat to low and cook them gently until they are a deep golden colour. Add 4 tablespoons of water and continue simmering until it evaporates.

- Meanwhile, place the fish in a steaming basket and set it into a pan over 2.5 cm (1 in) of boiling water. Cover and steam for 4–5 minutes.

- When the onions are ready, add the ground and fresh coriander, stir for a few seconds and add the pine nut and *tahini* mixture. Bring to the boil, stirring, then turn the heat off before the sauce thickens too much.

- Place the sauce in a warm serving dish, spread the fish over it, sprinkle with the cayenne and serve.

Poultry and Eggs

UNTIL A FEW DECADES AGO chickens were highly valued and raised particularly for eggs. Older ones were sacrificed for the cauldron, to make a meal for a festive occasion or an eminent visitor. After childbirth, a mother used to be fed for 40 days on traditional chicken soup or stuffed chicken until all her strength was regained. The belief that the soup is invigorating and curative is an old one. It is said that centuries ago Maimonides, the Jewish philosopher and scholar, used it to treat Saladin's son for asthma.

When the battery rearing of chickens became customary in the 1960s the quality dropped but so did the price, with the result that chicken was cheaper than other meat and it became popular. Various recipes then evolved, for chicken is versatile and adopts the flavours derived from the spices, aromatic herbs or vegetables of any given recipe.

It has been demonstrated that health is closely linked with diet; certain foods strengthen the immune system and protect the body from degenerative diseases. Chicken has regained favour as a good source of protein with a low fat content. According to the Arabic philosopher Ibn Jazlah, it is an excellent food for all. The Arabic poet Ibn er Rumi (d. 896) described foods he craved. He presented them to the reader as paintings. He compared the yellow colour of chickens to the gold of a dinar, and said that once they are skinned their flesh is like silver, while their plumpness in his eyes can be compared with that of a goose. Chickens may not be gold or silver, but they are certainly delicious.

The following recipes are simple, enjoyable to experiment with, and most of all constitute good nourishment. Chicken is combined with rice, spices, aromatic herbs, vegetables, pine nuts or almonds, and is baked, grilled, simmered or sautéd. All the dishes are prepared with a small quantity of olive oil. Some recipes are elaborate and suitable for special occasions, others are quick to put together for everyday dinners, with the great advantage that they can be prepared ahead of time.

A chicken can carry harmful bacteria, which thorough cooking destroys. Freshly cooked, it can be kept in the refrigerator for up to two or three days.

The secret of good cooking lies in buying good quality produce, preparing all the ingredients needed beforehand, and tasting and checking the food halfway through cooking so you can adjust the seasonings and liquid.

Free-range chickens are generally best because they are allowed to grow freely and are fed on natural food; I also use corn–fed ones, which are flavourful, and which have a distinctive yellow colour derived from the corn. Nowadays both varieties are widely available and for our convenience they are sold in individual pieces. Some of my recipes call for pieces of chicken. I mostly use the white meat, but if you wish you can select the dark meat or mix the two.

In most of the recipes the skin is removed to cut down on fat; in roasting, however, the skin and fat protect the flesh from drying out.

Cleaning a chicken

REMOVE ALL VISIBLE FAT around the neck and tail, remove the giblets from the cavity, sprinkle the chicken generously with salt and rub inside and out with half a lemon to rid it of any rank odour. The use of lemon is essential for me in this process. This is the way my mother used to prepare chicken and for some people in Lebanon it is customary. Next wash the chicken inside and out with cold water, pulling out and discarding all bloody bits. Remember to wash your hands, surfaces and utensils with hot soapy water after preparing raw chicken and before handling or touching other ingredients. Proceed with the cooking.

Turkey Stuffed with Rice
Habash mihshi bi–roz

CHICKENS FORM the major part of Lebanon's livestock. Turkey, on the other hand, is rather alien to Lebanese cuisine, except that it is enjoyed during the festive seasons of Christmas and the New Year as tradition indicates. However, it is not a recent addition to the Lebanese table, but was imported into Lebanon from Cyprus at least as long ago as the nineteenth century.

The turkey in this dish is filled with a highly flavoured stuffing, which adds a lot of taste to its meat and vice versa. Nevertheless, it can be prepared without stuffing. The bird is marinated overnight in yoghurt to keep it moist before being stuffed. The following day it is wiped out with kitchen paper and prepared as mentioned below, to be baked in the oven, breast down, and turned for the last half hour to brown. To keep maximum moistness my mother used to poach the turkey first, rub it with a little yoghurt and then finish it off in the oven to brown. The broth from the poaching was used for rice. I serve this dish with a honeyed quince preserve. They go together perfectly.

Serves 8–10
1 x 4.5–5.5 kg (10–12 lb) turkey
Lemon wedges
Good pinch of salt
Freshly ground black pepper
½ teaspoon white pepper
60 g (2 oz) unsalted butter, softened (optional)
Yoghurt

For the stuffing:
2–3 tablespoons extra virgin olive oil
450 g (1 lb) lean mince, preferably lamb
1 small onion, grated
550 g (1 lb 4 oz) long grain white rice, preferably basmati
2 teaspoons ground cinnamon
2 teaspoons allspice
½ teaspoon freshly ground black pepper
½ teaspoon freshly grated nutmeg
¼ teaspoon ground cloves
1 apple, peeled, cored and very finely chopped
16 chestnuts, peeled
1.2 litres (2 pints) chicken stock or water
2 teaspoons salt or to taste

For the garnish:
1 tablespoon extra virgin olive oil
85 g (3 oz) blanched almonds
85 g (3 oz) pine nuts
85 g (3 oz) pistachio nuts, soaked

- Preheat the oven to 180°C/350°F/Gas Mark 4.

- Make the stuffing. Heat the oil in a pan over medium heat, add the mince and sprinkle with the onion. Sauté until the mince changes colour and cooks through (about 5–6 minutes), then sprinkle with the cinnamon, allspice, pepper, nutmeg and cloves. Add the apple and rice. Stir for a few minutes to bring out the flavours. Add the chestnuts and chicken stock or water and add the salt. Bring to the boil, reduce heat to low and cook until rice is soft and all liquid has been absorbed (about 10–12 minutes).

- Meanwhile make the garnish. Heat the oil in a frying pan, add the almonds and sauté until golden brown in colour; remove and drain on kitchen paper. Add the pine nuts to the same oil in the pan, sauté until golden in colour, remove and drain. Alternatively, bake in the preheated oven until the nuts are golden in colour. Leave for later use. Peel the pistachios.

- Rub the turkey with lemon wedges and salt to remove impurities; rinse under running cold water and pat dry with kitchen paper. Sprinkle the turkey inside and out with salt and the black and white peppers, spread the yoghurt all over and refrigerate overnight. The following day wipe out the yoghurt and then gently loosen the breast skin and fill with the butter, if using. Loosely stuff the cavity and neck with some of the stuffing, and set the remaining rice aside. Sew all openings, truss, and place the turkey, breast down, in a roasting tin. Roast for about 2–2½ hours, turning the bird over for the last half hour to brown the breast side. To check whether it is done, prick the knee joint. If the juices run clear, transfer the turkey to a large warm serving dish. Pile the remaining rice around it and scatter with the almond, pine nuts and pistachios.

- Serve with Special Christmas Salad (see page 12).

NOTE: If desired, before stuffing the turkey sprinkle the rice with 3 tablespoons rose water.

Stuffed Chicken
Djej mihshi

THIS OLD-TIME CLASSIC is special to Lebanese Christians at Christmas. They serve both the chicken and its stock, to which they add rice and parsley; it is said that the white of the rice and the green of the parsley bring luck and happiness to the family. *Djej mihshi* is also served to honour guests or for lunch on Sunday. When chicken was rare and expensive this dish was considered a delicacy by the Lebanese. Nowadays it has become more accessible. Nevertheless, it somehow maintains its aura and remains one of the special dishes to prepare, although it may seem time-consuming, especially for anyone who has never come across this kind of cooking. However, it is worth trying.

The stuffing is aromatized with rose water which produces a special festive flavour, and which I favour to the flower water that is generally used. After stuffing the chicken it is fried in olive oil – traditionally in *samneh* (generally sheep fat) – to enrich its taste. The one recipe produces two delightful dishes: soup and chicken with rice. You can prepare the chicken and, if preferred, freeze the soup to use later. On the other hand, you could make more rice and use most of the stock.

3–4 tablespoons extra virgin olive oil
30 g (1oz) whole blanched almonds or almond flakes
30 g (1oz) pine nuts
225 g (8 oz) minced lamb
225 g (8 oz) long grain white rice, preferably basmati
½ teaspoon ground cinnamon
¼ teaspoon allspice
¼ teaspoon freshly ground black pepper
1–2 ground cloves
1½ teaspoons salt or to taste
2 tablespoons rose water
1 kg (2lb 2oz) chicken, skin on, cleaned (see page 122)
1 medium-size onion studded with 6 cloves
2 cinnamon sticks
2 bay leaves
Orange peel (optional)
30 g (1oz) short grain white rice
30 g (1oz) chopped parsley
Lemon juice, to sprinkle (optional)

• Heat half the oil in a pan and when it is hot but not smoking add the whole almonds (if using flaked almonds add these with the pine nuts). Stir constantly for a few seconds or until they start to change to pale yellow. Add the pine nuts and continue stirring until both are a golden colour. Remove to a side dish. Add the mince to the pan and stir until it changes its colour and cooks through, gently breaking any lumps with the sides and back of a wooden spoon. Add the long grain rice, ground cinnamon, allspice, pepper, cloves and half the salt and gently stir for a few seconds. Turn off the heat and stir in the rose water and nuts.

- Fill the cavity of the chicken up to the neck with a little less than a quarter of the rice mixture (about 4 tablespoons), and reserve the remaining rice. Truss the chicken using string or skewers. Bring the skin loosely over the neck and under the back of the bird and secure with a skewer pin, to allow the liquid to seep through the rice and cook it.

- Heat the remaining oil in a pan large enough to take the chicken comfortably. Brown the chicken on one side, then gently turn it to brown the other side (altogether about 7–10 minutes). Add 2 litres (3½ pints) water, or enough to cover chicken, and the onion, cinnamon sticks, bay leaves and orange peel, if using. Bring to the boil, skimming the foam from the surface of the water. Cover, reduce the heat to medium and simmer. After 30 minutes reduce the heat further and simmer for a further 40 minutes or until chicken is tender.

- About 10 minutes before the end of the cooking time measure 300–450 ml (½–¾ pints) of the broth and place in a pan. Add the remaining rice mixture and bring to the boil. Reduce the heat to low, cover and simmer for about 7–8 minutes or until the water is absorbed. Meanwhile, remove about three-quarters of what remains of the broth and sieve it into a pan to make the soup. Add the short grain rice and parsley, bring to the boil and simmer until the rice is tender.

- To serve, transfer the chicken to a serving dish and surround it with the cooked rice. Serve the soup in bowls. If desired, sprinkle with a few drops of lemon juice.

Chicken Rice and Tomatoes
Djaj bi-roz wa banadoura

IN THIS TASTY DISH chicken, onions, garlic and tomatoes simmer
until the chicken is tender and the sauce acquires a rich consistency and
wonderful aroma. The sauce, with the spices and tomatoes, is forced
through a sieve, and the rice is cooked in this fragrant, velvety liquor. Serve
a bowl of it so that people can pour some over their rice and chicken.

  4 chicken breasts, skinned
  ½ teaspoon ground cinnamon
  ½ teaspoon ground black pepper
  ½ teaspoon allspice
  1¼ teaspoons salt or to taste
  2–3 tablespoons extra virgin olive oil
  30 g (1 oz) whole or flaked almonds
  2 medium-size onions, coarsely chopped
  6 garlic cloves
  2 medium-size ripe tomatoes, coarsely chopped
  1 heaped teaspoon double concentrated tomato purée
  1 bouquet garni: 1 cinnamon stick, 6 black peppercorns,
     1 bay leaf, 4 cardamoms
  225 g (8 oz) long grain white rice, preferably basmati

- Season the chicken breasts all over with the ground cinnamon, pepper,
  allspice and salt; leave to stand. Meanwhile, heat ½ tablespoon of the oil
  in a medium-size pan and when it is hot but not smoking, add the
  almonds and sauté until golden in colour. With a slotted spoon remove
  and set aside. Add remaining oil; when hot add the chicken pieces, and

sauté to seal their juices, for about 5 minutes or until nicely browned on both sides. Remove and add the onions and garlic to the same pan. Stir occasionally until they are a nice golden brown colour. Add the tomatoes and tomato purée. Give them a good stir, return the chicken to the pan, and add the bouquet garni and 1 litre (1¾ pints) water scraping the juices in the pan. Bring to the boil, reduce the heat to medium, cover and simmer for 40–50 minutes or until chicken is tender.

- Transfer the chicken to a plate. If desired, slice into medium-size pieces and discard the bones and bouquet garni. Place the tomatoes, onions and garlic in a blender with a little stock and blend until creamy. Add to the liquid in the pan and stir well. From this resulting sauce measure 400 ml (14 fl oz), thin this with 4 tablespoons water and place in a pan. Add the rice and bring to the boil. Reduce the heat to medium-low, cover and simmer for about 8 minutes. Halfway through cooking taste and if necessary add a little salt. Return the chicken to the remaining sauce in the pan to keep warm.

- To serve, spread the rice in a warm serving dish. Arrange the chicken over it and sprinkle with the almonds. Place some sauce in a small bowl for spooning over the chicken and rice. *Bon appetit.*

Chicken with Potatoes
Djaj bi-batata

THIS IS MY DAUGHTER Nour's favourite recipe, and can be prepared very quickly. The unpeeled potatoes absorb the flavours of the chicken, spices, lemon juice and oil as they cook. The flavour is dense and the aroma very appetizing. Eat with *tabbouleh* (Cracked Wheat Salad, see page 4) and aubergine dip (see page 36) for a very health-giving meal.

4 medium-size chicken supremes, skinned
2 medium-size potatoes, unpeeled, scrubbed and cut into
   2.5 cm (1 in) cubes
1 medium-size onion, sliced
3 garlic cloves, crushed
1½ teaspoons salt or to taste
½ teaspoon ground cinnamon
¼ teaspoon freshly ground black pepper or to taste
½ teaspoon allspice
3–4 tablespoons lemon juice
3–4 tablespoons extra virgin olive oil

- Combine the chicken, potatoes, onion, garlic, salt, cinnamon, pepper, allspice, lemon juice, oil and 2 tablespoons water in a baking dish. Mix thoroughly to blend well. Marinate for 2 hours or overnight in a cool place. Allow to reach room temperature before baking.

- Preheat the oven to 180°C/350°F/Gas Mark 4. Bake for 1 hour 20 minutes or until the chicken and potatoes are nicely browned.

Chicken Kebab
Djaj bi-chiche meshwi

BEFORE THE 1975 Lebanese war my brother used to bring home the most delicious of sandwiches, a baguette filled with chicken and an ample amount of *toum* (garlic) cream and *kabis khiar* (pickled cucumber). This was pressed between two hot plates, producing a most appetizing meal from relatively modest ingredients.

The kebab is good with *fattouche* (Bread Salad, see page 6) and *mtabbal u. batinjan* (Aubergine Dip, see page 36), or with *salatet malfouf* (Cabbage Salad, see page 8). This recipe can also be made with lamb fillet.

> **450 g (1 lb) chicken breasts, cut into 1.5 cm (½ in) cubes**
> **1 garlic clove, crushed**
> **¾ teaspoon salt**
> **½ teaspoon yoghurt**
> **¼ teaspoon ground cinnamon**
> **¼ teaspoon freshly ground black pepper**
> **¼ teaspoon allspice**
> **2 tablespoons extra virgin olive oil**
> **3 tablespoons lemon juice**
> **1 large pitta bread**

- In a glass bowl combine the chicken, garlic, salt, yoghurt, cinnamon, pepper, allspice, oil and lemon juice. Mix well and marinate for 3 hours or overnight in the refrigerator. A little while before grilling remove from fridge and allow the chicken to reach room temperature.

- Preheat the grill. Place chicken pieces on skewers on a baking sheet and grill until brown (6–8 minutes), turning the skewers and basting the chicken with the marinade to keep it moist. Remove from heat and place the chicken inside a large pitta bread. Serve hot.

VARIATION: Thread unmarinated chicken pieces on to skewers and prepare a separate bowl of the marinade. Grill or barbecue, basting often with marinade.

You can also try an alternative marinade: dilute 1 teaspoon honey with 1 tablespoon cider vinegar, 1½ tablespoons lemon juice and 1 teaspoon yoghurt. Blend with 1 deseeded, chopped red chilli, 2 crushed cloves of garlic, 1 small onion, chopped, 1 tablespoon extra virgin olive oil, 1 teaspoon salt, and a pinch each of turmeric, paprika and black pepper, until the mixture is creamy. Place the chicken pieces in a plastic bag and pour over the marinade. Refrigerate overnight then follow the cooking instructions above. A whole chicken can be used instead.

❀ ❀ ❀

Chicken with Peppers
Djaj bi-flaifleh

COLOURFUL, with a subtle flavour, this dish is quick to assemble and can be prepared ahead of time. Chicken is so versatile that its taste is transformed by the ingredients that are added. *Djaj bi-flaifleh* is a good example; a combination of fresh green, red, orange and yellow peppers, ripe tomatoes and onions, all sliced to cover the chicken. This is sprinkled with aromatic spices and baked in the oven so that the meat is impregnated with a myriad juices. Water is used here, but to enrich the flavour you can substitute chicken stock.

4 chicken supremes
Pinch of allspice (optional)
½ teaspoon ground cinnamon
½ teaspoon freshly ground black pepper or to taste
2 teaspoons salt or to taste
2 garlic cloves, finely crushed
3 small onions, quartered
1 small green pepper, cored, deseeded and coarsely sliced
1 small red pepper, cored, deseeded and coarsely sliced

1 small yellow pepper, cored, deseeded and coarsely sliced
1 small orange pepper, cored, deseeded and coarsely sliced
2 large ripe tomatoes, quartered
2–3 tablespoons extra virgin olive oil
2–4 tablespoons hot water

- Preheat the oven to 180°C/350°F/Gas Mark 4. Place the chicken in a deep baking dish (with a lid) and sprinkle evenly with the allspice, if using, cinnamon, black pepper and half the salt. Add the garlic, onions and peppers and mix thoroughly with the chicken pieces. Top with the tomatoes and sprinkle with the remaining salt. Drizzle over the oil and water. Bake covered for 1½ hours, then uncover and cook for a further 30 minutes or until browned.

- Serve with roasted potatoes.

Chicken, Flamed Green Wheat, Chillies and Pistachios
Djaj bi-freekeh, har wa fustok halabi

THE NAME IS SO APPEALING. The *freekeh* (flamed green wheat), green chillies and pistachios are interlaced to produce a pretty gradation of pale greens. The colour so much resembles Lebanon's trees and fields that I can't help but think of The Cedars of Lebanon painted by Edward Lear.

Kama are a kind of truffle but their flavour is nothing like that of truffles found in the West. They are much appreciated in the Levant and grow in the deserts of Syria and Iraq. I have substituted the more readily available chestnut mushrooms which have nearly the same bite.

Serves 8–10

1 x 2 kg (4 lb 8 oz) chicken, cleaned (see page 122)
1 bouquet garni: 2 bay leaves, 2 cinnamon sticks,
    4 cardamoms
1 onion studded with 2 cloves, plus 350–400 g (12–14 oz)
    onions, finely chopped
1½ teaspoons salt or to taste
2–3 tablespoons extra virgin olive oil
450 g (1 lb) *freekeh*, rinsed once
4 green chillies, deseeded and sliced
90–120 g (3–4 oz) pistachio nuts, shelled
60 g (2 oz) butter
2–3 tablespoons unbleached plain white flour
2–2½ tablespoons lemon juice
225 g (8 oz) *kama* or chestnut mushrooms, halved

- Place the chicken in a large pan with about 2.4–3 litres (4–5 pints) water to cover, and bring to the boil, skimming the foam from the surface of the water. Add the bouquet garni and whole onion, bring to the boil again, cover and simmer over medium heat for 1 hour. About 10 minutes before the end of the cooking time add 1 teaspoon salt.

- Meanwhile, heat the oil in a wide non-stick pan, and add the onions. Sprinkle with ½ teaspoon salt and sauté until the onions are a yellowish golden colour. At this point add the *freekeh*, stir and add 1.2–2.4 litres (2–2½ pints) of the chicken broth. Bring to the boil, cover and simmer over low heat for about 12–15 minutes or until the broth is fully absorbed. About 5 minutes before the end of the cooking time add the chillies and pistachio nuts.

- In the meantime, melt 45g (1½ oz) of the butter in a medium-size non-stick pan, add the flour and cook until it reaches a pinkish colour. Gradually add about 450–600 ml (¾–1 pint) of the broth while whisking, and cook to a velvety consistency. Stir in the lemon juice. Sauté the mushrooms with the remaining butter for a few minutes and add to the sauce. Cut the chicken into bite-size pieces.

- If the pan in which you cooked the *freekeh* is presentable, leave it there. Place the chicken in a serving dish and pour the sauce into a sauce boat. Serve the *freekeh* with the chicken and the sauce.

Spiced Chicken
Shawarma djaj

THE LEBANESE like to indulge in very tasty food. *Shawarma djaj* is one such dish, although its reputation is less than that of the great meat *shawarma* (Spiced Meat, see page 184), and it is frequently eaten in Lebanon. Vendors wrap their vertical spits with the chicken, which is turned slowly close to open heat to be ready by lunch time, so that hurried passers-by can grab a most delicious and cheap sandwich.

> 4 boneless chicken breasts
> 2 garlic cloves, pounded until creamy
> 120 ml (4 fl oz) lemon juice
> 1½–2 tablespoons extra virgin olive oil
> 1½ teaspoons cider vinegar
> 2 bay leaves, halved
> 1 cinnamon stick, quartered
> 2 shreds of orange peel
> 1 ¼ teaspoons salt
> 2 cloves
> 4 cardamoms, whole or crushed

¼ **teaspoon ground cinnamon**
¼ **teaspoon white pepper**
Pinch of freshly grated nutmeg
2 *miskee* pieces (see Glossary under mastic, page 302),
  gently ground with a little salt
1 large Lebanese bread

- In a glass bowl, combine the chicken, garlic, lemon juice, oil, vinegar, bay leaves, cinnamon stick, orange peel, salt, cloves, cardamoms, ground cinnamon, pepper, nutmeg and *miskee*. Toss thoroughly, cover and refrigerate overnight.

- Preheat the oven to 180°C/350°F/Gas Mark 4 and remove the chicken from the refrigerator 5–10 minutes before cooking. Place the chicken in a roasting tin with the marinade. Bake for 30 minutes, turning the chicken once or twice with a spoon to coat it evenly with the juices.

- Remove the chicken, discard the cloves, cinnamon sticks and cardamoms and leave until cool enough to handle. Carve over a wooden board into thin strips. Preheat the grill and return the strips to the roasting tin. Mix them thoroughly with the pan juices and finish them off under the hot grill for about 2–5 minutes or until the strips are golden brown; turn them once and make sure they do not become dry.

- Remove the chicken strips and place them inside Lebanese bread pockets to keep warm. Eat with *Tahini* Sauce (see page 300), pickles, sliced tomatoes and a dish of fried potatoes.

VARIATION: Use skinless chicken breasts, sliced into 5 cm (2 in) long strips. Mix thoroughly with the remaining marinade ingredients, cover and marinate overnight. Follow the instructions in the recipe above.

Chicken and Basil
Djaj bi-habak

BASIL WAS PLANTED in huge pots on our veranda and was within easy reach of my mother while she was cooking. Its scent, which is soothing and invigorating, is at its strongest in the early morning and at sunset. Basil aids digestion and is said to turn cooks into poets. *Djaj bi-habak* is very low in fat and is ideal for people who are short of time.

> 450 g (1 lb) chicken breasts, skinned and cut into 2.5 cm
>   (1 in) pieces
> 1 large garlic clove, crushed
> 1 onion, thinly sliced
> 1 teaspoon extra virgin olive oil (optional)
> 45 g (1½ oz) fresh basil leaves, coarsely chopped
> ½ teaspoon salt or to taste
> ¼ teaspoon freshly ground black pepper
> Pinch of white pepper

- Place the chicken, garlic, onion, oil if using, and half the basil in a medium-size pot over moderately high heat. Cook for about 3 minutes. Reduce the heat to low, cover and simmer, allowing the chicken pieces to cook in their juices for about 15 minutes. Add the remaining basil and the salt, black and white peppers. Cover and simmer for 3–5 minutes more. Towards the end of the cooking time, turn the heat up to moderately high and cook until the juice has reduced to less than half and the chicken is slightly golden in colour.

- Transfer to a serving dish and serve with Aubergine Dip (see page 36).

Chicken with Thyme
Djaj bi-zaatar

ZAATAR (THYME), an aromatic herb that greatly elevates the taste and satisfies the palate, is an important spice for the Lebanese and is used fresh or dried (*zaatar* mix is a blend of dried *zaatar*, *sumac* and sea salt). *Djaj bi-zaatar* makes a magnificent main meal accompanied by fried potatoes and *mtabbal al-batinjan* (Aubergine Dip, see page 36).

4 chicken supremes, skinned
½ teaspoon ground cinnamon
¼ teaspoon freshly ground black pepper
½ teaspoon salt or to taste
2 tablespoons extra virgin olive oil
I large onion, chopped
I garlic clove, crushed
2 teaspoons *zaatar*

- Rub the chicken breasts all over with the cinnamon, pepper and salt. Heat the oil in a deep frying pan and when it is is hot but not smoking, add the chicken. Cook for 6–8 minutes, turning once. When the breasts are browned on both sides transfer to a plate with a slotted spoon, allowing the oil to drip back into the pan. Add the onion to the remaining oil in the pan, reduce the heat to medium and cook until pale golden in colour, about 2–3 minutes. Add the garlic, cook for a few seconds and add the *zaatar*. Stir once, return the browned chicken to the pan and finally add 350 ml (12 fl oz) water. Bring to the boil, cover and simmer over medium heat for 10 minutes. Reduce the heat to medium-low and continue cooking for a further 30 minutes or until the chicken is tender and the liquid has reduced and thickened slightly. Transfer to a warm serving plate and spoon over the remaining juices.

• Serve on its own or with fried potatoes (see page 25).

VARIATION: Mix together all the ingredients except the water (if desired add ½ tablespoon lemon juice) and grate the onion instead of chopping it. Marinate for few hours then barbecue the chicken breasts or bake them in the oven.

❀ ❀ ❀

Chicken with Almonds
Djaj bi-loz

DJAJ BI-LOZ is quick to prepare and pleasing to the palate. As the chicken, almonds and spices are simmered their flavours merge to produce a sweet, rich-tasting dish with a nutty texture, a beautiful deep gold colour and a moist meat. The combination of chicken and almonds is one of the many recipes in a medieval Arabic treatise on food entitled *Kitab al-Wusla-il al-Habib*.

This is a good recipe for simple entertaining. I like to serve it with a selection of fried or grilled vegetables, such as aubergines, and roasted potatoes which complement the dish.

4 chicken supremes
2 large cinnamon sticks
2 bay leaves
2 tablespoons extra virgin olive oil
1 large onion, chopped

I large garlic clove, crushed
2 teaspoons unbleached plain white flour
60 g (2 oz) almond flakes
¾–I teaspoon ground cinnamon
Pinch of freshly ground black pepper
½ teaspoon salt or to taste

- Place the chicken, cinnamon stick and bay leaves in a medium-size pan with 450 ml (¾ pint) and bring to the boil over medium-high heat, skimming the foam from the surface of the water. Add the cinnamon sticks and bay leaves. Reduce the heat to medium, cover and simmer for 20 minutes.

- Meanwhile, heat the oil in a non-stick frying pan, add the onion and sauté until golden in colour. Add the garlic and stir constantly for a few seconds, then add the flour, almonds, ground cinnamon, pepper and salt. Keep stirring for I minute longer, then add this mixture to the chicken and cook for a further 30 minutes or until the chicken is tender. Transfer to a deep serving dish, spooning the juices over the chicken, and serve immediately.

❀ ❀ ❀

Chicken Rice, Aromatic Herbs and Yoghurt
Fattet djaj

THE LEBANESE EXPECT a dish to satisfy their hunger and also pleasure their senses. For most, economy is another important issue. These combined requirements are behind the Lebanon's cleverly concocted dishes, many of which use basic ingredients.

The chicken here is not fried in butter nor in oil; neither is the bread as is traditional. Instead, chicken breasts are poached with aromatic herbs and spices which eventually enrich the broth. In this broth, rice simmers gently to give a lovely fresh clean taste to the meal. Bread is lightly brushed with oil, and cut into small squares or broken after it has been toasted. All are layered, to be topped with the soothing yoghurt; the taste is heightened with pine nuts, parsley or mint and spring onions. Therefore there are a few preparations to be made before assembling the dish.

Fattet djaj is remarkable, nourishing and presents beautifully at dinner or lunch parties. It is also an excellent option when you have leftover chicken. I've never tried it with turkey, but why don't you?

2 large chicken supremes
I bouquet garni: I large cinnamon stick, a few black
    peppercorns, I bay leaf, 2 stems of parsley with leaves
I small onion studded with I clove
1¼ teaspoons salt or to taste
I–2 medium–size Lebanese or pitta breads, split in two
Extra virgin olive oil
I garlic clove
I tablespoon *tahini*
I teaspoon lemon juice
500 g (I lb I oz) tub of yoghurt or to taste
225 g (8 oz) long grain white rice, preferably basmati
3–4 spring onions, thinly sliced
Handful of chopped mint or I–2 large handfuls of chopped
    parsley
I–2 tablespoons clarified butter or extra virgin olive oil
3–4 tablespoons pine nuts

- Place the chicken in a large pan with 750 ml (1¼ pints) water and bring to the boil, skimming the foam that forms on the surface of the water. Add the bouquet garni and onion. Cover and reduce the heat to medium. Cook for 50–60 minutes or until the chicken is tender. Five minutes prior to the end of the cooking time sprinkle with 1 teaspoon of the salt.

- Preheat the oven to 180°C/350°F/Gas Mark 4. Lightly brush the breads with the oil, place in the oven and cook until they are golden brown, about 5 minutes. Remove them from the oven, leave to cool and then break into bite-size pieces.

- Pound the garlic with the remaining salt until creamy and mix well with the *tahini* and lemon juice. Gradually stir in the yoghurt; if the mixture is too thick add about 2–3 tablespoons water. Beat it in well – the consistency should be like single cream.

- Place 475 ml (16 fl oz) of the chicken broth in a pan with the rice and bring to the boil. Reduce the heat to low, cover and simmer for about 5–7 minutes or until the broth is absorbed but the rice is not too dry. Separate the chicken meat from bones and carve into strips lengthwise, discarding the skin and bones.

- Now that everything is ready, spread the bread pieces over a hot, deep rectangular or round serving dish and sprinkle with 2 tablespoons of the remaining chicken broth. Place the rice over the bread, and sprinkle with the spring onions and half the mint or parsley, then add the chicken pieces. Top with the yoghurt mixture.

- Heat the butter or oil in a pan, add the pine nuts and sauté them only until they are golden. Remove the pan from the heat and quickly stir in the remaining mint or parsley. Pour over the yoghurt and serve.

Poussin Stuffed with Flamed Green Wheat
Farkhet djej

FREEKEH IS A FRESH green wheat that is picked and flamed to give
it an exceptional burnt smoked flavour. It is much appreciated by the
Lebanese, and more so in the south of Lebanon and in the Bekaa Valley.
This is an exotic dish with a unique and special flavour. In general,
I don't like to add any seasonings to *freekeh*, so that nothing affects its
smoky flavour. A stuffed poussin makes an elegant presentation for
special occasions. Poussin can be poached ahead of time and the final
cooking is done in the oven. *Freekeh* is on sale in Lebanese shops and
isn't expensive.

2 poussin
1 bouquet garni: 1 cinnamon stick, 1 parsley stem, 1 small
    piece of celery
1 small onion studded with 2 cloves, plus 150g (5 oz)
    onion, finely chopped
1 teaspoon salt
1 tablespoon extra virgin olive oil
Knob of butter
1 large garlic clove, crushed
225 g (8 oz) *freekeh*
1 teaspoon oregano
¾ teaspoon finely chopped fresh thyme
½ teaspoon finely chopped fresh marjoram
¼ teaspoon *miskee* (see Glossary page 302)
Pinch of sugar

½ **teaspoon ground cinnamon**
Good pinch of allspice
Good pinch of freshly ground black pepper
1 teaspoon salt or to taste
1 teaspoon yoghurt

- Preheat the oven to 180°C/350°F/Gas Mark 4. Place the poussin in a pan and cover with about 600–750 ml (1–1¼ pints) water. Add the bouquet garni, whole onion and half the salt and bring to the boil, skimming the foam from the surface of the water. Reduce the heat to medium, then medium-low. Cover and simmer for 20 minutes.

- Heat the oil and butter in a medium-size non-stick frying pan and when they are hot but not smoking add the chopped onion. Sauté for a minute or until lightly golden. Add the garlic (be careful it doesn't burn), stir for few seconds then add the *freekeh*, oregano, thyme, marjoram and 450 ml (¾ pint) of the poussin broth. Bring to the boil, cover and simmer over low heat for 10 minutes or until the broth is absorbed.

- Meanwhile, gently pound the *miskee* with the sugar and stir it into the *freekeh* a few seconds before the end of the cooking time. Quickly turn the heat off and leave to cool. Stuff the poussin with as much *freekeh* as they can take. Tie their legs with string and fold back their wings. Mix the cinnamon, allspice and pepper into the yoghurt and rub the mixture thoroughly into the breast, front and sides of each bird. Place in a roasting tin and bake in the oven for 15–20 minutes or until nicely browned. Remove and serve with the remaining *freekeh*.

VARIATION: You can use coarse *burghol* or rice instead of *freekeh*.

Chicken in a Walnut and Pomegranate Syrup
Fasenjun

THIS VERY FAMOUS Persian dish came to Lebanon with Lebanese Shia scholars who studied at Najaf, one of the holiest cities of Shia Muslims and the site of the tomb of Ali Ibn Abi Taleb, the cousin and son-in-law of the prophet Mohammad. The perfect party dish, *fasenjun* is served at festive times, and for celebratory lunches and dinners. Here it is made with chicken but pheasant is also excellent.

I medium chicken, cleaned (see page 122) and cut into
    6 pieces
I teaspoon ground cinnamon
Good pinch of freshly ground black pepper
Pinch of allspice (optional)
3 tablespoons extra virgin olive oil or butter
I large onion, finely chopped
1.1 litres (2 pints) hot water
I bouquet garni: I large stick cinnamon, 3 cardamoms,
    2 bay leaves, handful of parsley stems
120 g (4 oz) shelled walnuts, finely ground
300 ml (½ pint) freshly squeezed pomegranate juice
    (in season)
3–4 tablespoons pomegranate syrup or to taste
2 tablespoons lemon juice
1½ teaspoons salt or to taste

• Season the chicken pieces with the cinnamon, pepper and the allspice, if using. Heat I tablespoon of the oil or butter (or a mixture of the two) in a pan, add onion and sauté until a golden brown colour. Remove to a side dish and reserve. Heat the remaining oil and/or butter in the same pan, add the chicken pieces and sauté until golden brown on all sides. Add the water and bring to the boil. Skim then add the reserved onion and bouquet garni and bring to the boil again. Cover and simmer over medium heat for 1 hour or until the chicken is tender. Remove the chicken and when it's easy to handle discard the skin and cut the meat into bite-size pieces. Discard the bouquet garni. Stir the walnuts, chicken pieces, pomegranate juice and syrup, and lemon juice into the broth. Season with the salt. Simmer for a further 15–20 minutes. If it needs thinning add more broth. Serve with rice or bread.

LEBANESE EGG DISHES are tasty and straightforward. Omelettes are generally cooked through and are presented flat, unlike the folded European ones with their uncooked centres. Whenever I come back home hungry to find an almost empty fridge, eggs solve the problem. They give me the necessary protein and fill me without a high intake of calories. In addition, they are perfect for outdoor eating, suitable for picnics and children's lunch boxes. You shouldn't worry about eating too many eggs; balance is what it takes.

Eggs, Olive Oil and Sumac
Baid mikli bil-sumac

FRIED EGGS WITH *SUMAC* are irresistible, at least for me. In the mountains of Lebanon it is a meal in itself, eaten with Lebanese bread while picking on a side dish of olives. Sachets of *sumac* are sold in Lebanese, Iranian, Turkish and Cypriot shops and I have a feeling they will soon invade the supermarkets.

> **Serves 1**
> **2–3 tablespoons extra virgin olive oil**
> **2 eggs**
> **Pinch of salt**
> **1 heaped teaspoon** *sumac*

- Heat the oil in a small frying pan and when it is hot but not smoking crack first one egg then the other into it. They should sizzle. Sprinkle with the salt and *sumac* and leave until the base sets, less than 30 seconds. Hold the handle of the frying pan with one hand and tilt the pan to the side so that the oil runs and accumulates. With the other hand hold a spoon, take some of the oil and pour it over the yolks of the eggs. The white that clings to the yellow will become opaque. The whole operation will take about 3 minutes unless you want the yolks to be very well cooked. Remove with a spatula and serve with Lebanese bread.

Eggs, Garlic and Spices
Baid bil-toum wa bharat

THIS IS another tasty way to fry eggs and the spice helps to keep clean 'internal flora' – or this is what is believed in the Lebanese mountains. Not long ago, when someone complained of a stomach pain – known as *tiini*, meaning 'groaning' – this dish was considered to be the best remedy. Garlic is regarded as an excellent antibiotic and this is real food; so much better for the body than feeding it expensively with pills.

> *Serves 1*
> **2 tablespoons extra virgin olive oil**
> **8 small garlic cloves**
> **2 eggs**
> **Pinch of salt**
> **1 heaped teaspoon *sumac***
> **½ teaspoon ground cumin**

- Heat the oil in a small frying pan and when it is hot but not smoking add the garlic and sauté until lightly golden in colour. To prevent it burning, take the pan off the heat now and then and swirl. The garlic will keep on cooking but will not burn. Crack the first egg over the garlic, then the second. Sprinkle with the salt and then the *sumac*. Allow a little time for the base to set, then sprinkle with cumin. Hold the handle of the frying pan with one hand and tilt the pan to the side so that the oil runs and accumulates. With the other hand hold a spoon, take some of the hot oil and pour it over the yolks of the eggs. Repeat a few more times and turn the heat off. Remove the eggs with a spatula.

- Serve with Lebanese or any other bread.

Yoghurt, Onions, Garlic and Eggs
Shamamit

THIS UNUSUAL DISH is prepared in Marjeyoun, a small Christian town in south-east Lebanon. Simple to make and very nutritious, it is prepared with goat's yoghurt, which does not need cornflour or egg to stabilize it. It generally has a thick consistency and is eaten with bread. If preferred add 4 more eggs.

2-3 medium-size onions, coarsely sliced
8 garlic cloves
I teaspoon salt or to taste
900 g (2 lb) goat's yoghurt
4 eggs

- Place the onions and garlic in a medium-size pan with 350–450 ml (½–¾ pint) water. Add the salt and bring to the boil. Reduce the heat to medium-low, cover and simmer for 30–40 minutes. Sieve the yoghurt into another pan and 5–6 minutes before the cooking time for the onion mixture is up, place it over medium-low heat and bring to boil stirring. Add the onions and garlic and their reduced liquid. Keep stirring, bring to the boil again. Break the eggs, one after the other, into the yoghurt and onion mixture. Bring to the boil, then reduce the heat to low and simmer for 10–12 minutes.

- Serve hot with coarse *burghol* or Vermicelli Rice (see page 54), olives, radishes and spring onions.

Meat

WHEN THE NINETEENTH CENTURY was about to draw to a close, a number of
the inhabitants of Lebanon escaped an increasingly harsh Ottoman rule
and found refuge in Egypt. There, they materially contributed to the
Arab renaissance, in the literary field and in the world of journalism.
If the intellectual contribution of those expatriates was welcomed in
their adopted home, this was not the case for one of their culinary
habits, namely the preparation of *kibbeh*, what is perhaps regarded as *the*
national dish of Lebanon. I was told by one of my great-uncles that
whenever a Lebanese family sought lodgings, the Egyptian landlord
invariably said that the use of a mortar for pounding meat (a crucial part
of the making of *kibbeh*) would not be allowed on the premises.
Fortunately, the restrictive and vexatious terms of autocratic landlords
did not stop the flow of immigrants coming from Lebanon and the
literary renaissance was not compromised by such inconvenience.
Who knows, mortars left idle along the Nile may have contributed to
the invention of the Moulinex meat-grinding machine that is nowadays
used by most inhabitants of Lebanon's towns to prepare *kibbeh* and
recipes that include minced meat. Yet in the boroughs and villages of
the mountains, *kibbeh* is still prepared the traditional way. I saw this for
myself during a recent visit to Becharreh, a large borough perched high
in the mountains at the foot of the Cedars of Lebanon. Flaubert, the 19th
century French novelist, made his way through the valley and was
amazed by its beauty, likening its natural cascades among the rocks and
waterfalls to those in the paintings of Poussin, and describing Lebanon
as 'Pays vraiment fait pour la peinture et qui semble même fait d'après elle' (A
country truly made for painting and which seems to be made from it).

Becharreh was the home of the great American-Lebanese author and poet Khalih Gibran, and is the site of his mausoleum and a charming museum of memorabilia and paintings. After a dutiful visit to both I was the guest, for lunch, of the most hospitable people. Part of the feast was *kibbeh nayeh* (see page 152), which was prepared in front of us. A thin, nervous woman, her hair tidily covered by a scarf, sat on a low wooden stool in front of a large mortar made of stone. With a sizeable wooden pestle she started pounding raw meat. After a while she added to the battered meat cracked wheat, onions and spices, and resumed her pounding in a rhythmical way that could well be mistaken for a mysterious message on a tom-tom.

When she finished we ate the most delicious *kibbeh*, prepared with goat meat as that is what is used for the table in this part of the country. In other parts and in towns lamb is used instead. Lebanon has no proper grazing grounds and meagre livestock. Goats are found in the heights, mainly in the north of the country, whereas lambs and cows are scarce and mostly imported.

Before distances became unimportant, and before frozen meat shipped from Australia and New Zealand became readily available, as the next local produce, the Lebanese did not rely on meat for their daily diet. Whenever they ate local meat it had to be prepared in an elaborate way to make it more edible. In the process they made a delicacy of their concoctions. Lamb meat was parsimoniously used for some stews, or cooked in plenty of salt and preserved for the winter season. Beef steaks were rarely eaten. In spite of the poor quality of the meat, or maybe because of it, the culinary imagination of the Lebanese had no limits. Like *kibbeh*, *kafta* is a culinary triumph, not to mention the dozens of recipes where meat is not the main ingredient, but is used to lift the taste, to thicken the sauce and to provide the most needed protein in the peasant diet.

Raw Kibbeh
Kibbeh nayeh

A TRADITIONAL and very popular dish all over the country, *kibbeh* is a particular speciality in the mountainous region of north Lebanon and in the town of Zahle. In the south it is prepared a little differently, in that a few fresh basil leaves and some marjoram are pounded with the onions and spices to form a smooth paste, which is then mixed with the meat and *burghol* (cracked wheat). Both versions are delicious.

The secret to achieving a good *kibbeh* is good-quality meat, which should be trimmed of all fat and gristle and then be freshly and finely powdered or ground. Concern about the dangers of eating raw meat can make people uneasy about eating *kibbeh nayeh*. On the other hand, it seems to me that when the thinly sliced meat is pounded in a stone mortar with a heavy pestle, this generates enough heat to half-cook the meat.

I small onion, grated
1–2 good pinches of salt or to taste
¼ teaspoon freshly ground black pepper
¼ teaspoon ground cinnamon
¼ teaspoon white pepper
165 g (5½ oz) fine *burghol*
450 g (1 lb) ground meat, preferably from a leg of lamb
125 ml (4½ fl oz) iced water
Extra virgin olive oil, to drizzle
Mint leaves, to garnish

• Place the onion in a bowl, sprinkle in the salt, black pepper, cinnamon and white pepper and rub into the onion. Rinse the *burghol*, drain and quickly squeeze out excess water, add to the onion and combine thoroughly. Add the meat and work this mixture. Add as much of the iced water as necessary (not all) to achieve a smooth dough with a good consistency. Continue kneading until the *kibbeh* mixture blends well together. Taste and adjust the seasoning. Spread the *kibbeh* smoothly over a serving dish, drizzle generously with oil and garnish with mint.

- Serve with white or spring onions and Lebanese bread.

VARIATION: Place the onion in a blender with a medium-size red pepper and about 8–10 fresh mint leaves, fresh basil, ½ teaspoon grated orange zest and a little marjoram and combine with the meat and cracked wheat as above.

✾ ✾ ✾

Baked Kibbeh
Kibbeh bi-sayniyeh

THIS IS ONE of my favourite versions of *kibbeh* and reminds me of relaxed Sunday lunches at home. My father used to love pounding the meat in our large marble mortar, using a huge wooden pestle.

Kibbeh is traditionally baked with a liberal amount of olive oil and topped with large dots of *samneh* (fat from a sheep's tail); this gives it a rich, fine flavour and prevents it drying out in the oven. I bake the *kibbeh* in olive oil and, after removing it from the oven, discard about half the oil while it is still bubbling. I guarantee the *kibbeh* so treated is just as tasty.

Traditionally *kibbeh* is served as a hearty main course or as part of a buffet and, in restaurants, as a *plat du jour*. A soothing *salatet laban w'khiar* (Cucumber and Yoghurt Salad, see page 229), or *salatet malfouf* (Cabbage

Salad, see page 8) complements the *kibbeh* nicely. My daughter Nour finds *kibbeh* delicious straight out of the fridge.

Here the *kibbeh* is stuffed with a meat and pine nut mixture as is traditional. Another version uses *labneh* (a Lebanese cheese) instead of meat, as prepared in Zgarta, North Lebanon.

3–4 tablespoons extra virgin olive oil
30 g (1 oz) pine nuts
3 medium-size onions, finely chopped
150 g (5 oz) lean mince, preferably lamb
1 teaspoon ground cinnamon
½ teaspoon salt or to taste
Pinch of freshly ground black pepper (optional)
1 tablespoon lemon juice or sumac (optional)

For the kibbeh dough:
1 small onion, grated
1¼ teaspoons salt or to taste
½ teaspoon allspice
½ teaspoon ground cinnamon
½ teaspoon freshly ground black pepper
275 g (10 oz) fine *burghol*
450 g (1 lb) lean mince, preferably lamb
3–4 tablespoons iced water
75–120 ml (3–4 fl oz) extra virgin olive oil

• Preheat the oven to 180°C/350°C/Gas Mark 4 and grease a round 26 cm (10½ in) baking dish with 1 tablespoon of the oil.

• Heat the remaining oil in a heavy-bottomed frying pan and when it is hot but not smoking add the pine nuts and sauté, stirring constantly, until golden in colour. Remove with a slotted spoon, allowing the oil to drip back into the pan, and set aside. Add the onions to the pan, and sauté over medium-high heat until soft and pale in colour, about 2 minutes. Add the meat and cook until it is lightly browned, then return the pine nuts to the pan. Add the cinnamon, salt and the pepper, if using. Turn off the heat and add the lemon juice or sumac, if using. Stir well, remove the stuffing from the heat and set aside.

- Meanwhile, prepare the *kibbeh* dough. Place the onion in a bowl and mix with the salt, allspice, cinnamon and pepper. Rinse the *burghol* and quickly squeeze out excess water. Add to the onions and mix thoroughly. Add the meat and work with the *burghol* mixture, adding iced water as necessary to achieve a smooth *kibbeh* dough with a good consistency. Knead until the *kibbeh* mixture blends well (if necessary process in a blender for a few seconds). Take a portion of the kibbeh dough and flatten it thinly to a uniform thickness over the base of the baking dish (this layer should be thin).

- Spread the reserved stuffing evenly over the dough. To cover it, take small portions of the remaining dough, flatten them between your palms – they should be slightly thicker than the base layer – and cover the stuffing with them; moisten your hands with cold water as necessary. Press down and smooth the portions so that they are joined together. Drizzle all over with the oil and quickly run a thin-pointed knife around the edge of the baking dish. Then cut through the *kibbeh* and divide it into 8 portions (similar to pizza slices), allowing the oil to seep down. Make a criss-cross pattern on top of each portion.

- Bake for 40 minutes or until the *kibbeh* is nicely browned. Remove from oven and while the oil is still bubbling carefully pour some off.

- Arrange on a platter and serve with a salad.

Fried Kibbeh
Kibbeh mikli

SOME SKILL IS NEEDED to form an oval-shaped *kibbeh*, but do not be put off because with a little experience it becomes quite easy. A faster way is to make patties with the dough, wrap them around the stuffing and then make them into egg shapes. You can also use an egg cup. Rinse or oil it to prevent the dough sticking, then put a small portion of dough into it and work the inside with your finger following the shape of the cup. Add some stuffing and close the opening. Remove the dough and shape it like an egg. The *kibbeh* shells are fried in olive oil, which produces a crunchy texture and a very pleasing taste.

Kibbeh mikli are perfect as appetizers or as a first course. They remind me of Nabeh Mar Sarkis (Spring of St Sarkis), a famous restaurant in north Lebanon where delicious *kibbeh* is offered in various ways and with different stuffings. Lemon juice brings out a lovely tart flavour. However, *sumac* is also a delicious addition. You can replace some of the meat with more pine nuts if you wish. In Becharreh a dome-shaped *kibbeh* is stuffed with goat's cheese instead of meat, or *bulgari* white cheese, similar to the Greek feta cheese.

Makes about 14 pieces
1 quantity *kibbeh* dough, prepared as for Kibbeh in Tahini Sauce (see page 159)
Extra virgin olive oil, for deep-frying

For the stuffing:
3 tablespoons extra virgin olive oil
45 g (1½ oz) pine nuts

2 medium-size onions, finely chopped
150 g (6 oz) lean mince, preferably lamb
½ teaspoon ground cinnamon
1 teaspoon salt or to taste
1 tablespoon lemon juice or 1 teaspoon pomegranate
syrup
½ tablespoon *labneh* (optional)

- Heat ½ tablespoon of the oil in a frying pan, add the pine nuts and sauté until a light golden colour. Remove to a side dish and set aside. Add more oil and when hot add the onions and sauté until yellowish in colour. Add the meat and sauté until it changes colour. Sprinkle with the cinnamon and salt and stir. Return the pine nuts to the pan, stir in the lemon juice or pomegranate syrup and *labneh*, if using, and turn off the heat.

- Moisten your hands with cold water, take small portions of the *kibbeh* dough and roll each portion between your palms to form a ball. Hold the ball in one hand and with the index finger of the other poke a hole in the centre of the *kibbeh* ball and work around the inside with your finger until you have a very thin shell.

- Fill each *kibbeh* shell with 1½ tablespoons of the meat mixture (or less, depending on the size of the shells), then gently reshape and smooth it to enclose the stuffing into an oval shape; moisten your fingers as necessary with cold water to smooth the shells. Place the shells on a side dish after you fill and shape them.

- Heat some oil in a deep-frying pan. When it is hot but not smoking gently drop in the *kibbeh* and fry until they are golden brown on all sides. Remove and drain on kitchen paper.

- Serve warm with lemon wedges, *baba ghanouj* or *hummous*.

Mother's Milk
Laban ummoh

THE LEBANESE NAME for this melange is in some way a hint
to its goodness and digestibility. This dish is highly regarded by the
Lebanese though it is prepared as an everyday meal. It is relatively
expensive as it uses the meat from the best part of the lamb and is
simmered in goat's yoghurt which is regarded as top-notch, superior to
any other. Here I use cow's yoghurt, but I often combine cow's, sheep's
and goat's. As a general rule, when only goat's yoghurt is used there is no
need for the cornflour or egg to stabilize it. However, for it to be
effective it should be of superior quality and not mixed with water.
To make the sauce richer you can add a little fresh cream, though this is
not traditional.

> 500 g (1 lb 1 oz) meat from a leg of lamb, cut into 2.5 cm
>   (1 in) pieces
> 2 cinnamon sticks
> 4 medium-size onions, sliced
> 1 teaspoon salt or to taste
> 1 free-range egg or 1 egg white plus 1 teaspoon cornflour
> 1 kg (2 lb 2 oz) yoghurt
> 2 garlic cloves, pounded until creamy
> 1 teaspoon dried mint or a large handful of finely chopped
>   fresh mint

• Place the meat in a medium-size pan with 450–600 ml (¾ pint–1 pint)
water and bring to the boil, skimming the foam from the surface of the
water. Add the cinnamon sticks, onions and salt. Bring to the boil again,

reduce the heat to low, cover and simmer for 1 hour or until meat is tender. The stock should have reduced to about 150 ml (¼ pint) or even less; if not, ladle out some.

• Five minutes before the end of the cooking time beat the egg or the egg white and cornflour with a fork and combine thoroughly with the yoghurt. Strain through a sieve into a pan, set over medium-high heat and stir continuously with a wooden spoon in the same direction, otherwise the yoghurt will curdle. Bring to the boil. Add the meat and its reduced liquid. Discard the cinnamon sticks and add the garlic. Do this while you're still stirring. Bring back to the boil again, then reduce the heat to low. Add the mint and simmer uncovered for about 3–5 minutes.

• Serve hot with rice and radishes.

NOTE: If there is any leftover *kibbeh* and you want to reheat it, add 1–2 tablespoons water and reheat gently, stirring occasionally.

❀ ❀ ❀

Kibbeh in Tahini Sauce
Kibbeh arnabieh

KIBBEH ARNABIEH is normally prepared when Seville oranges are in season (winter). Because it is a seasonal dish and time consuming to prepare, it is definitely deemed a treat. Indeed, it has proud place on many tables on Sundays, especially in the coastal towns where citrus fruits grow. There are devotees of *kibbeh arnabieh* and of *mouloukhiyeh* (see page 169), and they argue about the superiority of their favourite.

This dish is not difficult to make but it is elaborate, so it is helpful to read the recipe several times before starting the preparation. Here the bones that come with the leg of lamb are used. They enrich the flavour and also the calcium content, an important mineral for strong bones. Some Lebanese omit the meat and refrain from poaching the *kibbeh*, instead cooking them with the *tahini* sauce.

Makes about 14–16 kibbeh *shells*
275 g (10 oz) meat from a leg of lamb, cut into 2.5 cm (1 in) pieces
1–2 bones from the knuckle end of the leg (optional)
1½ teaspoons salt or to taste
250 g (9 oz) onions, roughly sliced
2 bay leaves
2 cinnamon sticks
60 g (2 oz) chick-peas, soaked overnight, drained, rinsed and precooked until nearly tender

For the kibbeh *dough:*
1 small onion, grated
¼–½ teaspoon ground cinnamon
¼ teaspoon allspice
¼ teaspoon freshly ground black pepper
1 teaspoon salt
140 g (5 oz) fine *burghol*
225 g (8 oz) mince, preferably lamb
iced water

For the tahini *sauce:*
250 ml (8 fl oz) *tahini*

120 ml (4 fl oz) clementine juice
120 ml (4 fl oz) orange juice
120 ml (4 fl oz) grapefruit juice
250 ml (8 fl oz) Seville orange juice (in season) or about
    120 ml (4 fl oz) lemon juice or to taste

- Place the meat and bones in a pan with 750 ml (1¼ pints) water. Add the salt and bring to the boil over high heat, skimming the foam from the surface of the water. Add the onions, bay leaves and cinnamon sticks, reduce the heat to low, cover and simmer for 1 hour or until the meat is tender. Fifteen minutes before the end of the cooking time, add the precooked chick-peas.

- Meanwhile, make the *kibbeh* dough. In a bowl, mix the onion with the cinnamon, allspice, pepper and salt. Rinse the *burghol*, quickly squeeze out excess water, and rub into the onion. Add the mince and knead; if necessary add a little iced water to give the dough a smooth texture. Moisten your hands with cold water, take small portions of the dough and roll each one between your palms to make 5 cm (2 in) long shapes. Hold each shape in one hand and with the index finger of the other poke a hole in the centre of the shape and work around the inside until you have a medium-thin shell. Close this opening by bringing the dough together forming pointed ends with the inside empty. Using a cocktail stick, pierce the shells on both ends, then drop them in boiling salted water and cook for 2–4 minutes. Drain and set aside.

- Make the *tahini* sauce. Place the *tahini* in a bowl and gradually whisk in clementine, orange, grapefruit and Seville orange (or lemon) juices. Keep whisking to form a thin, cream-like sauce.

- Add the *tahini* sauce to the meat mixture and its reduced stock. Bring to the boil stirring constantly. Gently drop in the *kibbeh* shells, bring to the boil again and then reduce the heat to medium-low. Simmer for about 10–15 minutes, or until the sauce thickens slightly, stirring occasionally. Remove from heat, discard the bones and cinnamon sticks and transfer to a warm serving bowl.

- Serve immediately with Vermicelli Rice (see page 54) and radishes.

❀ ❀ ❀

Kibbeh in Yoghurt
Kibbeh labanieh

KIBBEH IN YOGHURT seem as the Lebanese mountains, described by the French writer Nerval as '... *chaine violé trés pàle noyé dans les nuages et tainté de lait* (a mountain chain, very pale purple, drowned in the clouds and tinted with milk). This savoury dish is one of the most sought after in Lebanon and at sophisticated dinners it crowns the table. In contrast, in some villages it is eaten along with bread as a simple everyday meal. I recall one trend that started in Beirut in the 1960s: to enrich the dish, chicken was added as an extra ingredient.

As with many other dishes, the preparation of *kibbeh labanieh* varies according to regional customs and economy, and the recipe changes and evolves from village to village. Traditionally, the meat shells that simmer in the yoghurt are empty. Alternatively, they are stuffed with meat and onions. Some people add pine nuts to the stuffing – and the options go on. But the shells still simmer in yoghurt. The resulting dish is served with rice – some prefer to simmer a handful in the yoghurt along with the *kibbeh* shells. Authentically, goat's yoghurt, which many prefer to cow's, is used. It does not need cornflour or egg to stabilize it, unlike cow's, but it must be made from genuine goat's milk.

2–3 tablespoons extra virgin olive oil

125 g (4 oz) mince, preferably lamb

30g (1 oz) grated onion

½ teaspoon ground cinnamon

1½ teaspoons salt or to taste

1 quantity *kibbeh* dough, prepared as for Kibbeh in Tahini
Sauce (see page 159)

1 large free-range egg or 1¼ tablespoons cornflour

1 kg (2 lb 2 oz) cow's or sheep's yoghurt

2 garlic cloves, crushed (optional)

1 bunch coriander, leaves and tender stems only, finely
chopped; or ½ bunch mint leaves, finely chopped;
or 1 teaspoon dried mint

- Heat ½ tablespoon of the oil in a small non-stick frying pan, and add the meat and onion. Sauté until the meat changes colour and the water it releases has nearly evaporated. Sprinkle with the cinnamon, ½ teaspoon salt, stir well and turn the heat off.

- Divide the *kibbeh* dough into 20 portions and do the same with the meat. Moisten your hands with cold water and take a portion of dough. Flatten into a round medium-thin disc. Hold the disc in the palm of your hand and fill with a portion of meat. Gently bring the dough together and smooth it to enclose the filling, then roll it between your palms into an oval or lemon shape. Repeat until all the *kibbeh* shells are completed. Drop the shells into boiling salted water, simmer for 2 minutes, then remove with a slotted spoon and set aside.

- Beat the egg and mix thoroughly with the yoghurt. Alternatively mix the cornflour into the yoghurt. Strain through a sieve into a stainless-steel pan. Place the pan over medium-high heat and bring to the boil while constantly stirring with a wooden spoon in the same direction.

Add the *kibbeh* shells and bring to the boil again, stirring gently. Reduce the heat and simmer over low heat for about 5 minutes, stirring occasionally.

- Meanwhile, wipe the frying pan with kitchen paper and add the remaining oil. When the oil is hot but not smoking add the garlic, if using, and the coriander or fresh mint and sauté for 10 seconds; if using dried mint, sprinkle it directly over the yoghurt just before serving. Add to the *kibbeh* shells and yoghurt in the pan or serve separately, spooning the mixture over individual dishes.

- Serve with plain rice.

NOTE: If you want to use empty *kibbeh* shells prepare them as in the recipe. Pierce both pointed ends of the shells with a cocktail stick, add to the yoghurt and continue as above.

VARIATIONS: To heighten the taste, stir or whip 1 tablespoon fresh cream into the yoghurt. You can sauté chopped coriander, with or without a little crushed garlic, in butter or oil and serve it separately. To keep the snow-white colour of the yoghurt replace the beaten egg with 1 egg white mixed with 1 teaspoon cornflour.

Stuffed Vine Leaves
Warak enab

WARAK ENAB OR YABRAK – a Turkish term/phrase meaning 'leaves of the tree' – is one of the most popular dishes in the Levant. It has travelled to the West and stuffed vine leaves, especially meatless ones cooked in oil, are for sale in many supermarkets and Middle Eastern shops.

Wrapping food in vine leaves is said to have started in ancient times and is referred to in the writings of the Greeks and Persians. Fresh vine leaves have a wonderful lemony flavour. They are wrapped artistically to form finger-like shapes that are most attractive when unmoulded.

In season fresh vine leaves are sold in Middle Eastern speciality shops. They need blanching in boiling water for a few seconds; when canned they need a slightly longer time, which also helps to rid them of salt. Today jars of vine leaves without brine are available.

Thin slices of shoulder or neck of lamb are sometimes layered between the stuffed leaves. Long ago my mother used *janarek*, unripened green plums, instead which gave the dish a pleasing sharpness. Most probably she used them because we had a *janarek* tree in our garden. Some people add the juice of unripened green grapes to *warak enab*, which also produces a lovely tartness. In Marjeyoun, a village in south Lebanon, *warak enab* and stuffed chicken are simmered with stuffed courgettes.

100 g (3½ oz) long grain white rice, preferably basmati
225 g (8 oz) mince, preferably from a leg of lamb
3 garlic cloves, finely crushed
¼ teaspoon ground cinnamon
¼ teaspoon allspice
¼ teaspoon freshly ground black pepper
1½ teaspoons salt or to taste
1 tablespoon extra virgin olive oil
4 lamb cutlets (optional)
30 vine leaves
5–7 tablespoons lemon juice

- Place the rice, meat, garlic, cinnamon, allspice, pepper and half the salt in a bowl with 6 tablespoons water. Mix thoroughly and set aside.

- Heat the oil in a medium-size pan, add the oil the lamb cutlets, if using, and sauté lightly on both sides. Turn off the heat. Blanch the vine leaves in batches of six for a few seconds in boiling water or steam them. Remove them carefully to prevent breaking and drain in a colander. Place 1 leaf at a time on a clean surface, stem end towards you with the shiny side facing down. Trim off the stem and spread 1½ teaspoons of the meat mixture evenly near the stem end. Roll once, fold in both sides of the leaf and continue to roll firmly into a sausage shape about 5 cm (2 in) long, depending on the size of the leaf. Repeat with the remaining leaves and meat mixture. Arrange them over the lamb cutlets in the pan, packing them tightly one next to the other. Season with the remaining salt, add 300–450 ml (½–¾ pints) water – just enough to barely cover the leaves – and place a small heavy dish on top of the leaves to prevent them opening while cooking.

- Bring to the boil over high heat, then reduce the heat to medium-low. Cover and simmer for about 1½ hours or until the leaves are tender; to check, remove 1 leaf roll and taste. About 5–8 minutes before the end of the cooking time add the lemon juice and cover the pan again. Remove the pan from the heat, carefully press on the dish with your fingers and empty the reduced liquor into a bowl to ease unmoulding the leaves. Remove the dish, place a large serving plate over the pan and turn the pan upside down.

- Serve immediately with the liquor spooned over. Eat with yoghurt.

Stuffed Cabbage
Malfouf mihshi

AN ATTRACTIVE and homely delight, *malfouf mihshi* is prepared with
cabbage leaves wrapped around a succulent mixture of mince, rice or,
as is traditional, coarse *burghol*, and spices. Stuffed cabbage is served hot
on its own as a main dish or is accompanied by a bowl of yoghurt and
wholemeal Lebanese bread. Adding Seville orange juice works wonders.
To lock in as many nutrients as possible, steam the cabbage instead of
boiling it.

    I x 900 g (2 lb) head of green cabbage
    120 g (4 oz) long grain brown rice
    275 g (10 oz) mince, preferably from a leg or
        shoulder of lamb
    ½ teaspoon ground cinnamon
    ½ teaspoon allspice
    ¼ teaspoon freshly ground black pepper
    1¼ teaspoons salt or to taste
    4 tablespoons hot water
    ½ tablespoon extra virgin olive oil
    12 garlic cloves
    15 g (½ oz) butter
    1–1½ teaspoons dried mint
    6 tablespoons lemon juice or 300 ml (½ pint) Seville
        orange juice

* Cut out and discard the core of the cabbage, then gently remove the
  leaves one at a time. Put them in a pan with just enough boiling water

to cover and leave to stand for a few minutes until limp and easily pliable. Drain. Alternatively, place the head of cabbage in a steaming basket and set into a pan over 2.5 cm (1 in) boiling water. Cover and steam until tender, then gently separate the leaves.

- In a bowl, combine the rice, mince, cinnamon, allspice, pepper, half the salt and the hot water. Set aside.

- Place several cabbage leaves on a clean surface, thick vein sides up. Trim the middle thick vein of each leaf or flatten it with your thumb. Put about 1 tablespoon of the meat mixture on the stem end of each leaf. Roll once, fold in both sides of the leaf and continue to roll the leaf around the meat mixture. Repeat with all the leaves. Set aside.

- Heat the oil in a pan over medium-high heat until hot but not smoking. Add 8 of the garlic cloves and stir until golden brown, about 1 minute. Remove from the heat and arrange the cabbage rolls, seam sides down, in the pan. Place the garlic at intervals between the rolls. Pour in enough water to just cover the cabbage, season with the remaining salt and bring to the boil. Reduce the heat to medium-low, cover and simmer for 30–40 minutes.

- Meanwhile, crush the remaining garlic until smooth, heat the butter in a small frying pan and lightly sauté the garlic for a few seconds. Turn off the heat and quickly stir in the mint. Add to the cabbage rolls along with the lemon juice. Cover the pan and continue to simmer for a further 30 minutes.

- Serve hot with plain yoghurt and Lebanese bread.

Jew's Mallow
Mouloukhiyeh

THE JEW'S MALLOW PLANT is said to have originated in the Jewish community in Aleppo; it then travelled to Lebanon and Egypt and in the process was used by the locals. The legend says that the Fatimid Egyptian sultan, Hakim bi amr Allah, deified by the Druse, prohibited his congregation from eating *mouloukhiyeh*. Some say that it was owing to its aphrodisiac virtues, while others claim that the sultan wished to punish his undisciplined people, who were fond of *mouloukhiyeh*, for improprieties. Whatever the truth, many Druse, and definitely the religious sheikhs, even now, refrain from eating it. The preparation is lengthy but this dish is worth trying for its rich, aromatic taste.

I x 900 g–1.35 kg (2–3 lb) free-range chicken, skin removed
350 g (12 oz) meat from a leg of lamb, cut into 3 cm (1¼ in) cubes
2 bones from the knuckle end of the leg
I whole onion, plus I large onion, very finely chopped
2 large cinnamon sticks
1½ teaspoons salt or to taste
3–4 bunches fresh *mouloukhiyeh*, leaves only, rinsed and patted dry
175 ml (6 fl oz) organic cider or red wine vinegar
2 medium-size pitta breads, toasted and broken into small pieces
I bunch coriander, leaves and tender stems only, finely chopped
¼ teaspoon ground coriander

8–10 garlic cloves, crushed
Heaped ¼ teaspoon ground cinnamon
Heaped ¼ teaspoon freshly ground black pepper

- Place the chicken, lamb and bones in a large pan with 2 litres (3½ pints) water and bring to the boil over high heat, skimming the foam from the surface of the water. Add the whole onion, cinnamon sticks and salt, then reduce the heat to medium, cover and simmer for 50–60 minutes or until both chicken and meat are tender.

- Meanwhile, pack together small handfuls of the *mouloukhiyeh* leaves and slice them very finely, or place them in a food processor (make sure they are dry) and run the motor on and off, 2–3 times only otherwise the *mouloukhiyeh* will become too mushy. Set aside.

- Combine the chopped onion and vinegar in a serving bowl and place the bread in a dish. Set aside.

- Remove the chicken from the broth and debone it. Cut its meat into serving pieces and place on one side of a serving dish. Remove the meat from the broth and place next to the chicken pieces. Remove the bones and discard, along with the cinnamon sticks and onion. To the broth in the pan add the fresh and ground coriander and garlic and bring to the boil, then reduce the heat to medium, cover and simmer for 5–6 minutes. Add the reserved *mouloukhiyeh*, season with the ground cinnamon and pepper. Bring to the boil again and simmer for 2 minutes. Taste and adjust the seasonings.

- Serve the *mouloukhiyeh* in a soup bowl with a side dish of plain cooked rice, the onion and vinegar and the toasted bread. To eat, put about 2 tablespoons of the rice in a soup plate, top with a little chicken, some meat pieces and a little bread, then ladle over some *mouloukhiyeh*. Cover with onions and vinegar to taste and eat with a spoon.

Aubergines with Pine Nuts and Tomato
Sheikh al-mihshi

THIS IS A PLEASANT VARIATION on cooking aubergine, the queen of vegetables. A Lebanese story is told in praise of aubergines. Traditionally, when they were in season a wife was expected to know the vast array of dishes that can be prepared with them. When a husband came home after a long day and asked what was for dinner, the reply had to be instant. The wife in the story failed to reply and was sent back to her parents. I am not sure whether this tale was told in praise of the aubergine or to intimidate young brides. A friend of mine told me that whenever someone asked for her hand in marriage she asked him: 'Do you know how to cook aubergines?'

8 small aubergines
4 tablespoons extra virgin olive oil
1½ tablespoons pine nuts
1 onion, finely chopped
120 g (4 oz) mince, preferably lamb
1 tomato, finely chopped
1 teaspoon salt or to taste
¼ teaspoon allspice
¼ teaspoon freshly ground black pepper
Pinch of ground cinnamon
Pinch of white pepper
300–350 ml (10–12 fl oz) boiling water
2 tablespoons double concentrated tomato purée
1 tablespoon lemon juice

- Preheat the oven to 190°C/375°F/Gas Mark 5. Trim the green cap of each aubergine, leaving half the stem intact. Peel the aubergines leaving lengthwise strips of skin. Heat the oil in a medium-size frying pan over medium heat. When it is hot but not smoking, add the aubergines 4 at a time and cook until lightly browned and soft. Remove with a slotted spoon, allowing the oil to drip back into the pan, and leave to cool.

- Add the pine nuts to the pan and sauté until golden in colour, stirring constantly. Quickly add the onion and meat and cook until browned, about 5 minutes. Add the tomato and stir. Season with half the salt and add the allspice, black pepper, cinnamon and white pepper. Stir well and turn the heat off.

- Make a deep slit along the side of each aubergine and with your fingers or a spoon fill the slit with the meat mixture. Place in a deep baking dish. In a small glass bowl, combine the boiling water, remaining salt, tomato purée and lemon juice. Stir and pour over the aubergines. Bake for 30–35 minutes.

- Serve immediately with Vermicelli Rice (see page 54).

❋ ❋ ❋

Upside Down Aubergines
Makloubet al-batinjan

AN IMAGINATIVE and most enchanting dish cherished by aubergine lovers and many others throughout the Levant. *Makloubet* means upside down. Traditionally, it is prepared with repeated layers of meat, rice and aubergine, which are then simmered in the meat broth. When it is unmoulded it looks spectacular and is rendered more so if embellished with glistening pine nuts and almonds.

Here, for a quick and economical version, the procedure is shortened. Instead of cooking a half or whole leg of lamb, mince is used. I use white rice, but brown can be substituted (remember it will require more water and takes longer to cook). Another option is to prepare the dish with coarse *burghol* (cracked wheat), which cooks quickly.

750 g (1 lb 10 oz) aubergines
Extra virgin olive oil
Handful of pine nuts
Handful of whole almonds or almond flakes (optional)
500 g (1 lb 1 oz) lamb mince
1 medium-size onion, grated
1 teaspoon ground cinnamon
¼ teaspoon freshly ground black pepper
¼ teaspoon allspice
2 teaspoons of salt
1 medium-size tomato, peeled (optional)
750 ml (1¼ pints) hot water
225 g (8 oz) long grain white rice, preferably basmati

- Preheat the grill to high and a baking tray. Peel the aubergines leaving lengthwise strips of skin. Cut lengthwise into thin 5 mm (¼ in) slices. Brush both sides with oil and place on the baking tray. Grill until brown, then turn to brown the other side. Remove and set aside.

- Heat ½ tablespoon of the oil in a pan, add the pine nuts and sauté until golden in colour. Remove with a slotted spoon and set aside. Add the almonds, if using, to the same pan and if necessary add a little more oil. Sauté until golden in colour, remove and place with the pine nuts. Add the mince and onion to the pan, stir and cook until the meat changes colour, about 5–6 minutes or until browned. A liquid may appear and

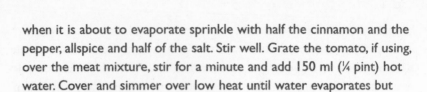

when it is about to evaporate sprinkle with half the cinnamon and the pepper, allspice and half of the salt. Stir well. Grate the tomato, if using, over the meat mixture, stir for a minute and add 150 ml (¼ pint) hot water. Cover and simmer over low heat until water evaporates but meat is quite moist. Turn the heat off.

- Meanwhile, place the rice, remaining salt and 300 ml (½ pint) hot water in a pan. Bring to the boil, cover, then reduce the heat to low and simmer for about 7 minutes or until water has been absorbed by the rice.

- Preheat the oven to 180°C/350°F/Gas Mark 4. Cover the base and sides of a medium-size, round baking tin with some of the aubergine slices. Place a layer of the meat mixture and reduced liquid over the slices, top with rice and then add another layer of aubergine slices. Repeat until all the meat, rice and aubergine slices are used. Cover with 150 ml (¼ pint) hot water mixed with the remaining cinnamon. Cover and bake for about 15–20 minutes, then remove and uncover the tin. Place a serving dish on top and carefully turn the baking tin upside down. Leave to stand for 2 minutes then remove the baking tin. Sprinkle with the reserved nuts.

- Serve with plain yoghurt or Spinach in Yoghurt (see page 237).

❀ ❀ ❀

Stuffed Artichokes
Ardi-chowki mihshi

STUFFED ARTICHOKES are a stylish delicacy that will impress family and friends. They are time-consuming to prepare but the result is worthwhile.

In Lebanon they are served as part of the daily home cuisine, and as a *plat du jour* in some restaurants. An aromatic combination of mince, onions, pine nuts and spices is packed into the artichoke hearts which are then simmered gently in water and sharpened with the lemon juice. Fresh artichokes are available all year in many outlets and good frozen or canned artichoke hearts are sold in supermarkets.

8 fresh globe artichokes
½ lemon
1½–2 tablespoons extra virgin olive oil
30 g (1 oz) pine nuts
90 g (3 oz) onion, finely chopped
175 g (6 oz) mince, preferably lamb
¼ teaspoon ground cinnamon
½ teaspoon allspice
¾ teaspoon salt
200 ml (7 fl oz) hot water
1 teaspoon plain flour
2–3 tablespoons lemon juice

- To prepare the artichokes, cut off the stem close to the base and snap off all the leaves one by one until you reach the base. With a sharp knife gently scoop out the choke and discard it, then trim the tough skin around the base and quickly rub with the lemon to prevent discolouration.

- Heat the oil in a frying pan over medium-high heat and when it is hot but not smoking add the artichoke hearts, four at a time. Sauté for 1–2 minutes, coating all sides with the oil. Remove to a plate with a slotted spoon, allowing the oil to drip back into the pan, and set aside. Add the pine nuts and sauté, stirring constantly, until pale golden in colour. Quickly add the onion and mince and stir well to prevent the pine nuts turning darker in colour. Cook until the meat is browned, about 3–5 minutes. Stir in the cinnamon, half the allspice and the salt, stir well and turn off the heat.

• Use a spoon to fill the artichoke hearts with the meat mixture, pressing in as much as possible. Place in one layer in a medium-size pan and carefully pour in the water. Mix the flour with the lemon juice and add to the water in the pan. Add the remaining allspice. Bring to the boil over medium heat, then reduce the heat to medium-low, cover and simmer for 20 minutes. Transfer the artichoke hearts to a serving dish, spooning the liquid over.

• Serve with Vermicelli Rice (see page 54) and a seasonal salad.

❀ ❀ ❀

Courgettes Farci and Pine Nuts
Kablama

THIS LOVELY VERSION of stuffed baby courgettes was the first savoury dish I prepared. I remember that I fried the courgettes, which made it easier to slit them for stuffing. Lebanese ones are tiny, about the size of a finger, so this was possible. Here I steam the courgettes and then sauté them. In general, they are hollowed out which may seem easier and more straightforward than making a slit. Nevertheless, slitting them gives the dish a distinctive appearance.

8 baby courgettes
1 tablespoon extra virgin olive oil
120 g (4 oz) lamb mince
30 g (1 oz) grated onion

2 tablespoons pine nuts
Pinch of ground cinnamon
Pinch of white pepper
Pinch of allspice
¾ teaspoon salt
150 ml (¼ pint) hot water
1–2 tablespoons lemon juice
Juice of 1 sour pomegranate

- Place the courgettes in a steamer and set into a pan over 2.5 cm (1 in) boiling water. Cover and steam until just soft, about 3–5 minutes; press the courgettes with your fingers to see if they are done. Remove and leave for a few minutes until they are cool enough to handle.

- Meanwhile, heat ½ tablespoon of the oil in a non-stick frying pan. Add the mince and onion and sauté until meat changes colour. If a liquid appears wait until it has nearly evaporated then stir in the pine nuts, cinnamon, pepper, allspice and half of the salt. Stir well and turn the heat off.

- Trim the courgettes and make a lengthwise slit in each of them, without puncturing the other side; it becomes a pocket for the filling. Divide the meat mixture into 8 portions and push these inside the courgettes. Wipe the frying pan with kitchen paper, add the remaining oil and place over medium heat. When the oil is hot add the courgettes, filling sides up. Sauté for 1 minute or until lightly browned. Gently add the hot water and the remaining salt. Bring to the boil, then reduce the heat, cover and simmer for about 15 minutes. Add the lemon and pomegranate juices and simmer until the liquid has reduced by half, about 10 minutes.

- Serve hot with plain basmati rice.

Lamb Dumplings in Yoghurt
Chiche barak

ONE OF THE MOST APPRECIATED dishes in Lebanon, especially among Armenians, *chiche barak* reflects its Ottoman origins. A recipe known as *manti* in Turkey is similar, but its flavour and preparation are different. Small, stuffed parcels are simmered in yoghurt, to which coriander is added, to make a beautiful, economical lunch or dinner dish.

Makes 70 pieces
2 tablespoons extra virgin olive oil
200 g (7 oz) lamb mince
½ medium-size onion
Good pinch of ground cinnamon
Pinch of allspice
Pinch of freshly ground black pepper
½ teaspoon salt
1 kg (2 lb 2 oz) cow's or sheep's yoghurt
1 egg white
1 teaspoon cornflour diluted with ½ tablespoon water
1 tablespoon fresh cream (optional)
2–3 garlic cloves, pounded until creamy
1 small bunch coriander, leaves and tender stems only,
    finely chopped

For the dough:
200 g (7 oz) unbleached all-purpose white flour
½ teaspoon salt or to taste
½ teaspoon organic cider vinegar

- Make the dough. Combine the flour, salt and vinegar, gradually add about 150 ml (5 fl oz) water, and mix and knead for about 3–4 minutes to form a pliable dough. Cover with a clean cloth and leave to rest for 30 minutes.

- Meanwhile, heat ½ tablespoon of the oil in a non-stick frying pan, add the mince and grate the onion over it. Cook until the meat changes colour, about 4 minutes. If a liquid appears wait until it has nearly evaporated then stir in the cinnamon, allspice, pepper and salt. Turn the heat off.

- Divide the dough into two portions. Roll one portion thinly over a lightly floured surface and, with a biscuit cutter, cut it into 2.5 cm (1 in) rounds. Place about 1 teaspoon of the meat mixture in the centre of each. Bring the opposite sides together to make a half-moon shape, pinch to secure, then bring the two pointed ends together and pinch to seal, leaving a hole in the middle. Place on waxed paper to prevent them from sticking.

- Thoroughly mix the yoghurt with the egg white and cornflour paste and sieve into a pan. Place over medium heat and stir constantly with a wooden spoon in one direction until boiling. Stir the cream, if using, into the yoghurt. Add the dough parcels and bring to the boil, then reduce the heat to low and simmer for about 5–8 minutes, stirring occasionally.

- Meanwhile heat the remaining oil in a non-stick frying pan. Add the garlic and coriander and sauté for a few seconds only. Pour this over the yoghurt in the pan and leave for 1 minute (or serve separately).

- Serve hot with plain or Vermicelli Rice (see page 54).

NOTE: You can add fresh or dried mint to the yoghurt instead of coriander. The dough parcels can be baked in the oven until they are just dry, before being added to the yoghurt. The dough parcels also freeze well.

VARIATION: Small *kibbeh*, as in Kibbeh in Yoghurt (see page 159) can be added with the dough parcels.

❀ ❀ ❀

Fried Meat Patties
Kafta mikli

PICTURE A CROWD of people in an olive grove resting on blankets thrown over the grass. Some men are playing backgammon while others are smoking the *nargileh* (hubble bubble). Children run around and hide behind trees. A little further away, smoke emanates from the *kafta* being grilled over glowing red embers. From a distance the people seem like flowers of different colours, a garden of happiness and peace. How often I have seen this on spring and summer Sundays. Today I so long for it.

Kafta is a popular Middle Eastern version of the hamburger, made of ground meat combined in abundance with richly flavoured parsley and a blend of spices.

This medley is the basis of numerous recipes cooked in a variety of ways. *Kafta* is excellent fried, as below, or pressed on to skewers to be grilled or barbecued; it is often accompanied by fried potatoes and *mtabbal al-batinjan* (Aubergine Dip see page 36), which goes particularly well with it.

I onion, finely chopped
Large handful of parsley, tough stems removed
8–10 mint leaves
450 g (I lb) mince, preferably lamb
½ teaspoon ground cinnamon
¼ teaspoon freshly ground black pepper
¼ teaspoon allspice

1 teaspoon salt or to taste

90–120 ml (3–4 fl oz) extra virgin olive oil

- Place the onion, parsley and mint in a food processor and blend until smooth. Mix thoroughly with the mince, cinnamon, pepper, allspice and salt, and shape into a ball. Take small portions and flatten them between the palms of your hands to form medium-size patties about 5 cm (2 in) in diameter; moisten your hands with water as necessary. Arrange the *kafta* patties over a lightly floured dish and set aside.

- Heat the oil in a frying pan over medium-high heat and when it is hot but not smoking add the patties. Cook over medium heat until browned on both sides, about 6–8 minutes. Remove with a slotted spoon, drain on kitchen paper, arrange on a dish and serve.

NOTE: To cut back on frying, place the *kafta* patties on a lightly oiled baking tray and grill on both sides until browned.

VARIATION: Use chopped chicken breast instead of minced meat and follow as above, adding a little ground cumin instead of mint.

Baked Kafta
Kafta saynieh

THIS HOMELY and delicious dish is found throughout Lebanon. *Kafta saynieh* is easy to prepare and is baked with a selection of fresh vegetables, producing an interesting deep yet subtle flavour and colourful presentation. Here the meat is spread over the pan. Some people prefer to make patties. Traditionally, the potatoes and meat are both fried in oil; in this recipe frying is omitted with no noticeable change in the taste.

> **1 quantity *kafta* mixture, prepared as for Fried Meat Patties (see page 180)**
> **1 tablespoon extra virgin olive oil**
> **550 g (1¼ lb) potatoes, unpeeled and cut into medium-thin slices**
> **200 g (7 oz) onions, cut into medium-thin slices**
> **2 large ripe tomatoes, sliced**
> **¾ teaspoon salt or to taste**
> **¼ teaspoon freshly ground black pepper or to taste**
> **¼ teaspoon ground cinnamon**
> **Pinch of allspice**
> **2 tablespoons double concentrated tomato purée**
> **300 ml (½ pint) boiling water**

- Preheat the oven to 180°C/350°F/Gas Mark 4 and brush a medium-sized round tin with oil. Spread the *kafta* mixture over the base of the tin and smooth it to a depth of about 5 mm (¼ in). Preheat the grill and grill the *kafta* until lightly browned, about 2–4 minutes. Spread the potatoes over the *kafta*, then add the onions followed by the tomatoes. Combine the salt, pepper, cinnamon, allspice and tomato purée with the boiling water and pour over the vegetables in the baking dish.

- Bake until the potatoes are tender, about 1½ hours, basting twice with the pan juices.

- Serve with a seasonal salad.

Meatballs in Tomato Sauce
Dawood Pasha

DAWOOD PASHA was the first governor of Mount Lebanon appointed by the Ottomans with the approval of the Western powers, after the war between the Druse and the Christian Maronites in 1860. Meatballs in tomato sauce served with rice was said to be one of his favourite dishes and the recipe took his name. Traditionally, its main ingredients, onions and meatballs, are fried with *samneh* (sheep fat). Nowadays this is less acceptable. Here the onions and meat are not fried but still retain their succulence while being lighter to digest. Also, a small amount of meat is used; this can be doubled along with the spices and without having to double the amount of sauce. Just check the level of the water and add more if necessary.

225 g (8 oz) lean mince
¼ teaspoon ground cinnamon
¼ teaspoon freshly ground black pepper
Pinch of allspice
½ teaspoon salt

For the sauce:
3 onions, thinly sliced
3 tablespoons double concentrated tomato purée
¼ teaspoon salt or to taste
¼ teaspoon ground cinnamon
¼ teaspoon allspice
45 g (1½ oz) pine nuts
1 teaspoon plain flour
1 tablespoon lemon juice

- In a bowl, combine the mince, cinnamon, pepper, allspice and salt and mix thoroughly. From this mixture form mini-meatballs 2 cm (¾ in) in diameter. Preheat the grill and a baking tray. Arrange the meatballs over the tray in a single layer, place 10 cm (4 in) away from heat and grill until browned, about 4–5 minutes. Quickly remove the meatballs to a dish to prevent them from sticking.

- Put the onions in a pan with 750 ml (1¼ pints) water, bring to the boil, cover and simmer over medium heat for 10 minutes. Add the tomato purée, salt, cinnamon, allspice, pine nuts, flour and mini-meatballs. Stir well, bring to the boil again, then reduce the heat to medium-low, cover and simmer for about 20–30 minutes. Stir in the lemon juice – do not boil – and turn the heat off. Leave for a few minutes to allow the flavours to blend.

- Serve with Vermicelli Rice (see page 54) and a side salad.

VARIATION: A different and interesting sauce is prepared by the Greek Orthodox Christians of Beirut who blend 200 g (7 oz) pine nuts with water and lemon juice to the consistency of single cream. The onions are chopped and fried, and the mince is also fried. The sauce simmers gently with the meatballs until all the flavours blend.

Spiced Meat
Shawarma

A HEALTHIER TAKE on a very popular Middle Eastern speciality. Lamb meat and fat are marinated for 12–24 hours, then layered alternately on a large skewer and placed in front of an upright grill while the skewer turns slowly. As the outside of the meat browns it is thinly sliced over a split Lebanese bread to serve as a takeaway or to eat in a restaurant, and this is repeated until all meat is consumed. *Shawarma* is rich in saturated fats, but this home-made version uses a leaner meat and is marinated in olive oil, a monounsaturate that is known to improve the balance of HDL (friendly cholesterol). The meat is first baked, then browned under the grill. I believe its flavour is as good as that of the real *shawarma*. *Shawarma* is delicious, very easy to prepare and suitable for an exotic dinner or to add variety to a buffet.

675 g (1½ lb) meat, preferably from a leg of lamb or beef fillet, cut into 5 mm (¼ in) strips
½ teaspoon ground cinnamon
1¼ teaspoons freshly ground black pepper
½ teaspoon allspice
¼ teaspoon white pepper
¼ teaspoon freshly grated nutmeg
¼ teaspoon ground cardomoms or 4–5 whole cardamoms
Pinch of ground cloves or 2–3 whole cloves
2–3 pieces *miskee* (see Glossary page 302), gently crushed to a powder with a little salt
4 tablespoons lemon juice
5 tablespoons organic cider vinegar
2 tablespoons extra virgin olive oil
½ teaspoon salt or to taste
¼–½ teaspoon grated orange zest
1 small tomato, peeled and very finely chopped or shredded
1 small onion, finely grated
1 large Lebanese bread, split

For the tahini *sauce*:
5–6 tablespoons lemon juice
120 ml (4 fl oz) *tahini*
¼ teaspoon salt or to taste

- Place the meat in a glass bowl. Season with the cinnamon, black pepper, allspice, white pepper, nutmeg, cardamoms and cloves. Add the *miskee* and toss with the lemon juice, vinegar, oil and salt. Add the orange zest, tomato and onion, mix thoroughly and leave to marinate, covered, in the fridge for 12–18 hours, tossing 2–3 times.

- Preheat oven to 180°C/ 350°F/Gas Mark 4. Remove the meat from the fridge and allow it a little time to reach room temperature. Arrange the meat mixture in one layer on the base of a baking dish. Bake for about 30–40 minutes or until cooked through.

- Meanwhile, prepare the *tahini* sauce. In a bowl, gradually whisk the lemon juice into the *tahini*. Before the liquid thickens and while you are whisking add up to 5–6 tablespoons water (or you can use orange juice, if liked) and the salt; the sauce should look like cream, neither too thin nor too thick. Taste and adjust the seasoning.

- Preheat the grill. Remove the meat from the oven, place it 10 cm (4 in) away from the heat and grill for about 2–3 minutes or until nicely browned, turning the strips to brown both sides. Split a large Lebanese bread and place the meat inside its pocket.

- Serve immediately with the *tahini* sauce or *hummous*, home-made pickles, and with thinly sliced red onions sprinkled with 1 tablespoon of *sumac* and topped with a handful of coarsely chopped parsley leaves.

Marinated Lamb with Spices, Yoghurt and Rice

Lahmet ganam wa roz

IN THE MIDDLE EAST lamb is often cooked whole and presented with beautifully glistening rice and browned nuts, especially during the religious feasts of Id al Kabir and Id al Saghir (big and small feasts) and when pilgrims return from the hajj (pilgrimage to Mecca). Marinating the meat in yoghurt is a very Arabic way of tenderizing it and gives the lamb a special flavour and colour. Every country has its own mixture of spices to rub into it. In Lebanon cinnamon is the most commonly used. Nevertheless, every region, if not every household, has its own touch. The lamb can be prepared ahead of time and is suitable for parties. If you don't fancy making the rice, bake the lamb until browned and cooked through (about 3 hours) and serve with roasted potatoes. This recipe calls for a leg of lamb, but you can use a lamb shoulder instead. Ask your butcher to debone the lamb and keep the bones to use with the stock. This recipes serves 6–8 people.

    I x 3 kg (6½ lb) leg of lamb, boned
    I–2 bones from the leg
    8–10 tablespoons sheep's yoghurt
    2–3 tablespoons extra virgin olive oil
    I onion studded with 2 cloves
    I bouquet garni: 5 cardamoms, 3–4 cinnamon sticks, few
        parsley stems, I slice of orange peel, I piece of celery
    1.8 litres (5 pints) hot water
    I teaspoon salt
    450 g (I lb) lamb mince

I teaspoon ground cinnamon
¼ teaspoon allspice
¼ teaspoon freshly ground black pepper
Good pinch of freshly grated nutmeg
Pinch of white pepper
450 g (I lb) long grain white rice, preferably basmati
Large handful of almonds, toasted
Large handful of pine nuts, toasted
Large handful of pistachio nuts (optional)
I *markouk* bread (optional)

For the spice mixture:
2½–3 teaspoons ground cinnamon
I–I½ teaspoons allspice
¼ teaspoon ground cumin
¼ teaspoon ground coriander
¼ teaspoon ground caraway seeds
4 cloves, finely ground
3 cardamoms, finely ground
½ teaspoon salt
I garlic clove, pounded until creamy
Good pinch of freshly ground black pepper

- Make the spice mixture. Place the cinnamon, allspice, cumin, coriander, ground caraway seeds, cloves, cardamoms and salt in a small bowl. Gradually add ¾ tablespoon water, stirring until you have a creamy consistency. Stir in the garlic.

- Open up the lamb to reveal the meaty side and make 3–4 slits, then rub some of spice mixture all over the meat and inside the slits so that the spices are well absorbed. Fold the lamb over and rub the remaining

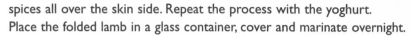

spices all over the skin side. Repeat the process with the yoghurt. Place the folded lamb in a glass container, cover and marinate overnight.

- Gently heat 1 tablespoon of the oil in a large pan and add the marinated lamb, skin-side down. It should sizzle. Also add the bones and the onion. Sauté for about 5 minutes until brown but not burnt. Turn the lamb over. If a white liquid appears continue cooking until it darkens in colour and has nearly evaporated; this enhances the flavour of the meat and stock. Add 1.8 litres (5 pints) water and bring to the boil, skimming the foam from the surface of the water. Add the bouquet garni and salt. Bring again to the boil. Make sure the water covers the meat, otherwise weigh it down with a heavy heatproof dish. Cover, reduce the heat to medium-low and cook for 2½–3 hours or until the meat falls apart.

- Preheat the oven to 180°C/350°F/Gas Mark 4. When the cooking time of the lamb is up, heat ½–1 tablespoon of the oil in a frying pan, add the mince and sauté until browned. If a liquid appears, wait until it has nearly evaporated then stir in the cinnamon, allspice, black pepper, nutmeg and white pepper. Stir well and ladle in 300 ml (½ pint) of the stock from the lamb. Cover and simmer over medium heat until stock has evaporated but the mince is still moist.

- Meanwhile, place the rice and about 1 litre (1¾ pints) of the lamb stock in a medium-size pan. Bring to the boil, then reduce the heat, cover and simmer over low heat until the stock has been absorbed (about 8–10 minutes). Halfway through check the flavour of the rice. It may need a little salt; if so add it at this point before the stock evaporates.

- Rub your hands with olive oil, coat the almonds and pine nuts and place them in the oven. Allow about 10–12 minutes for them to reach a deep golden colour. Turn the heat off and leave for 2 minutes more or as necessary. They will brown beautifully. Remove and cool.

- When the lamb, rice and mince are ready, place the *markouk* bread, if using, in a wide serving dish. Cut the lamb into bite-size pieces or chunks. Spread the rice over the bread, then the mince and finally the lamb. Sprinkle with a few tablespoons of the stock and top with the nuts and pistachios, if using. Fold over the bread and place in a hot oven for 2–5 minutes before serving.

NOTE: For a quick-fix supper just serve the mince mixture with the rice.

❀ ❀ ❀

Dervish's Beads
Masbahat al-derwich

THE NAME OF THIS RECIPE is connected with the dervish practice of incessantly repeating prayers, since the dish was elaborate and needed patience to prepare, with its endless layers representing the endless beads. Traditionally, the meat and vegetables, with the exception of the tomatoes, are fried separately in butter. This is a simpler version.

285 g (10 oz) meat from a leg of lamb, preferably the fillet, sliced medium-thin
2 tablespoons extra virgin olive oil
I onion, sliced, or pearl onions
I aubergine, sliced
I courgette, cut into 5 mm (¼ in) slices
I orange pepper, cored, deseeded and sliced
2 potatoes, unpeeled, scrubbed and cut into 1.5 cm (½ in) cubes
500 g (I lb I oz) ripe tomatoes, peeled and quartered
2 teaspoons salt

Pinch of ground cinnamon
¼ teaspoon freshly ground black pepper
4 tablespoons hot water
I tablespoon double concentrated tomato purée

• Preheat the oven to 180°C/350°F/Gas Mark 4. Place the meat and
  I tablespoon of the oil in a heavy-bottomed ovenproof dish. Add the
  onions or pearl onions. Then in successive layers spread the aubergine,
  courgette and pepper slices and potato cubes. Finally, cover with the
  tomatoes. Sprinkle with the salt, cinnamon and pepper. Mix the hot
  water with the tomato purée and remaining oil and pour all over the
  vegetables. Bake, covered, for 2 hours or until cooked through. Uncover
  the dish for the last 20–30 minutes to allow the contents to brown.

❀ ❀ ❀

Lebanese Couscous
Moghrabiyeh

DON'T BE MISLED by the name *moghrabiyeh*, which means Moroccan:
this is a couscous with a difference and, although it may have originated
in North Africa, it has little to do with the many dishes prepared in that
region. Towards the end of the fourteenth century many pilgrims from
North Africa passed through Lebanon on their way to and from Mecca.
Some liked the weather, others needed to make money or were ill and
had to rest. Many stayed for good and their food, principally couscous,
was prepared according to local preferences and available ingredients.
The taste and flavour of Lebanese *moghrabiyeh* is very distinctive. It is
particularly popular in Tripoli, the second largest town in Lebanon; and
can be bought in Lebanese shops in the UK.

1 x 1 kg (2 lb 2 oz) small chicken, cleaned (see page 122)
   or pieces of chicken

225 g (8 oz) meat from a leg of lamb, cut into 4 cm (1½ in)
   pieces

2 cinnamon sticks

2 cardamoms

2 bay leaves

1½ teaspoons salt or to taste

60 g (2 oz) chick-peas, soaked overnight, drained and
   rinsed

12–14 baby onions or pearl onions, peeled

1–1½ teaspoons ground cinnamon

1–1½ tablespoons ground caraway seeds

3 tablespoons extra virgin olive oil

225 g (8 oz) *moghrabiyeh* grains

30 g (1 oz) butter

¾ pint (15 fl oz) stock from chicken and meat

- Place the chicken and lamb in a large pan with 1.75 litres (3 pints)
  water and bring to the boil over high heat, skimming the foam from the
  surface of the water. Add the cinnamon sticks, cardamoms, bay leaves
  and 1 teaspoon of the salt. Reduce the heat to medium and cook for
  about 1 hour or until the chicken is tender (it cooks faster than red
  meat). Remove and debone the chicken and cut it into medium-large
  pieces. Cover with some broth and keep warm until serving time.
  Continue to cook the meat until it is tender.

- Meanwhile, place the chick-peas in a pan, cover with water by 5 cm
  (2 in) and bring to the boil, skimming the foam from the surface of the
  water. Reduce the heat to low, cover and simmer until tender, about
  1–1½ hours (the time will depend on the brand; organic chick-peas take

longer to cook). Add the onions and simmer for a further 30 minutes. Five minutes before the end of the cooking time, season with ¼ teaspoon each of the cinnamon and caraway, and the remaining salt. Stir and set this chick-pea sauce aside.

- Add 1 tablespoon of the oil to a pan of salted boiling water. Drop in the *moghrabiyeh* grains and cook for 5–7 minutes, then drain them and rinse under cold running water. Place in a colander to drain. Season with the remaining cinnamon and caraway, thoroughly coating the grains.

- Melt the butter in a deep frying pan and add the remaining oil. Set over medium-high heat and when hot add the seasoned grains. Reduce the heat to low and stir the grains for about 3 minutes. While stirring, gradually add 450 ml (¾ pint) stock from the chicken and lamb. Cover and simmer over low heat for about 10 minutes or until the grains are tender and moist, not dry. Taste and adjust the seasonings. Combine chick-pea sauce with about 300 ml (½ pint) or less of the stock and reheat. Arrange the *moghrabiyeh* on a serving dish and spread the chicken and lamb over it.

- Serve hot with the chick-pea sauce.

NOTE: Any leftover stock can be frozen and used for soups.

Stuffed Meat Pot Roast
Rosto madkouka mihshi

THIS SPLENDIDLY DELICIOUS pot roast comes from my parents' kitchen. The finely pounded or minced meat is wrapped around a tasty and nutritious mixture of carrots, fresh herbs, spices and pine nuts and moulded into a baguette shape. It is then browned all over in olive oil and left to simmer in water until it reaches its utmost tenderness and flavour. It is an excellent dish for serving during the festive season or to enrich a buffet table.

450 g (1 lb) lean mince, preferably from a leg of lamb
¼ teaspoon allspice
¼ teaspoon ground cinnamon
¼ teaspoon freshly ground black pepper
¾ teaspoon salt or to taste
1½ tablespoons extra virgin olive oil
300–450 ml (½–¾ pint) hot water
1 bouquet garni: 1 bay leaf, 1 cinnamon stick, 3 black
   peppercorns
1 small onion studded with 1 clove
½ teaspoon plain flour or cornflour

For the stuffing:
1 carrot, very finely diced
Handful of fresh coriander or parsley, leaves and tender
   stems only, finely chopped
2–3 garlic cloves, finely diced
30 g (1 oz) pine nuts, coarsely crushed
¼ teaspoon freshly ground black pepper
¼ teaspoon allspice
¼ teaspoon ground cinnamon
½ teaspoon salt

• Make the stuffing. Combine the carrot, coriander, garlic and pine nuts, season with the pepper, allspice, cinnamon and salt. Mix well. Set aside.

- In a bowl, combine the mince, allspice, cinnamon, pepper and salt. Knead for a minute and set aside. On a lightly floured surface flatten the meat into a long rectangular shape with a uniform thickness of about 5 mm (¼ in). Spread the reserved stuffing along the side nearest to you and roll up the meat, enclosing the mixture. Pack it tightly and form it into a log-shape roll. Heat the oil in a medium-size pan and when it is hot but not smoking add the meat and brown the roll on all sides.

- Gradually add 300–450 ml (½–¾ pint) water and the bouquet garni and onion. Bring to the boil, cover and simmer over medium-low heat for about 45–50 minutes. Remove the meat from the liquor in the pan and leave to rest for 10 minutes or until it reaches room temperature. Cut it into 1 cm (½ in) slices with a sharp carving knife and spoon the liquor over it; if necessary thicken the liquor with ½ teaspoon flour or cornflour and bring to the boil.

- Serve with *mtabbal al-batinjan* (see page 36).

Fried Liver
Kasbeh mikli

KASBEH is one of the numerous appetizers that come with a *mezzé*. Small cubes of lamb's liver are served raw to be eaten with allspice (*bharat*), onion, bread and, believe it or not, *shahm* (fat). They are also enjoyed grilled or fried. I use either lamb's liver or calf's, which has a most delicate, delicious flavour. *Kasbeh mikli* is quick to prepare, healthy and needs no planning ahead except for buying the liver. I like to add the juice of a clementine or orange. However Seville oranges shouldn't be shunned when in season.

2 tablespoons extra virgin olive oil
2 medium-size onions, thinly sliced
4–5 garlic cloves, coarsely slivered
450 g (1 lb) lamb's liver
Good pinch of salt or to taste
¼ teaspoon ground cinnamon
¼ teaspoon freshly ground black pepper
Pinch of allspice
3–4 fl oz (100–120 ml) hot water
4–5 tablespoons lemon juice
1 teaspoon pomegranate syrup (optional)
Juice of 1 orange (optional)

- Heat the oil in a non-stick frying pan and when hot add the onions and garlic. Sauté over medium heat until soft, about 3 minutes. Stir gently and add the liver. Cook until nicely browned and cooked through, about 5–8 minutes. Season with the salt, cinnamon, pepper and allspice, shake the pan and add the hot water. Cover and simmer over medium-low heat until the water has nearly evaporated but not dried out. Remove the lid, stir in the lemon juice, pomegranate syrup and orange juice, if using. Cook for a few more seconds. Transfer to a warm serving dish.

- Serve with bread.

❀ ❀ ❀

Lebanese Spiced Sausages
Maquaneq

ALTHOUGH THEY ARE NOT a common feature in all Lebanese restaurants a *mezzé* table cannot be considered complete without sizzling *maquaneq*. They arrive in an earthenware dish, announcing themselves by their appetizing smell. *Maquaneq* are highly seasoned and of the utmost simplicity. Traditionally, a piece of fat is added to the meat. Here I use mince from a leg of lamb. However, neck or shoulder of lamb would also give a lovely flavour. If you wish, you can add a tablespoon of white wine to the mixture. After frying, *maquaneq* are finished with a splash of lemon juice, and you can also use pomegranate syrup. I like to add a little clementine juice, though this is not customary, for more sauce and a subtle taste.

500 g (1 lb 1 oz) lamb mince
2 teaspoons ground coriander
1 teaspoon ground cinnamon
1 teaspoon ground ginger
1 teaspoon ground cumin
½ teaspoon freshly ground black pepper
½ teaspoon allspice
¼ teaspoon white pepper
Good pinch of freshly grated nutmeg
5–6 cloves
¾ teaspoon salt
1 garlic clove
½–1 tablespoon cider vinegar
15–30 g (½–1 oz) pine nuts
2 tablespoons extra virgin olive oil
2 tablespoons lemon juice
Juice of 1–2 clementines or 1 teaspoon pomegranate syrup
    (optional)

- Place the mince in a mixing bowl with the coriander, cinnamon, ginger, cumin, black pepper, allspice, white pepper and nutmeg. Grind the cloves well with the salt, then add the garlic and mince thoroughly until the mixture is very fine. Add to the meat mixture in the bowl, then add the vinegar. Knead well for about 5 minutes. Add the pine nuts and mix well. Refrigerate for 16–20 hours.

- Shape the meat mixture into short finger-like sausages. Heat the oil in a frying pan and add the sausages. Sauté for 1 minute then reduce the heat to medium-low and cook until the sausages have browned and are cooked through, about 5–7 minutes. Add the lemon juice, and the clementine juice or pomegranate syrup, if using. They will sizzle. Cook for 1 minute then serve.

NOTE: Traditionally, a funnel is used to push the meat mixture into a lamb casing which is twisted and knotted every 5 cm (2½ in). The sausages are left to dry for several hours or a day before they are used.

❋ ❋ ❋

Meat, Potatoes and Red Wine Vinegar
Lahmeh, batata bi khal ahmar

IN THIS COMFORTING DISH, long prepared by the Sunni Muslims of Beirut, the ingredients are brought harmoniously together. Though the expectation is that the vinegar and lemon juice will strongly sharpen the flavour, surprisingly they add a delightful subtle note. To enrich the dish, some people add a spoon of *samneh* (fat) or butter towards the end of cooking. I believe this is unnecessary as the ingredients are rich enough and olive oil complements their flavour.

2–3 tablespoons extra virgin olive oil
500 g (1 lb 1 oz) diced meat, preferably from a leg of lamb
½–¾ teaspoon ground cinnamon
Good pinch of allspice
1 small onion (optional)
600 ml (1 pint) hot water
2–3 tablespoons aged red wine vinegar
1–2 tablespoons lemon juice
1 teaspoon salt or to taste
3–4 medium-size potatoes, peeled and cut into 3–4 chunks

- Heat ½–1 tablespoon of the oil in a medium-size pan and when it is hot but not smoking add the meat. It will sizzle. Stir for 30 seconds and sprinkle with the cinnamon and allspice. Grate the onion, if using, over the meat. If a liquid appears wait until it evaporates but stir the meat now and then for about 10 minutes. As the liquid dries out add 600 ml (1 pint) hot water and the vinegar, lemon juice and ½ teaspoon salt. Scrape the meat juices from the base and sides of the pan and bring to the boil. Reduce the heat to low, cover and simmer for about 30 minutes.

- Heat the remaining oil in a non-stick frying pan large enough to hold the potatoes. Dry the potatoes with kitchen paper and add them when the oil is hot. Sprinkle with the remaining salt and sauté the potatoes over medium heat until they are a nice golden brown colour, about 10 minutes. Add the potatoes to the meat. Bring to the boil, then reduce heat to low, cover and simmer for a further 30 minutes or until the meat and potatoes are tender.

- Serve hot with a salad of rocket leaves, onions, olive oil and lemon juice.

Leg of Lamb
Fakhdet ghanam bil-forn

THE LEBANESE AND ARABS generally like their lamb to be well
cooked and falling apart. This dish was prepared in my parents' kitchen
to crown the table at Christmas time and I still make it during the
festive season as it evokes warm memories. With this dish, as with
turkey, my mother had an accompaniment, a speciality of hers. I have
included it though it is not typical of the Lebanese kitchen. She added
blanched almonds to it, and wine instead of the vinegar I use. A very
tasty but simple dish, *fakhdet ghanam bil-forn* presents very well for a party
or Sunday lunch.

 1 x 1.3 kg (3 lb) knuckle end of a leg of lamb
½ teaspoon ground cinnamon
½–¾ teaspoon salt
¼ teaspoon freshly ground black pepper
¼ teaspoon allspice
½ tablespoon yoghurt
Leaves from 4 stems of thyme

For the accompaniment:
2 tablespoons extra virgin olive oil
2 medium-size onions, sliced
45 g (1½ oz) sultanas
½ teaspoon ground cinnamon
2 medium-size tomatoes, peeled and finely chopped
½–¾ teaspoon salt or to taste
2 large handfuls of parsley, finely chopped

150 ml (¼ pint) hot water
½ tablespoon double concentrated tomato purée
1 teaspoon cider vinegar
1 medium-size sweet potato, cut into 1.5 cm (½ in) cubes
10–12 green olives, stoned

- Preheat the oven to 180°C/350°F/Gas Mark 4. Place the lamb in an oven dish. Put the cinnamon, salt, pepper and allspice in a small cup and dilute them to the consistency of a smooth paste with 1 teaspoon water. Rub the paste all over the lamb and leave it to stand for 15–30 minutes before baking it for 1 hour. Remove the lamb from the oven, baste it with its juices and rub it all over with the yoghurt. Spread the thyme over the lamb. Return it to the oven, lower the heat to 150°C/300°F/Gas Mark 2 and bake for a further 1½–2 hours, basting it frequently with its juices. Remove the lamb from the oven and leave to stand for 5–10 minutes.

- Meanwhile, prepare this special accompaniment. Heat the oil in a non-stick frying pan, add the onions, and sauté until transparent and golden in colour. Stir in the sultanas and after 30 seconds sprinkle in the cinnamon. Add the tomatoes and salt and stir a few times. Add the parsley and stir well. Add the hot water, tomato purée, vinegar and sweet potato. Bring to the boil, then reduce the heat to very low, cover and simmer for about 8–10 minutes or until the potato has softened. Finally, add the olives and simmer for 1–2 minutes. The consistency of the mixture may be slightly thick but should not be dry. Serve with the lamb.

❁ ❀ ❁

Meat with Olives
Lahm bi-zaitoun

FOR GENERATIONS many Tripolitans (people of Tripoli) in the north of Lebanon have prepared this dish using chicken or meat and olives, preferably green but black if that is what is available in their larders. Either way, the end product is one of those dishes that you wish would never end. The traditional recipe does not call for too much sauce, but I have stretched the one in this recipe by adding more water in order to have enough of its delightful flavour, and the pleasure of dousing a piece of bread or a roasted potato in it. Maybe I have been influenced by what I read in the ninth-century *Kitab Al-Bukhala* (The Book of Misers) by the satirist Al-Jahiz. The preamble to one of its short stories mentions that, 'The Prophet said: "When you cook the meat add to it a lot of water, so that if one of you did not find any more meat in the plate, at least there will be the sauce."'

2 tablespoons extra virgin olive oil
500 g (1 lb 1oz) meat from a leg of lamb, cut into 2.5 cm
    (1 in) pieces
675 g (1½ lb) onions, chopped
3 garlic cloves, pounded until creamy
¾ teaspoon salt or to taste
½ teaspoon ground cinnamon
¼ teaspoon freshly ground black pepper
Pinch of freshly grated nutmeg
1 bouquet garni: 1 large cinnamon stick, 2 bay leaves,
    3 cardamoms, 3 black peppercorns
140 g (5 oz) black olives, rinsed and stoned

- Heat the oil in a pan and add the lamb. It will sizzle. Sauté for 1–2 minutes over medium-high heat. Add the onions and stir occasionally. If a liquid appears give it a few minutes until it reduces and caramelizes. Stir in the garlic (make sure it doesn't burn), and season with the salt, cinnamon, pepper and nutmeg. Stir well and add the bouquet garni and 600 ml (1 pint) water. Scrape the base and sides of the pan with a wooden spoon so that the meat juices blend with the water. Bring to the boil, then reduce the heat to low, cover and simmer for 50 minutes or until the meat is tender.

- Remove only the meat to a side dish. Discard the cinnamon stick, bay leaves, cardamoms and peppercorns and place the stock and onions in a blender. Blend to a creamy consistency. Alternatively, pass through a vegetable mill or sieve. Return the stock and meat to the pan and add the olives. Bring to the boil, then reduce the heat to low, cover and simmer for 15–20 minutes.

- Serve hot with bread and roasted potatoes.

Potato Cake with Aromatic Meat Filling
Kaleb batata

IN LEBANON THERE ARE ENDLESS recipes for the humble potato. *Kaleb batata* is a warming, wintry dish that is easy to make and provides a multitude of nutrients for both young and old. All it needs as an accompaniment is a good salad. I have cut down on the butter that usually smothers the top of the potato cake without losing the lovely flavour of the traditional dish. The combination of aromatic spices,

meat and pine nuts in the filling sandwiched between the two layers of
potato purée contributes to its deliciousness.

I kg (2 lb 2 oz) potatoes, unpeeled, scrubbed and halved
8–10 tablespoons milk
I teaspoon salt or to taste
Pinch of ground cinnamon
Pinch of freshly grated nutmeg
Small knob of butter
3 handfuls of breadcrumbs
**Handful of *kashkaval* cheese or other yellow cheese,
    grated**

For the filling:
½ tablespoon extra virgin olive oil
250 g (9 oz) lamb mince
120 g (4 oz) onions, grated
Large handful of pine nuts
¼ teaspoon ground cinnamon
¼ teaspoon freshly ground black pepper
Pinch of allspice
I teaspoon double concentrated tomato purée

• Preheat the oven to 180°C/350°F/Gas Mark 4. Place the potatoes in a
  steaming basket and set into a pan over 2.5 cm (1 in) of boiling water.
  Cover and steam until cooked, about 20 minutes. Cool the potatoes
  slightly then peel and, while they are still hot, mash until smooth.
  Place in a pan over medium heat and gradually stir in the milk. After
  a minute sprinkle with half the salt, and the cinnamon and nutmeg.
  Add the butter. Stir well. Remove from heat and leave to cool slightly.

- Meanwhile, make the filling. Heat the oil in a non-stick frying pan and add the mince and onions. Sauté over medium-high heat until the meat changes colour. If some liquid appears wait until it has evaporated. Add the pine nuts, cinnamon, pepper and allspice. Stir well and add the tomato purée and 5 tablespoons water. Stir again and simmer over low heat until the water has nearly evaporated, about 5 minutes.

- Lightly oil or butter a 20 cm (8 in) round baking tin. Sprinkle with half the breadcrumbs. Divide the potato dough into two portions. Place chunks from one portion over the breadcrumbs in the pan. Moisten your hands and gently press down on the potatoes, at the same time spreading them to cover the base of the pan. You may need to moisten your hands more than once as the potato dough is soft and may stick to them. Spread the meat filling over the potato. Cover the filling with the other potato portion, as before. Sprinkle with the remaining breadcrumbs and the cheese. Bake for 30–40 minutes or until the top of the potato cake has browned.

- Serve with Purslane or Cabbage Salad (see pages 10 and 8).

VARIATION: Vegetarians can replace the meat by sautéing sliced onions in olive oil until they are a deep golden colour, and stirring in crushed walnuts, a good pinch of cinnamon and, if available, 1 teaspoon *sumac*.

❈ ❈ ❈

Meat in Vinegar
Lahm bi-khal

A HEARTY DISH with a strong tasty flavour, this was reputedly a favourite of the Prophet Mohammed. When I was reading the ninth-century Book of Misers by Al-Jahiz I came upon an anecdote about a meal that, to my surprise, resembled this one, particularly so as I had thought about adding carrots for colour. This proves that *lahm bi-khal* has been prepared for many centuries.

The account describes a man who said: 'Ever since I had the money, I never missed eating meat. When Friday comes, I buy cow's meat for one dirham, and the onions, the aubergines and the marrow, each for one-sixth of a dirham. And if it is the season of the carrots, then I'll buy some and cook all in a *sikbaj* [in vinegar]. Saturday we dip the bread in the stock, Sunday we eat the onion, Monday the carrots, and Tuesday the marrow. For Wednesday, it is the aubergine that we eat, and Thursday the meat.' Try this delicious dish but please don't follow the miser's way!

Traditionally, in most Middle Eastern cooking the meat and sometimes also the vegetables are sautéd before being simmered. Here, it would be a pity to allow any butter or oil to interfere with the delicacy of the dish.

450 g (1 lb) meat from a leg of lamb, cut into 2 cm (¾ in) cubes
1–2 bones from knuckle end of the leg
225 g (8 oz) baby onions or pearl onions
1 cinnamon stick
10 garlic cloves
1¼ teaspoons salt or to taste
225 g (8 oz) aubergines, trimmed and cut into 2.5 cm (1 in) cubes
225 g (8 oz) courgettes, trimmed, and cut into 2.5 cm (1 in) cubes
2–3 tablespoons cider vinegar
½ tablespoon plain flour
2 teaspoons dried mint

¼ teaspoon ground cinnamon
¼ teaspoon freshly ground black pepper
¼ teaspoon allspice

- Place the meat and bones in a pan, cover with 600 ml (I pint) water, and bring to the boil over medium-high heat, skimming the foam from the surface of the water. Add the onions, cinnamon stick, garlic and salt. Reduce the heat to medium, cover and simmer for about 40 minutes or until the meat is tender. Add the aubergines, courgettes, vinegar, flour and mint. Add the ground cinnamon, black pepper and allspice, and bring to the boil. Reduce the heat, cover and simmer for 15 minutes longer. Transfer to a warm serving dish.

- Serve with rice, preferably brown.

Minced Meat, Bread and Yoghurt
Fattet al kafta

A DELICACY NOT TO BE MISSED. *Fattet al kafta* is simple to prepare and will glorify the table without bankrupting you. Above all, it can be prepared a day ahead and assembled just before serving. *Kafta* is generally a combination of minced meat, parsley, onions and spices. Here I add mint, one of my favourite herbs – it aids digestion and tastes beautiful. Lebanese are hospitable and their buffet tables are works of art; the devastating war of 1975 didn't affect their love of entertaining. When I was in Beirut Mona Jreige, a friend, produced the most charming dinner. *Fattet al kafta* adorned the table among fish and other dishes.

450 g (1 lb) lamb mince
60 g (2 oz) onion
¼ teaspoon ground cinnamon
Pinch of allspice
Pinch of freshly ground black pepper
8 fresh mint leaves, finely chopped
1 teaspoon salt or to taste
1 tablespoon double concentrated tomato purée
1–2 medium-size Lebanese breads

For the yoghurt:
450 g (1 lb) yoghurt
½–1 tablespoon *tahini* (optional)
½ teaspoon lemon juice (optional)

For the garnish:
1–1½ tablespoons extra virgin olive oil
Handful of pine nuts

- Place the mince in a mixing bowl, grate the onion over and add the cinnamon, allspice, pepper, mint and salt. Mix thoroughly and make small patties about 3.5 cm (1½ in) in diameter.
- Make the garnish. Heat ½ tablespoon of the oil in a medium-size non-stick frying pan, add the pine nuts and sauté until they are golden. Remove with a slotted spoon, allowing the oil to drip back into the pan, and set aside.
- Add the remaining oil to the frying pan, heat and add as many meat patties as possible. Sauté for 1–2 minutes and turn to brown the other side. Repeat with all the patties. Cram them together into the pan.

Dilute the tomato purée with 5–6 tablespoons water and add to the patties. Bring to the boil, then reduce the heat, cover and simmer over very low heat for about 5 minutes or until the water has somewhat evaporated but the patties are moist.

- In the meantime, split the bread or breads in two and bake in a hot oven until a deep golden colour. Remove and leave to cool. Break into small pieces, spread over a serving dish and scatter with the meat patties. Mix the yoghurt thoroughly with the *tahini* and lemon juice, if using, and pour over the meat patties. Sprinkle with the pine nuts.

VARIATION: For extra taste and aesthetic purposes, heat 30 g (1 oz) butter in a frying pan, add a large handful of chopped mint and sauté for less than a minute or until the aroma of the mint is released. Pour over the yoghurt.

Courgettes, Mince and Mint
Mtabaket al koussa

WHEN YOU ARE IN NEED of something satisfying and tasty there can be nothing simpler to prepare than this lovely warming dish. *Mtabaket al koussa* is light on the stomach and has a soothing aroma. It is a good basic dish if you wish to experiment with seasonal vegetables; it would be nice to try it with aubergines or carrots instead of courgettes.

500 g (1 lb 1 oz) courgettes
½–1 tablespoon extra virgin olive oil
450 g (1 lb) lamb mince

2 large garlic cloves, finely minced
I large red tomato, peeled and coarsely chopped
I teaspoon salt
I teaspoon dried mint

- If the courgettes are long, halve them and then slice each half lengthwise into quarters. Heat the oil in a medium-size pan over medium-high heat and add the meat. Sauté, stirring occasionally, until browned, about 5 minutes. Stir in the garlic then add the tomato and courgettes. Add 250 ml (8 fl oz) water, sprinkle with the salt and bring to the boil. Reduce the heat to low, cover and simmer for about 30 minutes. Sprinkle with the mint and swirl the pan. Serve with rice or coarse *burghol* or Vermicelli Rice (see page 54).

Stews

LEBANESE STEWS (*yakhneh*) are simple to prepare and make vegetables more interesting. They are different to Western stews, and although they are good to eat they are not yet as well known as *mezzé*. Traditionally, they are prepared with more vegetables than meat, which generally comes from lamb shanks; the bones are also used to add more flavour. Nowadays, with the growing awareness of health issues, many people prefer their stews meatless. *Yakhneh* are enjoyed all over the country as everyday meals and these homely stews are, in general, served with bread and a side dish of boiled rice, Vermicelli Rice (see page 54) or coarse *burghol* (cracked wheat).

Lebanese stews, or one-pot meals, are a joy to any cook who is wondering what dish to prepare. They use seasonal vegetables, provide good nutrition and comforting feelings of warmth, and feed large families for little money. Stews are inviting and suitable for all ages.

Green Bean Stew
Yakhnet al-loubieh one

STEWS ARE STRAIGHTFORWARD to prepare. They are relished by the Lebanese, who use what the seasons have to offer, and *yakhnet al-loubieh* is one of the tastiest ones. Here I do as my mother did and throw in a couple of slices of green pepper. They add to, and enhance, the flavour of the stock.

2–3 tablespoons extra virgin olive oil

1 onion (about 115 g/4 oz), finely chopped

4–5 garlic cloves, slivered

225 g (8 oz) meat from a leg of lamb, cut into 3 cm (1¼ in)
**   pieces and trimmed of excess fat**

450 g (1 lb) green beans, topped, tailed and strings
**   removed, cut diagonally**

¼ teaspoon allspice

1 teaspoon salt

¼ teaspoon ground cinnamon

¼ teaspoon freshly ground black pepper

2 medium-size tomatoes cut into 2.5 cm (1 in) slices

2 tablespoons tomato purée

2 slices of green pepper

- Heat the oil in a pan over medium-high heat and when it is hot but not smoking add the onion, garlic and lamb and cook until slightly browned, 3–4 minutes. Reduce the heat to medium-low and add the beans, allspice, salt, ground cinnamon and pepper. Cover and leave to sweat for 10–15 minutes. Turn the beans twice without disturbing the onions, or shake the pan.

- Add the tomatoes, tomato purée and 450–600ml (¾–1 pint) water, bring to the boil then reduce the heat to medium-low. Cover and simmer for 40 minutes or until the meat is tender.

- Serve hot with rice.

Cauliflower Stew
Yakhnet arnabit

STEWS ARE A MAJOR PART of the Lebanese diet and are prepared
with very little meat. This one is delicious, provided you use a good
quality tomato purée. Traditionally, the florets are boiled and then fried
before being simmered with the remaining ingredients. This practice
greatly enriches the flavour but is time consuming and can be omitted;
the cauliflower still keeps its lovely taste and retains its nutrients.
Cauliflowers are rich in vitamin K, which helps blood to clot, and in
many minerals. They are excellent for the hair, skin and bones and
contain substances that may reduce the risk of cancer, particularly of
the colon and stomach. It is therefore a good idea to include them in
your diet, both raw and cooked.

2½ tablespoons extra virgin olive oil
1 medium-size onion, finely chopped
350 g (12 oz) lamb mince
3 garlic cloves, crushed
2 heaped tablespoons double concentrated tomato purée
½ teaspoon ground cinnamon
¼ teaspoon freshly ground black pepper
1¼ teaspoons salt or to taste
1 medium-size cauliflower, cut into florets
2 carrots, sliced
2 handfuls of coriander, leaves and tender stems only,
    coarsely chopped
2–3 tablespoons lemon juice

- Heat the oil in a medium-small pan, add the onion and sauté until golden. Add the lamb and garlic. Cook until the meat is lightly browned, about 3–4 minutes. Stir in the tomato purée and add 450–600 ml (¾–1 pint) water. Sprinkle with the cinnamon, pepper and salt. Bring to the boil and add the florets and carrot. Reduce the heat to medium-low, cover and simmer for 30 minutes. After about 20–25 minutes add the coriander. Towards the end of the cooking time add the lemon juice and shake the pan to distribute the juices evenly.

- Serve with Vermicelli Rice (see page 54) and radishes.

Tomato Stew
Yakhnet al-banadoura

TOMATOES IN LEBANON burst with flavour; they are abundant and nice to eat uncooked, simply seasoned with salt, a splash of olive oil and some dried or fresh mint. No less tasty are the tomatoes in this stew – in fact, their flavour is even more pronounced. To peel the tomatoes, drop them into fresh boiled water for a few seconds before peeling them, or use a sharp knife if they are very ripe. If you like hot-flavoured stews slip in one or two green chillis.

1½ tablespoons extra virgin olive oil
1 onion, finely chopped
4 garlic cloves, finely chopped
450 g (1 lb) mince, preferably lamb
30 g (1 oz) pine nuts
675 g (1½ lb) ripe tomatoes, peeled and coarsely chopped
1 tablespoon double concentrated tomato purée

1½ teaspoons salt or to taste
½ teaspoon ground cinnamon
¼ teaspoon freshly ground black pepper
¼ teaspoon allspice
Handful of parsley leaves, chopped

- Heat the oil in a medium-size pan over medium-high heat and add the onion, garlic and mince. Sauté until lightly browned, about 6–8 minutes, breaking up any lumps with the edge of a wooden spoon. Add the pine nuts, tomatoes and tomato purée, reduce the heat to medium and season with the salt, cinnamon, pepper and allspice. Add 200 ml (7 fl oz) water and bring to the boil, then reduce the heat to medium-low, cover and simmer for 20–30 minutes. Five minutes before the end of the cooking time add the parsley.

- Serve hot with plain rice or Vermicelli Rice (see page 54).

❋ ❋ ❋

Jew's Mallow Stew
Yakhnet al-mouloukhiyeh

MOULOUKHIYEH (Jew's mallow) is an extremely popular herb, highly praised in the Levant and Egypt, and Lebanese are proud to serve it at dinner or lunch parties. What is interesting about *yakhnet al-mouloukhiyeh* is its simplicity compared to the Jew's mallow dish on page 169. The one thing that is not authentic about this recipe is the spinach. I find that it enhances the flavour. Vegetarians can omit the meat.

To make this stew, the *mouloukhiyeh* leaves are first pulled out of their stems, and are rinsed and drained. Traditionally they are then fried in generous amounts of butter with the aromatic fresh coriander and spices that give the dish its characteristic flavour. Here it is prepared with olive oil. Adding the lamb bones is optional but they do enrich the stock with calcium. *Mouloukhiyeh* is abundant in summer and bunches are sold by Lebanese, Turkish, Iranian and Cypriot grocers.

   2 tablespoons extra virgin olive oil
   500 g (1 lb 1 oz) meat from a leg of lamb, cut into 2.5 cm
      (1 in) pieces and trimmed of excess fat
   1–2 bones from the knuckle end of the leg (optional)
   1 bouquet garni: 1 bay leaf, 1 cinnamon stick, 4 black
      peppercorns
   1 teaspoon salt or to taste
   1 medium-size onion, finely chopped
   7–9 garlic cloves, crushed
   ½ teaspoon ground coriander
   ½–¾ bunch fresh coriander, leaves and tender stems only,
      chopped
   90 g (3 oz) spinach leaves, coarsely chopped
   2–3 bundles *mouloukhiyeh*, leaves only, whole or coarsely
      chopped
   ¼ teaspoon ground cinnamon
   Pinch of freshly ground black pepper
   Juice of ½ lemon or to taste

• Heat 1 teaspoon of the oil in a medium-size pan and when it is hot but not smoking add the lamb and the bones, if using. They will sizzle. Stir well until lightly coloured all over, about 1–2 minutes. Add 450–600 ml (¾–1 pint) water and bring to the boil, skimming the foam from the surface of the water. Add the bouquet garni and sprinkle with the salt.

Reduce the heat to low, cover and simmer for 1 hour or until the meat is tender and falling apart.

- Meanwhile, heat the remaining oil in a non-stick frying pan, add the onion and sauté until transparent and pale in colour, about 2 minutes. Stir in the garlic and ground coriander. After a few seconds add the fresh coriander. As it reduces in size add the spinach and allow time for it also to wilt. Add the *mouloukhiyeh* in batches, then add the cinnamon and pepper. The whole operation should take about 5–8 minutes. Add this mixture to the softened meat and reduced stock in the pan. Bring to the boil again, then reduce the heat to low, cover and simmer for 5–8 minutes allowing the flavours to bind together. Finally add the lemon juice and serve.

Courgette Stew
Yakhnet al-koussa

COURGETTES ARE VERSATILE and appear in many recipes; they can be stuffed, cooked along with yoghurt, added to omelettes and stews or diced to simmer in soups. Whichever way they are used they add a pleasant and delicate flavour to a dish. This stew is a favourite of mine, prepared meatless or with meat. If meat is used I add tomato purée; if not, I add more dried mint to accentuate its taste and enrich the sauce. Accompanied by rice *yakhnet al-koussa* makes a wonderful family meal.

450 g (1 lb) meat from a leg of lamb, cut into 2.5 cm (1 in) pieces and trimmed of excess fat
2 medium-size onions, sliced into half-moon shapes

½ tablespoon extra virgin olive oil
I large ripe tomato, peeled and quartered
I tablespoon double concentrated tomato purée
I teaspoon salt or to taste
500 g (I lb Ioz) courgettes, trimmed and quartered
¼ teaspoon allspice
¼ teaspoon ground cinnamon
¼ teaspoon freshly ground black pepper
I teaspoon dried mint (optional)

- Place the lamb in a pan with 350–400 ml (12–14 fl oz) water and bring to the boil, skimming the foam from the surface of the water. Add the onions, oil, tomato, tomato purée and salt. Bring to the boil again, reduce the heat to low, cover and simmer for 30–40 minutes. Add the courgettes. Season with the allspice, cinnamon, pepper and mint, if using. Return to the boil, cover and simmer for a further 20 minutes.

- Serve hot with Vermicelli Rice (see page 54) or *burghol*.

Broad Bean Stew
Yakhnet al-foul

IT'S BEST to prepare this stew when broad beans are in season. Nothing compares with fresh vegetables. The broad, or fava, beans are generally shelled, although young and tender ones are left in their pods, to be cooked in this way. Scented with fresh coriander and enhanced with a touch of lemon, this stew is nourishing and has a strong flavour. Traditionally, the meat, onions and garlic in most stews are sautéed with butter. Here I use a negligible amount of olive oil.

350 g (12 oz) meat from a leg of lamb, cut into 2.5 cm
   (1 in) pieces and trimmed of excess fat
1–2 bones from the knuckle end of the leg (optional)
1 cinnamon stick
1 teaspoon salt or to taste
1 medium-size onion, finely chopped
2 large garlic cloves, crushed
4–5 sprigs of coriander, leaves and tender stems only,
   chopped
675 g (1½ lb) young broad beans, topped, tailed and strings
   removed
½ teaspoon ground cinnamon
¼–½ teaspoon allspice
¼ teaspoon freshly ground black pepper
1 teaspoon extra virgin olive oil
2–3 tablespoons lemon juice

- Place the lamb, bones if using, and cinnamon stick in a pan with 600 ml
  (1 pint) water and add the salt. Bring to the boil over medium-high
  heat, skimming the foam from the surface of the water. Add the onion,
  reduce the heat to low, cover and simmer until the meat is nearly soft,
  about 20–30 minutes. Add the garlic, coriander and beans, then the
  ground cinnamon, allspice and pepper. Add the oil. Bring to the boil
  again, then reduce the heat to medium-low, cover and simmer for a
  further 30–40 minutes. A few minutes before the end of the cooking
  time add the lemon juice.

- Serve hot with brown rice or with bread and yoghurt.

Spinach Stew
Yakhnet al-sabanekh

SPINACH, WHICH IS SAID to have originated in Persia, was introduced into North Africa via Syria and Arabia, and the Moors took it to Spain in the twelfth century. *Yakhnet al-sabanekh* can also be made without meat. Here mince is used, rather than pieces of meat.

1½ tablespoons extra virgin olive oil
1 onion, finely chopped
225 g (8 oz) mince, preferably lamb
450 g (1 lb) spinach, coarsely chopped
1 teaspoon salt
¼ teaspoon ground cinnamon
¼ teaspoon freshly ground black pepper
2–3 garlic cloves, pounded until creamy
15–30 g (½–1 oz) coriander, leaves and tender stems only, coarsely chopped
Handful of pine nuts
½ lemon

- Heat the oil in a pan over medium-high heat and when it is hot but not smoking add the onions and mince. Cook until browned, about 4–5 minutes, then add the spinach in batches. When it reduces in size, add the salt, cinnamon, pepper, garlic and coriander. Add the pine nuts and 200 ml (7 fl oz) water and bring to the boil. Cover and simmer over medium-low heat for 15–20 minutes. Transfer to a warm bowl and squeeze over a few drops of lemon juice to enhance the flavour.

- Serve with Vermicelli Rice (see page 54).

Aubergine Stew
Batinjan wa-lahm mafroum

AN OUTSTANDING STEW that bursts with tantalizing flavours. Boosted by tangy pomegranate syrup and chilli to add a mild piquant flavour, it is surprisingly delicious.

1½ tablespoons extra virgin olive oil
2 medium-size onions, finely chopped
450 g (1 lb) lean mince
30 g (1 oz) pine nuts
¼ teaspoon ground cinnamon
¼ teaspoon allspice
¼ teaspoon freshly ground black pepper or to taste
1–1¼ teaspoons salt or to taste
2 tomatoes, finely chopped
675 g (1½ lb) aubergine, cut into 2.5 cm (1 in) cubes
1–2 red chillies
150–175 ml (5–6 fl oz) hot water
2 tablespoons pomegranate syrup (optional)

• Heat the oil in a medium pan, add the onions and meat and sauté over medium heat until browned, about 3–4 minutes, breaking up any lumps with a wooden spoon. Stir in the pine nuts and add the cinnamon, allspice, pepper and salt. Add the tomatoes and stir well. Add the aubergine, chilli and hot water. Bring to the boil, then reduce the heat to medium-low, cover and simmer for 30–35 minutes. Ten minutes before the end of the cooking time stir in the fragrant pomegranate syrup.

• Serve hot with plain rice or Vermicelli Rice (see page 54).

Yoghurt

YOGHURT IS MADE when milk ferments, changing the nature of
lactose (a form of sugar), and is thought to have come about by chance
when nomads accidentally left their milk out in the heat of the steppes.
For centuries it has been used as a food and a panacea, and it is still
associated with purity and good health.. Ancient wisdom testifies to its
therapeutic benefits and its ability to restore and maintain youth. It is
said that in the sixteenth century a Jewish doctor travelled all the way
on foot from Constantinople to France with his herd to treat the
ailments of the French king Francis I with yoghurt.

Years back yoghurt was sold mostly in health food stores. Nowadays it
is becoming more and more popular. It is soothing and rich in protein,
B vitamins and calcium, all of which are essential for resistance to
infection, and for the bones, nerves and muscles. Its good bacteria are
instrumental in the assimilation of vitamins and minerals, and help the
intestines to defend the body against toxic matters that enter it via food.
It's no wonder that when I was a child I was given yoghurt while on a
course of antibiotics. There is more positive evidence to tempt you to
experiment with yoghurt, but if you are still in doubt about its curative
properties follow 'Le Pari de Pascal' (Pascal's wager), which advises:
'When chances are equal bet on the possibly more rewarding option.'

Yoghurt is highly regarded in the cuisines of the Arab world, Bulgaria,
Greece and Turkey, and plays a significant role in the Lebanese kitchen
where, as well as being freshly spooned over many dishes, it is also used in
cooking. It is versatile and combines happily with most vegetables, grains,
pulses and fruit. Its velvety note fills the mouth, producing a lovely,
comforting sensation on the palate. Traditionally, yoghurt is made by

adding a starter of live yoghurt to heated milk, which is left in a warm place to coagulate. The intensity and flavour of the end product depend on the temperature at which the yoghurt is kept, on the starter, and on the type of milk – whether it is full-fat, semi-skimmed or skimmed, and whether it comes from a cow, sheep or goat.

The nineteenth-century French romantic poet Nerval describes how when he was in the Lebanon a village woman asked him whether he wanted *laban* (yoghurt). He wrote that he remembered that in the German language the word means life, and that 'The Lebanon also takes its name from this word Laban and owes it to the whiteness of snow that covers its mountains.'

Yoghurt
Laban

NUTRITIOUS AND SOOTHING, yoghurt is luscious spooned over a hot dish of Vermicelli Rice (see page 54) and can also be combined with chopped vegetables like lettuce and tomatoes. To make home-made yoghurt non-pasteurized milk is boiled and then cooled slightly before a starter of live yoghurt from a previous batch is incorporated into it; if pasteurized milk is used it is heated to just below boiling point.

1.2 litres (2 pints) milk
2 tablespoons live yoghurt

• Place the milk in a stainless-steel pan and bring it to the boil if unpasteurized and to just below boiling point if it is pasteurized. Leave the milk until it reaches a temperature of 43°C (107° F), or until you can put your finger in it (carefully) and hold it there to a count of ten. It should sting slightly.

- Put the live yoghurt in a small cup, thin it with about 2 tablespoons of the milk and then stir it thoroughly into the milk in the pan. Cover and wrap in a woollen blanket. Leave to rest undisturbed for 8 hours. Thirty minutes before the required time is up uncover the yoghurt and leave until the half hour is up. Chill in the fridge.

NOTE: For a thicker, creamier yoghurt combine 1 tablespoon powdered milk with the milk.

Yoghurt Soft Cheese
Labneh

THIS IS ONE of the easiest and quickest cheeses produced by Lebanese in their homes. It has a creamy texture and a flavour that varies according to whether sheep's, cow's or goat's yoghurt is used; this depends on the region and availability. The yoghurt is wrapped in cheesecloth and hung to drain; the concentrated *labneh* is the result. This is spread on Lebanese bread or *markouk* bread, and topped with a little olive oil; sometimes it is flavoured with black or green olives and fresh mint leaves. In villages *labneh* is also mixed with onions and used as a filling that is folded into bread dough, cooked on a stove until done, and eaten hot. This is called *tlameh bi-labneh*.

900 ml (1½ pints) live yoghurt
1½ teaspoons sea salt or to taste

- Put the yoghurt in a mixing bowl, sprinkle with the salt and mix well. Pour the yoghurt into a cheesecloth bag, place it in a sieve set over a bowl and leave in a cool place to drain overnight. If cheesecloth is not available, place three thick pieces of kitchen paper in the sieve and fold them over the yoghurt.

- Remove the *labneh* from the cheesecloth bag and store in the refrigerator. It will last for up to a week.

NOTE: If the resulting cream is sour, measure the liquid in the bowl and discard. Then measure the same quantity of fresh drinking water. Incorporate with the *labneh* and drain again, as mentioned in the recipe.

Yoghurt Cheese Balls in Oil
Labneh makbouseh bi-zeit

LABNEH CHEESE BALLS can be prepared well in advance and are handy when you don't feel like cooking. Accompanied by good wheat bread, chopped tomatoes, cucumber, some fresh mint and olives, they make an inexpensive, comforting and nutritious meal. They can be prepared with cow's, sheep's or goat's yoghurt, but I have found that a mixture of sheep's and goat's yields a succulent flavour.

450 ml (¾ pint) live sheep's yoghurt
450 ml (¾ pint) live goat's yoghurt
2¼ teaspoons sea salt, free of additives
Extra virgin olive oil, for storing the cheese balls

- Place both yoghurts in a mixing bowl, season with the salt and mix thoroughly. Put the mixture in a cheesecloth bag, place in a sieve set over a bowl, refrigerate and leave to drain. Allow 2–3 days for the mixture to drain and dry. If cheesecloth is not available you can use three thicknesses of kitchen paper, folding them over the yoghurt; you may need to change the paper during the draining process.

- Remove the resulting *labneh* then take small portions and roll them into 2.5 cm (1 in) balls. Cover a baking tray with two layers of kitchen paper. Place the balls on the paper and put them in the fridge for 2–3 days to drain and dry. Change the kitchen paper twice during this time. Put the cheese in an airtight jar, fill with extra virgin olive oil and refrigerate. The *labneh* will last like this for several months.

Yoghurt Fermented Cheese with Dried Thyme and Red Pepper
Shankleesh

THIS IS A SPECIALITY of Accar, the hilly northern part of Lebanon, where it is often served as an accompaniment to a drink. In Lebanon balls of ready-to-eat *shankleesh*, the size of oranges, are on sale in supermarkets. They are prepared as follows: after the yoghurt curdles salt is stirred into it and it is then put in a cheesecloth bag to dry completely. Traditionally, the curdled yoghurt is dried in the sun for five days. Then it can be kneaded with the red (cayenne) pepper used in this recipe, but this is optional. What is important is that the dried matter is left in a jar until a mould forms. The *shankleesh* is then removed, the mould is peeled off and the ball is dredged with *zaatar* (dried thyme).

1.2 litres (2 pints) live cow's yoghurt
½ teaspoon cayenne pepper
¼ teaspoon white pepper
2½ teaspoons sea salt or to taste
4 tablespoons *zaatar* (dried thyme)

* Place the yoghurt in a stainless-steel pan, bring to the boil and cook until it curdles and the liquid (whey) separates from the curds. Draw out the curds from the whey, drain well and leave to cool. Season with the cayenne, pepper and salt to taste then put in a cheesecloth bag in a sieve set over a bowl and leave to drain and dry in a cool place for 3–4 days. Remove small portions of the *shankleesh* and roll into 4 cm (1¾ in) balls. Thoroughly coat each ball with the *zaatar*, then store in a sterilized jar in the fridge. Serve with olive oil and tomatoes.

Kishk

A POPULAR DISH among mountain people, *kishk* is eaten with bread for breakfast, especially in winter, to provide warmth and strength throughout the day. For a more substantial dish, a tablespoon of *kawarma* (see Glossary page 302) is added.

Kishk is prepared in several stages. *Burghol* (cracked wheat) is rinsed and topped with very hot water. When the water has been absorbed and the *kishk* is dry, a little milk is mixed thoroughly with the *burghol*. As the milk is absorbed *labneh* (see page 224), a derivative of yoghurt, is kneaded into the *burghol* mixture over a period of three days. The *kishk* is then dried in the sun to be crushed afterwards, either in the traditional way, between the fingers or, nowadays, using a machine. Making *kishk* is a lengthy operation and the mixture must be kneaded and rubbed several times and then be forced through a sieve. The resultant granular powder is kept ready for use as necessary. My favourite *kishk* is meatless, prepared with onions and garlic. Another recipe adds *kibbeh* balls and shredded cabbage to a *kishk* soup. This is highly nutritious and is still prepared in the mountains. Some people add a handful of chick-peas. Ready made kishk can be bought in Lebanese and Middle Eastern shops.

While travelling among the Druse the British explorer Gertrude Bell came across a sour soup called *kirk*. It was probably *kishk*. She didn't seem to like it, but trust me and try. It is very good. Probably the soup wasn't well prepared.

> 2 tablespoons extra virgin olive oil
> 1 medium-size onion, thinly sliced
> 7 garlic cloves, whole or halved
> ½ teaspoon salt
> 150 g (5 oz) *kishk*

- Heat the oil in a pan over medium heat and add the onion, garlic and salt. Stir well, cover and cook for 2 minutes, then uncover and stir for another 2 minutes or until the onion and garlic are soft and golden in colour. Add the *kishk* and stir continuously for 2 minutes. Gradually add 900 ml (1½ pints) water, still stirring, and bring to the boil. Reduce the heat to medium-low and simmer for 10–15 minutes. The resulting liquid should be medium-thick, like double cream. If it is too thick add a little hot water.

- Serve piping hot with bread.

Cucumber and Yoghurt Salad
Salatet laban w'khiar

THIS SALAD is a local interpretation of a well-known Turkish recipe, *cacik*. It can be prepared in seconds. Mint, native to the Mediterranean region, is added dry, to alleviate the sourness of the yoghurt. Since it can restore health-giving bacteria it is recommended for people who are taking some types of antibiotic. Cucumber is a natural diuretic, and is rich in mineral salts that aid hair growth.

In Lebanon, chilled *salatet laban w'khiar* is served with *kibbeh*, the national dish. It can also be eaten with fried aubergines. Here dried mint is added, as tradition dictates, but why not try fresh mint?

    1 large garlic clove
    1 teaspoon salt or to taste
    600 ml (1 pint) yoghurt
    3 baby cucumbers, thinly sliced or shredded
    ½–1 teaspoon dried mint

- In a salad bowl, pound the garlic and salt with a pestle until creamy. Add the yoghurt and whisk well. If it is thick add a little water and whisk again. Mix in the cucumber, taste and adjust the seasoning. Sprinkle with the mint.

- Chill or serve immediately.

Spaghetti with Yoghurt
Macaroni bi-laban

THIS IS AN ENJOYABLE and easily prepared meal. Combining spaghetti with yoghurt may seem strange at first, but wait until you try this lovely comforting spaghetti. *Macaroni bi-laban* is delicious, and handy when you are pressed for time. White spaghetti is fine but I like to use wholemeal, and most times I resort to rice or spelt spaghetti which is easy to digest. I prepared *macaroni bi-laban* during a demonstration and was told by a lady who attended: 'As an Italian I was sceptical, but having tasted it I like it very much indeed.'

250 g (9 oz) spaghetti
1 large garlic clove
½ teaspoon salt or to taste
600 ml (1 pint) live yoghurt

For the garnish:
½ tablespoon extra virgin olive oil
45 g (1½ oz) pine nuts
Large handful of coriander or parsley leaves, coarsely
  chopped
Good pinch of cayenne pepper (optional)

- Cook the spaghetti in boiling salted water until al dente following the instructions on the packet (or add boiling water and leave until soft).

- Meanwhile, in a serving bowl pound the garlic and salt with a pestle until creamy. Add the yoghurt and mix it thoroughly with the garlic. Heat the oil in a frying pan, add the pine nuts and sauté until golden in colour. Quickly add the coriander or the parsley and sauté for a few more seconds or until their aroma is released.

- When the spaghetti is cooked (or softened), drain it and plunge it into the yoghurt, cover with the pine nuts and coriander or parsley, and sprinkle with the cayenne, if using.

❀ ❀ ❀

Aubergines in Yoghurt
Batinjan moufassakh bi-laban

A WONDERFUL PREPARATION with soothing, velvety yoghurt and scented mint; it can be made in advance. Traditionally, the aubergine slices are fried but as they act as a sponge and absorb a lot of oil, grilling would be a better choice. The addition of *tahini* and lemon juice is not traditional but I find they act as a binder for the yoghurt and the other ingredients.

The wonderful purple colour of the aubergine reminds me of a story about the discovery of the colour purple in the city of Tyre. A dog came back to his master with a purple mouth, and after an extensive search it was found that the dog had bitten a murex, a type of mollusc. The Tyrians perfected the colour using a secret recipe, and sold dyed purple material to royalty and high priests thereafter.

675 g (1½ lb) aubergine
About ¼ pint (5 fl oz) extra virgin olive oil or as necessary
Olive oil for frying or grilling
2 garlic cloves
¾–1 teaspoon salt or to taste

300 ml (10 fl oz) yoghurt
1 tablespoon *tahini* (optional)
1 teaspoon lemon juice (optional)
1 tablespoon pomegranate syrup
A large handful of finely chopped parsley
A good pinch of paprika or cayenne pepper

- Trim both ends of the aubergine and peel leaving lengthwise stripes of skin. Cut lengthwise into thin slices. Heat the oil in a non-stick frying pan and when it is hot but not smoking add the aubergine slices and sauté over high heat until lightly brown on both sides. They will absorb the oil and then release it. Alternatively, preheat the grill and a baking tray and brush both sides of the slices with oil. Place them on the baking tray, set about 10 cm (4 in) from the heat, and grill until browned on both sides, about 6 minutes, turning the slices once.

- Meanwhile, in a bowl pound the garlic and salt with a pestle until creamy. Add the yoghurt, and the *tahini* and lemon juice if using, and whisk thoroughly.

- Sprinkle the browned aubergine slices with a little salt and mix with the pomegranate syrup and parsley. Arrange in one layer then pour the yoghurt mixture all over the aubergines. Sprinkle with paprika or cayenne pepper.

- Serve with wholemeal Lebanese bread.

Chick-peas with Yoghurt and Mince

Fatteh hummous bi-lahm

DISHES BASED on layers of cut-up toasted bread and a vegetable or a grain, with or without meat, and with yoghurt, are called *fatteh*. They are much loved in the Levant and are a meal in themselves. They should be eaten as soon as they are cooked, otherwise the bread will soak up the yoghurt and become soft, and the yoghurt will cool the warm dish.

This dish can be very rich in saturated fat if it is prepared the traditional way, which calls for a large quantity of hot butter to be poured over the yoghurt. I believe the dish is already rich in full-flavoured ingredients. Here mince is used, which is quick to prepare and marries well with the chick-peas, making a well-balanced meal. Vegetarians can omit the meat.

1½–2 medium-size wholemeal bread loaves, brushed with olive oil and cut into 2 cm (¾ in) cubes, toasted or deep-fried

120 g (4 oz) chick-peas, soaked overnight, drained and rinsed

275 g (10 oz) mince, preferably lamb

¼ teaspoon allspice

½ teaspoon ground cinnamon

¼ teaspoon freshly ground black pepper

½ teaspoon salt

Cayenne pepper to taste

For the yoghurt:

1 large garlic clove

½ teaspoon salt
600 ml (1 pint) yoghurt

For the garnish:
2 tablespoons extra virgin olive oil
45 g (1½ oz) pine nuts or almond flakes

- Spread the bread evenly over a deep serving dish and set aside.

- Place chick-peas in a pan with 900 ml (1½ pints) water and bring to the boil over medium-high heat, skimming the foam from the surface of the water. Reduce the heat to medium-low, cover and simmer for about 2 hours or until the chick-peas are very soft.

- Make the garnish. Heat the oil in a heavy-bottomed pan over medium-high heat and when it is hot but not smoking fry the pine nuts or almond flakes for a few seconds or until golden in colour; remove to a side dish with a slotted spoon, allowing the oil to drip back into the pan. Set aside.

- Cook the mince in the same pan for about 6–8 minutes or until nicely browned and crisp. Season with the allspice, cinnamon, pepper and salt, stir for a few seconds and turn off the heat.

- Prepare the yoghurt. In a bowl, pound the garlic with the salt using a pestle until creamy, add the yoghurt and whisk until smooth.

- To assemble the *fatteh*, place the chick-peas and 3 tablespoons of their cooking liquid over the bread in the serving dish and spoon the yoghurt over. Top with an even layer of the meat and scatter all over with the nuts. Sprinkle with the cayenne.

Broad Beans, Yoghurt and Fried Bread
Fattet el-foul bi-roz

FATTEH DISHES are among the tastiest. Made with a combination of varied textures and perfumes, they are substantial, satisfying and highly valued for their nutrients. *Fattet el-foul bi-roz* uses only a little oil in its preparation. To cut down further on oil, brush the bread with oil and toast it instead of frying it. Traditionally, coarse *burghol* (cracked wheat) was used, until rice (white) became less expensive. The onions and coriander are generally sautéd beforehand. Hazelnuts are not authentic but I find that their flavour blends wonderfully with the beans and rice – a heavenly marriage.

225 g (8 oz) brown rice
I medium-size onion, finely chopped
350 g (12 oz) broad beans, frozen or fresh and podded
4 sprigs of coriander, leaves and tender stems only,
finely chopped
1¼ teaspoons salt or to taste
½ teaspoon allspice
½ teaspoon ground cinnamon
¼ teaspoon freshly ground black pepper

For the yoghurt:
I large garlic clove
I teaspoon salt or to taste
400 ml (14 fl oz) yoghurt

For the garnish:
I tablespoon extra virgin olive oil
30 g (I oz) hazelnut flakes
Generous handful of coriander leaves, coarsely chopped

For the bread:
Extra virgin olive oil, for deep-frying
I½ medium-size Lebanese breads, split in two and cut into
  I cm (½ in) squares, brushed lightly with oil and toasted

- Place the rice in a heavy-bottomed pan with 600 ml (I pint) water and bring to the boil. Add the onion, reduce the heat to medium, cover and simmer for 25 minutes. Add the broad beans and coriander, then the salt, allspice, cinnamon and pepper. You may need to add a little more hot water. Stir well. Cover and simmer for 15–20 minutes longer or until the rice and beans are tender and the water has been absorbed.

- Meanwhile, prepare the yoghurt. In a bowl, pound the garlic and salt with a pestle until creamy, add the yoghurt and whisk until smooth.

- Make the garnish. Heat the oil in a non-stick pan and add the hazelnuts. Stir for a few seconds and add the coriander. Stir for another few seconds. Set aside.

- To assemble the *fatteh*, spread the rice and broad beans evenly over a serving dish, cover with the yoghurt and scatter with the hazelnuts and coriander. Top with the bread.

Spinach in Yoghurt
Fattet al sabanekh

THIS DELICACY CAN BE PREPARED with minced meat or with *kafta* (see page 180), which is tastier and nicer to present. Rich and lustrous, it is made with superb ingredients that promote good health and longevity. Give *fattet al sabanekh* a try; it is heavenly and makes an excellent starter or a main dish. If you want to finish it on an authentic note melt some butter and pour it over the yoghurt, as is done for all *fattet*. However, although this enriches the dish I believe it is not essential. Here the dish is prepared without meat.

2 medium-size Lebanese breads
1 teaspoon extra virgin olive oil, plus extra for brushing or deep-frying
1 medium onion, finely chopped
675 g (1½ lb) spinach, rinsed, tough stems removed, leaves coarsely chopped or cut into 1.5 cm (½ in) ribbons
1 teaspoon salt
¼ teaspoon ground cinnamon
¼ teaspoon freshly ground black pepper
2 garlic cloves, crushed
½ bunch coriander, leaves and tender stems only, finely chopped
30 g (1 oz) almond flakes

For the yoghurt:
1 large garlic clove
½ teaspoon salt or to taste
450 g (1 lb) yoghurt

2 tablespoons *tahini* (optional)
2 tablespoons lemon juice (optional)

For the garnish:
2 tablespoons extra virgin olive oil
2 large garlic cloves, finely crushed
2–3 large handfuls of coriander leaves, coarsely chopped

- Split the breads in two, brush with oil and bake until deep golden, or deep-fry. Place in a serving dish.

- Place the onion in a pan with 3–4 tablespoons water, set over low heat, cover and simmer for about 5 minutes. Remove the lid and add the spinach in batches. As it reduces in size, add the salt, cinnamon and pepper. Add the garlic, coriander and almond flakes. Stir well. Eventually a liquid will appear and at this point cover the pan again and simmer over low heat for 10–12 minutes.

- Meanwhile, prepare the yoghurt. In a bowl, pound the garlic and salt with a pestle until creamy, and add the yoghurt and the *tahini* and lemon juice, if using. Mix thoroughly to reach a smooth velvety consistency. Spread the spinach over the bread in the serving dish and pour the yoghurt over it.

- Make the garnish. Heat the oil in a non-stick medium-size pan, add the garlic and sauté for few seconds. Add the coriander and shake the pan to stir. Allow to cook for a minute, then spread the garnish over the yoghurt in the serving dish. Serve immediately.

NOTE: To keep the bread crunchy for longer, spread it evenly over the yoghurt instead of placing *under* the spinach, or serve in a separate bowl.

Beetroot in Yoghurt
Shamandar bi-laban

HERE IS A SOOTHING starter, simple and very nutritious. Beetroot and yoghurt salad is prepared all over the eastern Mediterranean and is worth trying. *Tahini* adds depth to the flavour. Whenever possible steam the beetroots to keep most of their nutrients. *Shamandar bi-laban* is a good accompaniment for barbecued meat and fried *kafta*.

4 medium-size beetroots
I garlic clove
I teaspoon salt or to taste
2 tablespoons *tahini*
I teaspoon lemon juice
500 g (I lb I oz) yoghurt or to taste
Handful of mint leaves, chopped

- Place the beetroots in a steaming basket and set into a pan over 2.5 cm (I in) of boiling water. Cover and steam for about 30–40 minutes or until tender. Leave to cool, peel and cut into I.5 cm (½ in) cubes

- Meanwhile, in a bowl pound the garlic and salt with a pestle until creamy. Stir in the *tahini* and lemon juice, then gradually add the yoghurt, mixing it thoroughly with the *tahini*.

- Pour the yoghurt into a slightly deeper dish and plunge the beetroot cubes into the yoghurt. Sprinkle with mint.

Conserves and Jams

Fresh fruits in season are not only full of flavour, they are also abundant in valuable vitamins and minerals. The Lebanese love all kinds of fruits, with their different colours, textures and flavours. Those that have a short season or are overripe are revived by cooking. Our grandmothers and mothers used to spend long, pleasurable hours making mouth-watering conserves and jams. Nowadays, few people have time for this and fruits tend to be identified as much with laboratory-made rejuvenating creams as with food. It is said that the Prince of Lebanon, Emir Beshir (d. 1850), always ate *mrabba* (see opposite) at sunset with a piece of bread.

Most fruits can be used to prepare jam but some set more easily than others because of their high pectin content – citrus fruits and quinces are an example – while others, such as strawberries, over–ripe plums and apricots, need some help. One method is to put the seeds of fruits such as lemons, oranges, apples or quinces in a muslin bag to simmer with the principal fruit.

The utensils you will need are a heavy-bottomed stainless-steel pan, a long-handled wooden spoon and sterilized jars. Strict cleanliness is essential throughout the process. Wash the fruits thoroughly to remove any harmful substances and wash the jars in hot, soapy water, rinse well and invert over a clean cloth. Prepare the fruit, cool and pour into sterilized jars, then cover with an airtight seal. To kill harmful organisms, set a wire rack in a large pan. Place the sealed jars on the rack and fill the pan with hot water. Bring to the boil, cover and leave to boil gently for 30 minutes. Carefully remove the jars, cool and store.

Seville Orange Preserve
Mrabba abou sfair

IN OUR FAMILY HOME we were surrounded by Seville orange trees adorning the alley in our garden and pleasuring the senses. Their juice enhanced the flavour of a multitude of fresh and cooked dishes and the bitter orangey taste of their skin enriched our preserves, while their delicate snow–white blossoms saturated the air with their reviving perfume. These are plucked off their branches to extract an essence used in most Lebanese desserts. Even when I was writing this recipe, these memories were so vivid that they aroused warm feelings and quickened my heart. I rose from my chair, reached for a Seville orange and bit into it. It satisfied my palate and eventually soothed my longings. Is the air laden still with lovely scents or is it nostalgia?

Mrabba abou sfair is one of the tastiest of all preserves. It is simple to make but takes time as the fruit has to be scrubbed and peeled, and then soaked. Nevertheless it is very satisfying to make. Dice the preserve and add to a sponge cake or vanilla ice cream, or eat it with rice pudding. The Seville orange season starts in January.

> 1 kg (2 lb 2 oz) Seville oranges
> 500 g (1 lb 1 oz) sugar
> 2½ tablespoons lemon juice
> 4–5 cloves

• Lightly grate the oranges, then cut the peel into quarters and put in a pan with water to cover. Bring to the boil then reduce the heat to medium and simmer for 5 minutes. Drain, then place in a bowl with cold water to cover. Leave to stand for 18–24 hours, changing the water at least three times daily to get rid of the bitterness. When soaking time is over, drain well, then take 1 piece of orange peel, roll it and squeeze out excess water. Use a needle to put a thread through it, to keep its rolled shape, and repeat with the remaining peel, attaching them to each other with the thread and packing them one against the other, to form a necklace. Set aside for a short while.

- Place the sugar in a pan, add 475 ml (16 fl oz) water and stir to dissolve the sugar completely. Bring to the boil over high heat, then skim any froth from the surface of the water. Add the lemon juice and stir. Reduce the heat to medium and simmer for 10 minutes or until the mixture thickens slightly. Place the reserved orange peel 'necklace' in the pan, bring to the boil, add the cloves and simmer over medium heat for 20–30 minutes longer or until the syrup has thickened. Towards the end of cooking turn up the heat for a few minutes, but be careful as the sugar may caramelize. Remove from the heat, then return to a high heat. Repeat this process until you get the desired syrup consistency. Turn the heat off, cool, and unthread the peel. Place the peel in sterilized jar, pour over the reduced syrup, seal and process for 30 minutes in boiling water (see page 240). Cool and store.

❀ ❀ ❀

Date Preserve
Mrabba al-balah

DATE PALMS have a graceful charm and produce delicious fruits, as do fig, pomegranate and Seville orange trees. One specific variety of palm produces a brilliant and dense blood-red date that is traditionally used in Lebanon to make date preserve. Dates are regarded as a gift from heaven in the Middle East. They are energizing and an excellent source of minerals. Their season is short, but any fresh, dark red or golden yellow ones are good for this preserve, so *mrabba al-balah,* with its abundant sweetness, can be made and enjoyed all year round. It is the ideal accompaniment to all versions of rice pudding.

50 fresh, red dates (ripe but firm), thinly peeled
50 blanched almonds
50 tiny strips of clementine zest (optional)
450 g (1 lb) sugar
8 cloves
2 tablespoons lemon juice
Juice of 1 clementine

- Place the dates in a pan and cover with water by 5 cm (2 in). Bring to the boil, skimming the foam from the surface of the water, then reduce the heat to medium and simmer until the dates are slightly soft and their stones can be easily removed, about 5–10 minutes. With a slotted spoon remove the dates to a side dish and turn the heat off, reserving the water in the pan. Hold one date in one hand and with the other hand insert a wooden cocktail stick in one end and gently push the stone out of the other end. Push one almond and one strip of clementine zest, if using, into the larger hole in the date. Repeat with the remaining dates.

- Reheat the reserved date water in the pan, add the sugar and stir until sugar has completely dissolved. Bring to the boil, skimming off the foam from the surface of the water, then drop in the stuffed dates one by one and the cloves. Add the lemon and clementine juices, bring to the boil again then reduce the heat and simmer for 50–60 minutes or until the liquid has thickened slightly. Ladle into sterilized jars. Cool, seal and process for 30 minutes in boiling water (see page 240). Cool and store.

NOTE: If the liquid doesn't thicken remove the dates and boil until it reduces by half. Return the dates to the pan and bring to the boil. Place in sterilized jars.

❀ ❀ ❀

Quince Preserve
Mrabba al-safarjal

QUINCES ARE DELICIOUS, especially when prepared as jam. In Greek mythology they were associated with love, marriage and fertility. Quince jams, pastes and preserve are much praised by the Lebanese.

> 1 kg (2 lb 2 oz) quinces, unpeeled
> 550 g (1¼ lb) sugar
> 2½ tablespoons lemon juice

- Halve and core the quinces and cut into cubes. Place in a pan with 600 ml (1 pint) water and bring to the boil over high heat. Reduce the heat to medium, cover and simmer for 10–15 minutes. Add the sugar, stir until it dissolves completely and bring to the boil again. Add the lemon juice and bring again to the boil. Reduce the heat to medium and simmer for 1 hour or until quinces turn red. For the last 2–5 minutes, turn the heat up to medium-high; reduce it if the mixture boils too vigorously. Ladle into sterilized jars. Cool, seal and process for 30 minutes in boiling water (see page 240). Cool and store.

Apricot Preserve
Mrabba al mish-mosh

APRICOTS ARE POPULAR in Lebanon and one variety, *mishmosh Baalbaky*, is designated as being the one that is best to make preserves. It is plump, has a succulent taste and a beautiful orange colour similar to that of the Levantine moon. In Lebanon, the preserve is left in the sun after being prepared, which helps to get rid of excess moisture. It is simple to prepare and can be added to ice cream, blended with cream to sandwich a sponge cake or mixed, with its syrup, into fresh or dried fruit salad.

I like to half-cover *mouhallabieh* (Creamy Pudding Rice, see page 262) with a heaped tablespoon of the preserve. Though it contains sugar, it is nutritious as long as it's consumed in strict moderation. Ibn er Rumi (d. 896), a great Arabic poet and satirist, had a burning desire for food. An artist who painted with words, in his eyes apricots were the doctor, meaning medicine: 'The time you see an apricot grove believe rightly it is a doctor.'

900 g (2 lb) apricots, ripe but firm
500 g (1 lb 1 oz) sugar

- Halve the apricots and remove the stones. Place them in a bowl, cover with the sugar and leave to stand overnight; this allows the apricots to release excess moisture. The following day put the apricot mixture into a pan over medium-low heat. Stir with a wooden spoon until the sugar is completely dissolved. Bring slowly to the boil until the mixture starts to bubble then reduce the heat and simmer for 30 minutes or until the mixture thickens. Ladle into sterilized jars. Cool, seal and process in boiling water for 30 minutes (see page 240).

NOTE: If the preserve isn't syrupy enough, remove the apricots to a side dish, using a slotted spoon. Reduce the syrup in the pan, then return the apricots, bring to the boil and finish as in the recipe.

❀ ❀ ❀

Dried Fig Jam
Mrabba lteen l'nashef

THE FIG is the mountain fruit *par excellence*. However, in Beirut and other cities some people are lucky enough to have a fig tree that embraces the front entrance of their house or stands in their garden. In summer fresh ripe figs are enjoyed for their amazing flavour; in general the Lebanese are fond of green figs and in particular a deliciously sweet variety with a thin skin and white flesh. Figs are also dried to keep through the winter. They are spread over large straw trays and laid on the roof or a terrace to dry in the sun. As the sun sets the figs are taken indoors daily to prevent the morning dew (*al-nada*) making them moist. A richly flavoured jam is simply and quickly made from dried figs each year as part of the preparation for the *munee* (provision). In the Shouf mountains, after the season of drying the figs, travellers may encounter the occasional street vendor selling home-made fig jam that a *shaikha* (a woman who has knowledge of religion or is very religious) has prepared.

Now that many women go out to work, home preparation has become less common. However, a home-made jam does not take long to prepare and you can be sure of its quality. It is also gratifying to carry on the tradition. For many, jam-making nurtures pleasant emotions and stimulates memories. If you crave something sweet, a teaspoonful of home-made jam is comforting and satisfying. Or, if you are feeling run-down, have some fig jam with a little *tahini* and a few walnuts. I was given the jam this way: some butter was heated and the fig jam was added, stirred for few minutes, then spread over a serving dish.

This is my mother's recipe, but on a much smaller scale. As children, watching my grandmother and uncle taking it in turns to stir the figs, and exchanging words, was most enjoyable theatre. We ran around the cauldron teasing them and laughing.

Figs are rich in fibre and pectin which aids digestion. They also have an a high concentration of calcium, magnesium and potassium. Believe me, when you make this jam you will be embarking on a culinary adventure.

1 kg (2lb 2oz) dried figs
500 g (1 lb 1 oz) sugar
2 tablespoons lemon juice
1 tablespoon aniseeds
50 g (2 oz) toasted sesame seeds
½ teaspoon *miski* (see Glossary page 302), gently pounded
    with ½ teaspoon sugar

• Make sure the figs are clean inside and cut out and discard their stems. Wash and drain the figs, then chop them roughly or blend them in a blender. Place the sugar in a pan with 750 ml (1¼ pints) water and bring to the boil. Wait about 30 seconds, skim the foam from the surface of the water then stir in the lemon juice. After a minute, and while the water is boiling, drop in the figs. Reduce the heat to medium-low and simmer for about 20 minutes until the water has been absorbed but figs are still moist. Now and then stir to prevent them sticking to the pan; use a long-handled wooden spoon – they may spatter. When the water has evaporated add the aniseeds and sesame seeds, and simmer stirring all the time for 7–10 minutes, or until the jam has thickened and easily coats the spoon. Turn off the heat and very quickly add the *miski*, stirring vigorously clockwise and back. Ladle into sterilized jars. Cool, seal and process for 30 minutes in boiling water (see page 240). Cool and store.

❀ ❀ ❀

Whole Cherries Preserve
Mrabba al karaz

MAKING PRESERVES AND JAMS was a ritual when family and sometimes friends got together to prepare huge amounts that would last for nearly a year. Tasty cherries grow in Lebanon and, in general, where they grow, preserves and jams are prepared. Here the preserve is made with sweet black cherries, using little sugar and more liquid for short-term consumption. The syrup can be added to fruit salads and yoghurt, or to meat or game when mixed with wine or any other alcohol. The flavour of the cherries and syrup develops after cooling, more so the following day.

500 g (1 lb 1 oz) black cherries, stalks removed
250–275 g (9–10 oz) sugar
1–2 cloves
1¼ tablespoon lemon juice

• Remove the stones from the cherries. Place the sugar in a small pan with 300–450 ml (½–¾ pint) water and stir over medium heat until the sugar has dissolved. Bring to the boil and leave for about 10 minutes. Add the cherries and cloves and simmer for 30–35 minutes or until the cherries have softened. A few minutes before the end of the cooking time add the lemon juice. Turn off the heat and leave to cool.

Sweets

Nearly all celebrations in Lebanon are religious and are deemed incomplete without a number of sweetmeats prepared especially for the occasion. Although all kinds of sweets are piled high in shops throughout the year, some varieties are only for a particular religious occasion, which may be paying homage to a real or legendary saint.

It is impossible to count all the sweets that can be found in Lebanon. This tiny country has an enormously varied range of climates and terrain from a mild coast to high, snowy mountains. Moreover, it is inhabited by more than 18 religious communities and sects, most of whom came to escape persecution, and some of whom kept links with their original religious centres. In addition, Lebanon was part of the Ottoman Empire for nearly 400 years. However, it was never cut off for long from Western influence. For all these reasons, Lebanese sweets are rich and varied.

The great fourteenth century traveller Ibn Battuta, who left his home town of Tangier at 21 years of age, came to Jabal Loubnan (Mountain of Lebanon) then to the city of Baalbeck, the sun city and the site of an important Roman temple. He tells us about *dibs enab* (grape molasses) and about a sweetmeat in which pistachio nuts and almonds were added, known as *al malban. Dibs enab* is still prepared in Mount Lebanon. Long ago it was used in certain desserts instead of sugar, which was expensive or unavailable. It is delicious and quite nutritious when used without the addition of sugar. Gertrude Bell, the nineteenth century writer and traveller, describes *dibs enab* as a kind of treacle made from boiled grape juice.

Another kind of molasses, and a great favourite with the Lebanese, is *dibs kharoub* (carob molasses); it is a delicacy, especially when eaten with *tahini* (sesame cream). *Dibs kharoub* was, and still is, used by some mountain people to make sweets such as turmeric cakes or macaroons. Rustic restaurants in the mountains serve it at the end of the meal with a bowl of *tahini*.

One way of identifying the origin of some of Lebanon's sweets is through the major religious feasts celebrated annually by, respectively, Muslims and Christians, who quite often join in a common celebration. A large concentration of the Muslim population lives in the coastal towns and was under direct Ottoman control and influence, much more so than the inhabitants of the mountains, mostly Christians and Druse.

The town dwellers were also more affluent than other communities and this is reflected in their traditional sweets. Those eaten during the month of Ramadan (the month of fasting for Muslims), Id-al-Fitr (a celebration of the end of fasting) and Id-al-Adha (the commemoration of Abraham's sacrifice of a ram) are of a distinct Ottoman inspiration and are more expensive to prepare than those consumed by the inhabitants of mountain villages. During Ramadan, and as soon as the sun has disappeared over the horizon, thick crêpes (*Kataef*, see page 252)filled with cheese, cream or crushed walnuts, covered with syrup, are laid on the table to tempt people who have been fasting during the hours of daylight. A salad of dried fruits with almonds, walnuts and pine nuts often adorns the dining table.

The new moon indicates the end of the fast and Id-al-Fitr is an occasion for joy, celebration and more sweets. A favourite is *kanafe bi-jibn*, which consists of layers of *akkawi* (a white cheese) and a semolina dough cooked in the oven and eaten with syrup and a layer of sesame bread. It is also a popular breakfast food; on their way to work people can buy individual portions from sweet shops or from the many eating houses and cafés in Beirut, Tripoli, Sidon and other places. It seems that *kanafe* has always been a delicacy; it is mentioned in *The Thousand and One Nights*.

At Id al-Adha and Easter pastries filled with dates reduced to a paste, or with crushed walnuts or pistachios, are enjoyed and offered to well-wishers together with *baklava* and sweets of Western origin. *Baklava* is also served to celebrate an engagement, a birth or some other happy event.

The two festive occasions celebrated by most Lebanese are Christmas, which does not have a religious connotation for Muslims, and New Year. The sweets served then include ones you would find on a French table, along with *mighli* (Spiced Rice Pudding, see page 272) which celebrates the birth of Christ and is traditionally served when a child is born. Christmas meant a lot to us as children – not only the occasion itself but the preparations for it. They started weeks before when wheat grains and lentils were spread on trays over a layer of cotton. They were kept in a dark place and sometimes watered. By Christmas Day the shoots would reach nearly 13 cm (5 in) and would be a beautiful green. They were put next to the tree, which was adorned with bags of raisins and sugar-coated chick-peas and almonds.

Indigenous recipes are found mainly during minor religious celebrations. Each mountain village has its patron saint, who is celebrated annually with a one- or two-day fair when sweets are abundantly on offer.

Sweet shops in Lebanon are bewitching, displaying wide trays piled high with interesting delicacies, amongst them *moushabak*, a dessert that I must have every now and then because it brings back childhood memories. It comes in a circular plaited shape, and glistens with the fragrant syrup in which it is dipped after being fried.

Most of us indulge in sweets at one time or another, and no cookery book is complete without recipes for them. However, they should be regarded as a special treat and consumed in strict moderation. Overeating foods high in fat and sugar may be harmful to health.

Crêpes
Kataef

CRÊPES ARE A POPULAR TREAT all over the country, but especially in coastal towns where, after sunset during the holy month of Ramadan, tables are laid out with several dishes including *kataef*. *Kataef* come with different fillings: the ones filled with *kashta* (cream) are eaten 'nature' (without further cooking) and those with cheese are fried, whereas *kataef bi-jawz* (*kataef* filled with walnuts) can be eaten either 'nature' or fried. Other crêpes are filled with pine nuts – a luxury today because of the high price of the nuts. This filling is a speciality of Druse families as pine trees grow abundantly in the regions where they live. Preparing *kataef* does not require any culinary experience and is quite fun. Grill or fry and use with mangoes, blueberries or strawberries. Drizzle with syrup.

Makes 8–10 kataef
1 teaspoon dried yeast
2 teaspoons warm water
1½ teaspoons sugar
130 g (4½ oz) plain flour
1½ teaspoons baking powder
1–2 teaspoons rose water (optional)
Groundnut oil, for greasing and frying

For the syrup:
275 g (10 oz) sugar
1 teaspoon lemon juice
1 teaspoon orange flower water
1½ teaspoons rose water

- Make the syrup. In a small pan, combine the sugar with 200 ml (7 fl oz) water. Stir until the sugar dissolves completely. Bring to the boil, add the lemon juice and simmer over medium heat for 7–10 minutes, or until the liquid thickens to a syrupy consistency. Add the orange flower and rose waters. Stir, simmer for a few seconds more, turn the heat off, pour into a serving jug and set aside.

- Dissolve the yeast with the warm water in a small cup. Stir in the sugar, cover and leave in a warm place for about 5 minutes or until frothy. Sift the flour into a deep mixing bowl and gradually add 250 ml (9 fl oz) water and the yeast mixture, whisking well to prevent any lumps forming, until it has the consistency of cream. Finally sprinkle with the baking powder and rose water, if using. Cover with a cloth and leave for 1½–2 hours to rise.

- When the batter has risen, lightly grease a small, thick-bottomed, non-stick frying pan with oil and set it over medium heat. Whisk the batter vigorously and measure about 3 tablespoons into a small cup (you can vary the amount if you want the *kataef* bigger or smaller). Pour into the centre of the pan and immediately tilt the pan slightly from side to side to distribute the mixture evenly. Cook for about 30 seconds or until the base is golden and the surface is relatively dry. Remove to a tray. Repeat with the remaining batter, using an oil-dampened piece of cotton wool to re-oil the pan after every three crêpes. Cover the crêpes with a damp cloth or cling film. If you are using them straight away fill them as soon as they have cooled; if not, stack them one on top of the other. Cover with clingfilm, otherwise they will dry and they will not seal properly to enclose the filling. Crêpes can be refrigerated for no more than 3–4 days.

- To add the filling, take one of the prepared crêpes and fill with about 1 tablespoon (more or less, depending on the size of crêpe) of your chosen filling (see below). Lift the edges of the crêpe and bring them together. Gently pinch to seal. Place on a side dish and cover with cling film. Repeat with the remaining crêpes.

- Heat the oil in a frying pan and fry the crêpes until golden brown. Remove and drain over kitchen paper. Serve with the syrup.

- Fill the crêpes with one of the following fillings:

Walnut Filling
120 g (4 oz) shelled walnuts, crushed medium-fine
½ tablespoon honey or ½ tablespoon sugar
¼ tablespoon orange flower water
¼ tablespoon rose water

- Place the walnuts in a small mixing bowl. Dissolve the honey or sugar in the orange flower and rose waters and combine thoroughly with the walnuts. Prepare the crêpes as described above.

Cheese Filling

Traditionally *akkawi*, a delicious white cheese, is used and is worth trying; it is sold in Lebanese shops. It needs to be soaked in several changes of water to rid it of its high salt content. Taste to make sure it's not salty before using. Mozzarella cheese is a good alternative.

150 g (5 oz) *akkawi* or mozzarella cheese, rinsed, drained
and very finely shredded
½ tablespoon orange flower water (optional)
Butter, groundnut or olive oil, for grilling

- If using orange flower water, mix this into the cheese. Prepare the crêpes as described above and grill as in variation, below.

  Cream Filling I
  130 g (4½ oz) ricotta cheese
  1 tablespoon fromage frais
  ½ tablespoon orange flower water
  2 tablespoons syrup or to taste

- In a blender, blend the ricotta with the fromage frais, orange flower water and syrup until smooth and creamy. Fill the crêpes and serve immediately with the syrup.

  Cream Filling II
  150 ml (¼ pint) double cream
  150 ml (¼ pint) single cream
  1½ teaspoons cornflour
  2 slices of bread, crusts removed, chopped
  1 teaspoon orange flower water
  1 teaspoon rose water
  Pistachio nuts

- Place the creams in a pan. Mix the cornflour thoroughly with 1 tablespoon of water and strain into the creams. Place over medium heat and stir constantly until the creams boil and thicken. Stir in the bread and the orange flower and rose waters and quickly turn the heat off. Chill and fill the crêpes as needed. Sprinkle with the pistachios and serve immediately with the syrup.

VARIATION: Instead of frying crêpes you can brush the generously filled crêpes all over with unsalted butter and grill them on both sides until golden and crisp. Remove and serve, spooning about 1–2 tablespoons of the syrup over each crêpe.

Wheat or Barley in Orange-flower Water
Kamhiyeh

KAMHIYEH is a mouth-watering sweet eaten during the celebration of St Barbara, which falls on 4 December. This saint, who lived in the fourth century, was the daughter of a heathen; she converted to Christianity and rejected all the suitors proposed by her father. She disguised herself and ran through wheat fields to a grotto to escape her father's cruelty. It is said that the wheat grew to hide her as she ran through it. Her father caught her and, at the moment he was about to strike off her head, a bolt of lightning killed him. St Barbara's festival is the opportunity for children to masquerade and go from door to door in their neighbourhoods, chanting, dancing and waiting for rewards, either of sweets or money.

Kamhiyeh is also prepared when a baby's first tooth appears, when it is called *snyniyeh*. Traditionally wheat is used, which how the dish got its name. However, you can use organic barley instead of the traditional wheat. Whole barley is full of flavour but takes a little longer to cook than the processed variety, from which all the bran has been removed.

200 g (7 oz) organic whole wheat grains or barley
Honey or sugar to taste

1½ tablespoons orange flower water or to taste
2 tablespoons rose water or to taste
30 g (1 oz) pine nuts, soaked for 1 hour and drained
30 g (1 oz) blanched almonds, soaked for 1 hour and drained
30 g (1 oz) pistachio nuts, soaked for 1 hour and drained
Seeds of 1 pomegranate (in season)

- If using whole wheat grains, place them in a medium-size pan with 1 litre (1¾ pints) water and bring to the boil over high heat. Reduce the heat to medium-low, cover and simmer for 60–70 minutes. If using barley, add an extra 75 ml (3 fl oz) water, bring to the boil and simmer for 35–45 minutes or until soft. Remove the wheat or barley and pour into a serving bowl, add the honey or sugar, orange flower and rose waters and stir to incorporate. Garnish with the pine nuts, almonds, pistachios and pomegranate seeds. Serve immediately or chill.

Flour and Rice Puffs in Syrup
Awamat

CHRISTIANS CELEBRATE the baptism of Christ on 6 January with the preparation of *awamat*. During the night a piece of bread dough, taken from a previous batch, is put in a fine, white cloth bag, which is suspended from a tree. Silver currency is sometimes inserted into the dough, in the belief that the dough, which helps bread to rise, will also expand money and other provisions in the household.

Awamat are really tasty and worth trying. Their golden glistening colour and plump round shapes take you back to the time of the sultans and

Arab banquets. They are beautiful to look at and embellish the table for a party. As a general rule the batter is made with flour mixed with water or yoghurt or cooked potatoes and has the consistency of a medium-thick yoghurt. Here ground rice is used. Whole rice can be cooked and blended.

> I teaspoon dried yeast
> 2 tablespoons warm water
> 45 g (1½ oz) finely ground rice
> 225 g (8 oz) plain flour
> Groundnut oil, for deep-frying
>
> *For the syrup:*
> 675 g (1½ lb) sugar
> I tablespoon lemon juice
> 1–1½ tablespoons orange flower water
> 2 tablespoons rose water

- Dissolve the yeast in the warm water in a small cup, cover and leave in a warm place for a little while. Put the rice in a small pan with 200 ml (7 fl oz) water and cook over low heat until the water is fully absorbed and the rice looks like porridge; keep your eye on it because the water is quickly absorbed. Cool slightly for 1–2 minutes.

- Meanwhile, sift the flour into a mixing bowl, add the yeasted water and cooked rice, and mix thoroughly. Gradually add 150 ml (¼ pint) water; the mixture should be like thick yoghurt. Cover with a clean cloth and leave in a warm place to rise for about 2–3 hours.

- While the dough is rising prepare the syrup, as it will need to cool thoroughly before it is used, otherwise the hot *awamat* will not absorb it properly. In a pan, combine the sugar with 350 ml (12 fl oz) water.

Stir over a low heat until the sugar dissolves completely. Bring to the boil, add the lemon juice and simmer over medium heat for about 7 minutes or until the liquid thickens to a syrupy consistency. Add the orange flower and rose waters. Stir, simmer for a few seconds, turn the heat off and leave to cool.

- When the dough has risen, prepare the *awamat* balls. Heat the oil in a small pan and have ready a teaspoon and a cup filled with water. To make 1–2 *awamat* balls, dip the teaspoon in the water, just to wet it (the film of water helps the dough to slide off without sticking to the spoon), then scoop out a level teaspoonful of dough and gently drop it into the oil. Prepare the balls in batches of 10–12. They will rise to the surface of the oil in a matter of seconds; stir and cook until they are deep golden in colour. Remove the balls into a sieve with a slotted spoon and then dip them well in the syrup; leave them there for 1 minute, then transfer to a side dish with a clean slotted spoon.

- Serve warm or, better still, at room temperature.

Walnut, Pistachio and Date Pastries
Maamoul

THESE FESTIVE PASTRIES are very special and were traditionally prepared only for Id al-Adha and Easter. Our consumer society has made such delicacies readily available all year round and, in the process, deprived us of the joyful expectation of their appearance on the table, and the knowledge that, although they wouldn't last long, they would be made again the following year. The flour is kneaded with *samneh* (sheep butter) and the aromatic essences of rose and orange flower waters. The amounts of these used vary from one person to another, and some people add powdered milk.

These are real favourites of mine. You can have three succulent fillings and, to differentiate between them, *maamoul* are traditionally moulded in three different shapes: round for dates, oblong for pistachios and dome-shaped for walnuts. Digressing slightly from tradition, I sweeten the filling with honey instead of sugar. *Maamoul* are not void of nutrients. Contrary to belief, they are rich in beneficial oils, D and B vitamins – and also calories, so a little goes a long way. Coarse semolina is on sale in Lebanese and Cypriot shops but if you can't find any the fine one will do. Wooden moulds in different shapes are specially designed to prepare these pastries and are available from Lebanese and Middle Eastern shops.

Makes 18–20
250 g (9 oz) medium-coarse semolina
45 g (1½ oz) plain flour or fine semolina, plus extra flour for dusting
120 g (4 oz) unsalted butter
3–4 tablespoons orange flower water
4 tablespoons rose water
½ teaspoon easy-blend yeast

For the walnut filling:
100 g (3½ oz) walnuts, crushed to medium-fine
2½ tablespoons clear honey or 5 tablespoons icing sugar
1 teaspoon orange flower water
1 teaspoon rose water
Icing sugar, for dusting

- Place the medium-coarse semolina and the fine semolina or flour in a mixing bowl. Put the butter in a small bowl and place this in a bowl of boiling water. When the butter has melted pour it over the semolina in the bowl. Mix thoroughly with your fingertips. Leave overnight.

- Make the filling. Mix the walnuts and the honey and icing sugar together and add the orange flower and rose waters.

- Preheat the oven to 180°C/350°F/Gas Mark 4. Warm the orange flower and rose waters over low heat for a few seconds, add to the semolina mixture with the yeast and knead for 2–3 minutes to form a dough. Cover with a clean cloth and leave to rest for about 20 minutes. Divide the dough into 18–20 equal portions, each about the size of a walnut. Take each portion and roll it between the palms of your hands to form a ball. Hold the dough in one hand and with the index finger of the other poke a hole into the centre until you form a medium-thin shell. Push in 1 teaspoon of the filling, bring the edges of the dough together and gently pinch them to enclose the filling. Press into the mould, smoothing the pinched side. Turn the mould upside down and tap it flat on the palm of your hand to remove the dough. Place on a lightly floured baking tray. Bake for about 15–17 minutes. Remove and while still hot dust with a little icing sugar. Cool before serving the *maamoul* or storing them in an airtight container. The flavour will be enhanced the following day. They will keep for 3–4 weeks.

For the pistachio filling:
90 g (3 oz) pistachio nuts, whole or roughly chopped
1½ tablespoons honey or 5 tablespoons icing sugar
2 teaspoons orange flower water
2 teaspoons rose water

- Mix the pistachios with the honey or icing sugar and the orange flower and rose waters. Prepare the *maamoul* as above, but make the dough portions into oblong shapes.

  For the date filling:
  15–30 g (½–1 oz) unsalted butter (optional)
  140 g (5 oz) dates, stoned and chopped
  ½–¾ teaspoon ground *mahlab* (see Glossary page 302)
  Pinch of ground cinnamon (optional)
  ½ tablespoon orange flower water
  ½ tablespoon rose water

- Place the butter, if using and dates in a pan with 2 tablespoons water or as necessary. Set over low heat and mash the dates to a smooth paste. Add the *mahlab* and the cinnamon, if using, and mix. Keep mashing until you have a soft mixture, then add the orange flower and rose waters, stir well and turn off the heat.

- Cool and prepare the *maamoul* as above, but make the dough portions into round shapes about 1.5 cm (½ in) thick and bake them for about 20 minutes or until golden brown. You can add 1 teaspoon yoghurt and ½ tablespoon icing sugar to the dough before kneading.

Creamy Pudding Rice
Mouhallabieh

This is a variation on the delicious Lebanese pudding prepared with whole rice. Instead, ground rice is used, which gives it a creamier texture and a soothing taste. Eaten with home-made jam or succulent dates in syrup, *mouhallabieh* is heavenly. It is often prepared at home, especially for large families, because it is nourishing, inexpensive and satisfying to those with a sweet tooth. It also provides all, including children who don't like milk, with some of the calcium they need.

Mouhallabieh prepared in the traditional way with ground rice (Method I) needs a lot of patience. Because only a little rice is used, it takes 25–30 minutes to thicken and requires constant stirring, but the result is rewarding. Make it when you are calm and have something pleasant to listen to. You may be hooked on the process – or never want to do it again. You can also make this with whole rice (see Fragrant Ground Rice and Milk, page 285)

Method I

75 g (3 oz) very finely ground rice
75 ml (3 fl oz) hot water
1.2 litres (2 pints) milk
100 g (3½ oz) sugar
1 tablespoon orange flower water
1 tablespoon rose water
¼ teaspoon *miskee* pieces (see Glossary page 302), ground with 1 teaspoon sugar
30 g (1 oz) whole or halved blanched almonds, soaked in water for at least 1 hour
30 g (1 oz) whole pistachio nuts or 2 tablespoons ground pistachio nuts

- Place the rice in a thick-bottomed stainless-steel pan and cover with the water. As the water is absorbed by the rice, add the milk gradually while whisking. Set over medium-high heat and allow to boil rapidly while stirring with a wooden spoon. Reduce the heat to medium and continue to stir until the pudding thickens. Be patient, this takes about 18–20 minutes. When the pudding coats the spoon add the sugar. Stir for 3–5 minutes more, then add the *miskee*, if using, and the orange flower and rose waters. Give it a few good stirs and quickly turn off the heat. Pour the pudding instantly (before it sets) into a deep 21 cm (8½ in) serving dish or individual serving cups. Garnish with the almonds or pistachios or a mixture of the two.

• Serve warm or chilled with apricot jam or date preserve.

VARIATION: For a quick *mouhallabieh* use 75 g (2½ oz) cornflour instead of ground rice. Dissolve cornflour with 5 tablespoons of milk then strain into 1.2 litres (2 pints) milk. Set the pan over medium heat and follow the recipe above.

Cheese Sweet
Halawet l'jibn

TRIPOLI, THE NORTHERN second city of Lebanon, is the undisputed origin of this refined and seductive delicacy. For me as a child, and for many others, it was a place of magnificent shops full of unfamiliar sweets. Forget about the majestic Crusaders' castle, the Mamluks' bustling *souks*, the colourful orchards and the deep blue sea: what we were after when we were taken for a drive to the north of Lebanon – usually just to run in a new car – was *halawet l'jibn*.

The preparation needs some effort and attention. *Akkawi* is the traditional white cheese used to make this *halwa* (sweet). Because it has a high salt content it has to be soaked for a long time in several changes of water. On the other hand, if you are in a hurry, mozzarella cheese is a satisfactory alternative. If you are a cheese-lover, are not averse to generous quantities of rose water, and have energy and time to spare, you will not regret trying this recipe. I believe its taste is reminiscent of that of the traditional dish.

The movement of the cheese stirred with the rose water provokes a faint picture of a serene whirling dervish. The resulting dough can be eaten plain or filled with *kashta* (cream).

500 g (1 lb 1 oz) *akkawi* **or mozzarella cheese**
225 g (8 oz) fine semolina
120 ml (4 fl oz) rose water
Ground pistachio nuts (optional)

For the syrup:
400 g (14 oz) sugar
1 teaspoon lemon juice
½ tablespoon orange flower water
½ tablespoon rose water

- If using *akkawi* cheese, soak it in several changes of water, then pat it dry and shred it. If using mozzarella, just rinse and dry before shredding.

- Make the syrup. In a pan combine the sugar with 250 ml (8 fl oz) water. Stir over low heat until the sugar dissolves completely. Bring to the boil, add the lemon juice and simmer over medium heat for 8 minutes or until the liquid thickens to a syrupy consistency. Add the orange flower and rose waters. Stir, simmer for a few seconds more, turn the heat off and set aside.

- Melt the cheese in a thick-bottomed pan (preferably non-stick) over low heat. Measure 110 ml (4½ fl oz) of the syrup and as the cheese melts pour the syrup into the pan and stir vigorously. Add the semolina and rose water, still stirring vigorously all the time, until the dough pulls away from the sides of the pan (you may need someone to help you). Spread some of the remaining syrup over a clean 45 cm (18 in) work surface.

- Remove the cheese mixture from the pan and, while still hot, place it on the syrup on the work surface. Moisten a rolling pin with a little syrup, roll the dough into a rectangular shape 3 mm (⅛ in) thick and leave to cool. Cut across the dough at 4 cm (1½ in) intervals, then cut lengthwise at 6 cm (2½ in) intervals. Roll each piece of dough into a bite-size, small fat sausage and place on a serving dish or roll in the ground pistachios, if using.

- Serve, or cover and chill.

NOTE: To fill the *halawet* with *kashta* (cream), as in the recipe for Crêpes (see page 252), or with a dollop of mascarpone, cut larger pieces of cheese dough and place the *kashta* or mascarpone on them. Tuck the sides over the filling and roll up the dough to encase it.

The Nights of Lebanon
Layali Loubnan

THIS IS AN ATTRACTIVE dessert that is quick to make and can be prepared ahead of time. *Layali Loubnan* consists of several layers: a semolina 'pudding', a cream mixture, a layer of bananas and another of pistachios and toasted flaked almonds. These are then drizzled with honey and scented with orange flower water. I also like to blend apricot preserve and its syrup and spread this between the semolina and the cream mixture.

½ teaspoon *miskee* (see Glossary page 302)
I tablespoon sugar
90 g (3 oz) fine semolina
600 ml (I pint) milk
I teaspoon orange flower water

*For the cream (*kashta*):*
I tablespoon cornflour
200 ml (7 fl oz) milk
300 ml (½ pint) double cream
2–3 slices of bread, crusts removed and processed until
    smooth
½ teaspoon orange flower water
I teaspoon rose water

For the topping:
I large ripe banana, sliced
Large handful of pistachio nuts, soaked overnight and
    peeled
Almond flakes, soaked for 2 hours and drained
Honey to taste
½ teaspoon orange flower or rose water

• Gently pound the *miskee* and sugar to a powder-like consistency and set aside. Place the semolina and milk in a medium-small pan and stir over medium heat until the mixture boils and thickens. At this point add the *miskee* to the semolina while stirring. Add the orange flower water, turn the heat off, stir well and pour over a deep serving dish. Leave to cool.

Make the cream. Dilute the cornflour with a little of the milk and strain into a pan. Combine with the remaining milk and add the cream. Place over medium heat and stir continuously until the mixture thickens. At this point stir in the breadcrumbs and the orange flower and rose waters. Turn the heat off, leave to cool slightly, then spread the cream over the cooled semolina mixture and refrigerate.

- Well before serving, spread the banana slices over the cream. Scatter with the pistachios and almond flakes. Mix the honey with the orange flower or rose water and drizzle all over. Refrigerate then serve.

❀ ❀ ❀

Baked Date or Walnut Cake
Maamoul mad

THIS CAKE IS DELICIOUS, simple to make and delightful to the palate. I associate it with winter, the time to stay indoors, sheltered from the wind and cold, and to enjoy a cup of tea. And what could better to accompany this than slices of *maamoul mad*; it softens in the mouth with a subtle sweetness that warms the heart. I like to add yoghurt to the pastry dough as it improves the flavour. I sometimes make small cakes with patterns that are different to the one described below.

300 g (11 oz) semolina
2 tablespoons plain white or wholemeal flour
120g (4 oz) butter, clarified, plus a knob of butter
    for greasing
2 tablespoons live yoghurt
2 tablespoons sugar or honey
½ teaspoon baking powder

2 tablespoons warm orange flower water
2½–3 tablespoons warm rose water

For the date filling:
200 g (7 oz) dates, finely chopped
I teaspoon ground *mahlab* (see Glossary 302)
2 tablespoons orange flower water

For the walnut filling:
175 g (6 oz) shelled walnuts, crushed medium-fine
2½–3 tablespoons honey or sugar to taste
I tablespoon orange flower water
I tablespoon rose water

- In a mixing bowl combine the semolina flour with the butter, working them well with your fingertips. Add the yoghurt, sugar or honey and baking powder, and mix well to form a crumbly dough. Add the orange flower and rose waters and knead well. Cover and leave to stand for at least 6 hours or overnight. When time is up prepare one of the fillings.

- For the date filling, place the dates in a pan with 6 tablespoons water. Set over medium-low heat and mash the dates with the back of a spoon until smooth and well mixed. Add the *mahlab* and orange flower water and continue mashing until smooth, then turn off the heat.

- For the walnut filling, place the walnuts in a small mixing bowl. Dissolve the honey in the orange flower and rose waters, add to the walnuts and mix thoroughly to blend.

- Preheat the oven 200°C/400°F/Gas Mark 6 and lightly grease a 20 cm (8 in) baking tin with oil. Place the dough on a clean work surface and knead; if necessary add 3 tablespoons of rose water. Divide into two equal portions. From one portion take small lumps, flatten between the palms of your hands and press down against the base of the baking tin until you have made a bottom layer. Spread the filling of your choice over this layer. Repeat the process with the remaining dough, placing on top of the filling and pressing to join together, forming a uniform top layer. (Alternatively roll the dough between two pieces of wax paper.) Use a fork to make a criss-cross pattern on the surface of the dough.

- Bake for 30–35 minutes or until nicely browned. Remove and leave to cool. Cut into 5 cm (2 in) or smaller squares and gently remove them with a spatula. Serve or store in an airtight container.

Sultanas and Raisins in Fragrant Water
Khusshaf

A REFRESHING, fragrant and pretty fruit salad derived from the traditional *khusshaf* (which includes dried apricots). This version consists of raisins and sultanas immersed in pleasantly scented water until they swell. A handful of nuts is added; and I have included pumpkin and sunflower seeds. All this provides energy and nutrients. Lychees marry delightfully with the texture and flavour of sultanas, the velvety juiciness of ripe papaya and the sweetness of bananas. This dessert salad sparkles like a collection of jewels. Let your imagination flow; you may think you've found Ali Baba's treasure.

> 175 g (6 oz) sultanas, rinsed
> 120 g (4 oz) raisins, rinsed
> 2–3 tablespoons honey or to taste
> 1½ tablespoons orange flower water or to taste

1½ tablespoons rose water or to taste

2 tablespoons sunflower seeds

2 tablespoons pumpkin seeds

30 g (1 oz) pistachio nuts, soaked in water and chilled for
30 minutes or overnight

30 g (1 oz) blanched almonds, soaked in water and chilled
for 30 minutes or overnight

30 g (1 oz) pine nuts, soaked in water and chilled for
30 minutes or overnight

50 g (2 oz) shelled walnuts, halved, soaked in water and
chilled for 1 hour or overnight

1 banana, sliced

8 lychees, shelled, left whole or cut in half and stones
removed

1 medium-size ripe papaya, cut into 2.5 cm (1 in) pieces

- In a serving bowl, combine the sultanas and raisins with 600 ml (1 pint) water and the honey. Stir until the honey is completely dissolved. Cover and chill for 12 hours.

- The following day add the orange flower and rose waters to the sultanas and raisins, stir, taste and, if necessary, adjust the flavourings. Add the sunflower and pumpkin seeds. Cover and chill.

- Just before serving, drain the pistachios, almonds, pine nuts and walnuts and mix lightly into the salad. Add the banana and top with the lychees and papaya.

Spiced Rice Pudding
Mighli

A FESTIVE SWEET that was traditionally prepared when a boy was born, *mighli* was offered to well-wishers and prepared freshly every morning for 40 days after the birth. It was also customary to distribute it among neighbours and close friends. Nowadays, baby girls are similarly honoured. The pudding is increasingly served at dinner parties, especially at Christmas to celebrate the birth of Christ. *Mighli* is a pudding rice, highly flavoured with exotic and apparently aphrodisiac spices, and simmered in water until it is brown and smooth. When cool it develops a velvety surface which is sprinkled with a touch of coconut and topped with a large handful of nuts. The amount and variety of these used to depend on the wealth of the family of the new-born baby, though families gladly made sacrifices in order to generously shower the dish with a rain of nuts.

A hot drink made in the same way, but without the rice, was given to nursing mothers during the 40-day period of *nafess*, in the belief that it helped her to produce milk.

> **175 g (6 oz) ground rice**
> **1 tablespoon ground cinnamon**
> **1 tablespoon ground aniseeds**
> **1 tablespoon ground caraway seeds**
> **225 g (8 oz) sugar or to taste**
>
> **For the topping:**
> **Desiccated coconut as necessary**
> **60 g (2 oz) pine nuts, soaked in water to cover**

60 g (2 oz) pistachio nuts, soaked in water to cover
60 g (2 oz) almonds, soaked in water to cover
90 g (3 oz) shelled walnuts, soaked in water to cover

- Meanwhile, in a pan combine the rice with the cinnamon, ground aniseeds and caraway seeds. Gradually add 1.75 litres (3 pints) water and set the pan over high heat, stirring all the time until boiling. Reduce the heat to medium and simmer uncovered for 15 minutes, stirring occasionally to prevent the rice sticking to the bottom of the pan. After the 15 minutes and, while stirring, add the sugar and simmer until the pudding thickens, about 10 minutes. It should coat the back of the spoon. Taste and adjust the sugar if necessary.

- Remove from the heat, and pour immediately into a serving dish, or separate, small bowls, and leave to cool completely. Chill in the refrigerator to allow the flavours to develop. Just before serving, sprinkle with the coconut. Drain the pine nuts, pistachios, almonds and walnuts and spread them evenly on top of the pudding.

VARIATION: This is a more strongly flavoured *mighli*, which my father much enjoyed and which I ate years ago in his village, Mukhtara.

15 g (½ oz) cinnamon sticks
15 g (½ oz) dried galangal
15 g (½ oz) dried or fresh ginger
1½ tablespoons caraway seeds
1½ tablespoons aniseeds
2 cardamoms
4 black peppercorns
2 bay leaves

1–2 cloves
175 g (6 oz) ground rice
1 tablespoon ground cinnamon
½–1 tablespoon ground caraway seeds
220 g (7½ oz) sugar

- Place the cinnamon sticks, galangal, ginger, caraway and aniseeds, cardamoms, peppercorns, bay leaves and cloves in a large pan with 1.75 litres (3 pints) water. Bring to the boil, then reduce the heat, cover and simmer for 10 minutes. Drain the liquid into another pan and add the ground rice, ground cinnamon and ground caraway. Place over medium heat and stir continuously until thickened. Add the sugar and cook for a further 5 minutes or until the mixture coats the back of the spoon. Remove from the heat, and pour immediately, before the *mighli* sets, into a serving dish or into separate small bowls. Leave to cool, then refrigerate and finish as in the recipe above.

Lebanese Pain Perdu
Khubz bil halib wal katr

WHEN WE WANTED something sweet as young children we had this delicious *pain perdu*, which reflects the influence of the French who previously ruled Lebanon. After being soaked in milk, bread is fried and then soaked in syrup. Here, to cut down on using too much oil, I bake the bread rather than frying it. It is simple, less calorific and extremely delicious as it is impregnated with the amazingly appetizing aromatic Lebanese syrup. It has a beautiful deep golden brown colour and is a lovely dessert for a lunch party. *Pain perdu* is perfect with ice cream.

Better still, pour a tablespoon of home-made preserved cherries over the bread and top with a little cream.

170g (6 oz) French baguette
300–350 ml (½–¾ pint) milk or as necessary
1 tablespoon butter (optional)

For the syrup:
225 g (8 oz) sugar
1 teaspoon lemon juice
1 teaspoon orange flower water
2 teaspoons rose water

- Preheat the oven to 200°C/400°F/Gas Mark 6 and, if you wish, lightly butter a baking tray. Cut the bread into 5 mm (¼ in) slices, place them side by side in a glass dish and pour the milk over them; it will be absorbed within a few minutes. Turn the slices over then place them on the baking tray. Bake for 30–40 minutes or until nicely browned.

- Meanwhile, prepare the syrup. In a pan, combine the sugar with 300 ml (½ pint) water. Stir over low heat until the sugar dissolves completely. Bring to the boil, add the lemon juice and simmer over medium heat for about 6–8 minutes or until the liquid thickens to a syrupy consistency. Add the orange flower and rose waters. Stir, simmer for a few seconds more, and turn the heat off.

- Remove the bread from the oven and pour about 1 tablespoon of the syrup over each slice. Leave for a few minutes or until the syrup is absorbed. Then use a spatula to transfer the bread to a warm serving dish, or serve on separate plates with syrup to taste.

Sesame and Hazelnut Candies
Soumsoumia wa boundoukia

THESE DELICACIES used to have prime place during festivities held in villages to mark a saint's day. Peddlars prepared them at home and brought them to the church courtyard where the annual fair took place. There they would place their candies on stalls among the candy-floss sellers, the showmen, entertainers and sweet vendors. The peddlars became a fixture in some locations, such as the alley leading to the famous Wadi Zahle; here restaurants line both sides of the Burdawni river and are busy with Beirutys and people from all over Lebanon, and from neighbouring countries, who have come to enjoy the finest Lebanese food. Although the candies are seldom prepared in domestic kitchens, I have decided to include the recipe in this book, for the benefit of expatriates and nostalgic Lebanese. Pistachios, cashews, almonds or toasted peanuts may be used instead of sesame seeds or hazelnuts.

Sesame Candies (*soumsoumia*)
185 g (6½ oz) sesame seeds
Butter, for greasing
120 ml (4 fl oz) honey
90 g (3 oz) sugar
½ tablespoon lemon juice

- If you wish to toast the sesame seeds (they can be left untoasted) place them in a frying pan and cook them over medium heat. Stir, at first occasionally and then constantly, until they become deep golden in colour; be careful as they burn quickly. Remove, spread over a tray and leave to cool.

- Meanwhile, generously grease a deep, medium-size rectangular dish with butter. In a pan, combine the honey, sugar and lemon juice with 2 tablespoons water. Set over medium heat and stir all the time until the sugar dissolves completely and the liquid thickens to a syrupy consistency. At this point add the sesame seeds and boil over medium heat for 4 minutes. Pour into the dish and leave to set and cool slightly. Cut into squares and store in a container, placing waxed paper between layers.

- To make hazelnut candies (*boundoukia*): heat the oven to 180°C/ 350°F/Gas Mark 4 and roast 250 g (9 oz) hazelnuts for 20–30 minutes or until nicely browned. Remove from oven, cool slightly and remove the outer skins by rubbing the nuts in the palms of your hands. Then follow the instructions above.

Feast Girdle Cakes
Kaak al-id

KAAK AL-ID ARE SWEET girdle cakes, bread-like when chewed and very much appreciated in Lebanon by mountain dwellers of all denominations. They are of great significance for the Druse who prepare them to celebrate Id al-Adha (the sacrifice of Abraham), and the Greek Orthodox community at Easter. As I recall, in my parents' home pieces of dough were rolled into the shape of long ropes and laid in a pan clustered one next to the other. They were also shaped into rounds or squares, each decorated with different patterns. The cakes were spectacularly pretty with a beautiful golden colour. We shared them with well-wishers during the *id* (feast) along with coffee or *sharabat el tout* (mulberry drinks). Though *kaak al-id* are richly scented they have a lovely subtle taste. The traditional patterns on the cakes suggest that this delicacy could well have its origins in Byzantium.

275 g (10 oz) plain flour
150 g (5 oz) fine semolina
1 tablespoon ground lavender
½ teaspoon easy-blend yeast
½ teaspoon baking powder
½ teaspoon ground *mahlab* (see Glossary page 302)
¼ teaspoon freshly grated nutmeg
¼ teaspoon ground cloves
150 ml (¼ pint) milk
1 bay leaf
Slice of root ginger (optional)
210 g (7½ oz) sugar
75 g (2½ oz) unsalted butter

- Sift the flour and semolina into a mixing bowl. Add the lavender, yeast, baking powder, *mahlab*, nutmeg and cloves. Set aside.

- Place the milk in a pan over medium heat, with the bay leaf and ginger, if using. When milk is warm add the sugar and butter, and turn the heat off. Stir until the sugar is completely dissolved, then pour the mixture over the ingredients in the mixing bowl. Discard the bay leaf and ginger. Mix well for about 3–5 minutes to form a smooth dough. Cover with a clean cloth and leave to rest for 4 hours.

- Preheat the oven to 180°C/350°F/Gas Mark 4. Divide the dough into small portions, each the size of a walnut. Roll each portion under the palm of your hand to form a medium-thick roll about 10 cm (4 in) long. Bring both ends together, pinch gently to seal and place on a baking tray. Bake for 15–18 minutes or until golden. Cool and place in an airtight tin.

❀ ❀ ❀

Anise Cakes
Kaak bi-yansoun

THESE CAKES are generally served with coffee or tea; they are simple to make and useful to have on hand for unexpected guests because they keep for a long time (up to 10 days) in an airtight container. They may be sweetened with honey or with sugar, as in the traditional recipe.

According to the eleventh-century Arabic physician Ibn Butlan, aniseed relieves flatulence. It definitely is carminative, and indeed relieves gas in the stomach and has antiseptic qualities. Long ago I knew of many mothers who diluted milk powder with aniseed-infused water. This helped to calm their babies' colic, enabling better sleep, but before following their example, check with your physician or nutritionist.

Makes 10–12
150 g (5 oz) plain flour, sifted
¼ teaspoon baking powder
1½–2 teaspoons whole aniseeds
60 g (2 oz) sugar
60 ml (2 fl oz) olive oil
2–3 tablespoons warm water

- Preheat the oven to 180°C/350°F/Gas Mark 4. In a mixing bowl combine the flour with the baking powder, aniseeds, sugar and oil.

Mix thoroughly. Gradually add the warm water and knead to form a smooth dough. Divide the dough into 10 portions and roll each one into a sausage shape about 7–10 cm (3–4 in) long; curve into a ring shape and press gently on the ends to seal. Place the rings on a baking tray and bake for about 18 minutes or until nicely browned. Cool and serve.

❀ ❀ ❀

Turmeric Cakes
Sfouf

THESE CAKES ARE A FEATURE of home cooking in the mountains. For some people the taste needs to be acquired because of the distinctive flavour of turmeric. *Sfouf* are simple and inexpensive to make, using ingredients that are standard in most kitchens. In addition, they have a light, spongy texture that makes them suitable for older people. When sugar was expensive – such as in times of war– *dibs kharoub* (carob) was used as a substitute. My grandmother told me this, adding, quite rightly as we now know, that molasses is healthier than sugar. For me, nothing can replace these amazing cakes. The problem is that when you eat one you want to have another and another. They are a nutritious accompaniment for your morning coffee. To make them more attractive I serve them in cupcake cases.

1 tablespoon *tahini*
185 g (6½ oz) plain flour, sifted
2 teaspoons baking powder
1½ tablespoons turmeric
250 g (9 oz) fine semolina

75 ml (3 fl oz) olive oil
2 tablespoons melted butter
300–350 ml (10–12 fl oz) milk
2 tablespoons water
225 g (8 oz) sugar
2 large handfuls of pine nuts

- Preheat the oven to 180°C/350°F/Gas Mark 4 and grease the base and sides of a 26 x 20 cm (10½ x 8 in) rectangular tin with *tahini*. Put the flour, baking powder and turmeric into a mixing bowl and combine with the semolina, oil and butter. In another, medium-size mixing bowl, combine the milk and sugar with 2 tablespoons water. Stir until the sugar is completely dissolved then gradually add to the ingredients in the other mixing bowl. Mix thoroughly to make a smooth batter. Pour into the *tahini* pan and scatter the surface with the pine nuts.

- Bake for 30–35 minutes. Remove, cool and cut into 5 cm (2 in) squares.

❈ ❈ ❈

Fragrant Pomegranate and Pine Nut Salad
Salatet al rumman bi-snoubar

IN THIS SALAD the jewel-like ruby-red seeds of the pomegranate gracefully cluster together and embrace the abundant pine nuts. The pomegranate is the symbol of love, beauty and good luck. Its red flowers blossomed on trees that adorned fabled gardens and the fruit crowned festive banquets. It was introduced to Spain by the Moors in 711 AD and became the emblem of the city of Granada where it grew in abundance. Its juice was fermented by the Egyptians to make wine.

120 g (4 oz) pine nuts
4 pomegranates
1¼ tablespoons orange flower water or to taste
Fresh mint leaves (optional)

- Cover the pine nuts with water and refrigerate until they plump up,
  about 30 minutes. Meanwhile, break up the pomegranates, remove the
  seeds and place them in a serving bowl. When the pine nuts have
  doubled in size, drain them. Sprinkle the orange flower water over the
  pomegranate seeds, mix thoroughly and chill. Just before serving
  carefully place the pine nuts over the seeds; do not mix as the seeds
  will tint the nuts. Sprinkle with mint, if using.

VARIATION: Pistachio nuts can be used instead of pine nuts.

Pastry with Cheese
Kanafe bi-jibn

I HAVE HEARD many Westerners complain about the excess of sugar
in Lebanese sweets. This recipe could be the answer to those critics.
In the Lebanon *kanafe*, more than any other sweet, is considered a real
treat; it is a mouth-watering delicacy that most people find irresistible at
any time of the day. Here is a succulent combination of semolina dough
and cheese which I believe matches the ones on offer in sweet shops.
Find cream of wheat if you can, otherwise semolina is fine.

300 g (11 oz) regular cream of wheat or coarse semolina
125 g (4½ oz) unsalted butter, melted

75 ml (3 fl oz) warm water
½ teaspoon easy-blend yeast
120 ml (4 fl oz) hot milk (not boiled)

For the syrup:
275 g (10 oz) sugar
1 teaspoon lemon juice
1½ teaspoons orange flower water
1½ teaspoons rose water

For the filling:
300 g (11 oz) *akkawi* or mozzarella cheese
1½ teaspoons orange flower water

- Place the cream of wheat or semolina in a bowl. Heat the butter until very hot but not smoking, then pour it into the bowl and mix well. Add the warm water and yeast, mix thoroughly, then gradually add the milk. Keep mixing to form a moist dough. Cover and refrigerate for 4 hours or overnight.

- Make the syrup. Combine the sugar with 200 ml (7 fl oz) water, bring to the boil, add the lemon juice and simmer over medium heat for 8–10 minutes or until the liquid thickens to a syrupy consistency. Add the orange flower and rose waters, boil and turn the heat off. Pour into a jug and set aside. If using *akkawi* cheese for the filling, soak it for several hours in several changes of water to rid it of excess salt. If using mozzarella, rinse and pat dry.

- Remove the dough from the fridge. Allow to reach room temperature, and knead it a little so that it becomes easily pliable. Take about half the dough, divide into small portions and, using both fingers and the heel of your hand, flatten and smooth each portion to make a very thin layer on the base of a 21.5 cm (8½ in) baking tin; moisten your hands with water as necessary. Repeat until the base of the dish and 2 cm (¾ in) of its sides are covered. This will protect the cheese from browning. Preheat the grill, place the baking dish under it and brown the dough well, taking care that it does not burn. Leave to cool.

- Preheat the oven to 180°C/350°F/Gas Mark 4. Make sure that the cheese for the filling does not taste salty, then shred it, mix thoroughly with the orange flower water and spread over the cooled dough in the baking dish. Press the cheese lightly and cover with remaining dough, preparing it as before. Bake for 20 minutes. Preheat the grill, remove the *kanafe* from the oven and place under the grill to brown the top (this will greatly enhance the flavour). Watch it as it can burn within seconds.

- Serve with the syrup.

Baked Kataifi with Cheese

This is a quick and delicious variation on *kanafe*.

75 g (2½ oz) *kataifi* (shredded wheat)
60 g (2 oz) unsalted butter, melted
200 g (7 oz) mozzarella cheese, rinsed, drained and finely
sliced
1 tablespoon orange flower water

- Preheat the oven to 200°C/400°F/Gas Mark 6. Gently loosen the *kataifi* and spread a little under a half of it over the base of a baking dish. This will protect the cheese from browning. Hold the *kataifi* in place with your fingers at one end and, with a brush, dot the *kataifi* threads with the butter to coat them; change the position of your fingers and keep dotting with the butter until all the threads are coated. Spread the cheese evenly over the threads and sprinkle with the orange flower water. Loosen the remaining *kataifi* to fully cover the cheese layer. Again, dot with butter to coat the surface of the *kataifi*. Bake until golden, about 12–15 minutes.

• Serve immediately with syrup (see page 283).

NOTE: For a golden brown top, place the dish under a hot grill for about 1 minute, no longer, or the top will burn.

❀ ❀ ❀

Fragrant Ground Rice and Milk
Moubataneh

THIS IS AN OLD-TIME dessert made with ingredients found in the storecupboard and costs little money. A layer of rice pudding and a spread of nuts are covered with a fragrant cornflour mixture. *Moubataneh* is unusual and looks pretty when presented in a glass bowl.

175 g (6 oz) long grain white rice, preferably basmati
450 ml (¾ pint) milk
2 tablespoons double cream (optional)
¼ teaspoon *miskee* pieces (see Glossary page 302) pounded
   with ½ tablespoon sugar (optional)
1½ tablespoons rose water

**90 g (3 oz) pine nuts, soaked in water just to cover and
    drained**
Large handful of walnuts, preferably freshly shelled

For the cornflour pudding:
40 g (1½ oz) cornflour
1½–2 teaspoons rose water

- Place the rice in a medium-small pan with 450 ml (¾ pint) water and
  bring to the boil over medium heat. Reduce the heat to very low, cover
  and simmer for about 6–7 minutes or until the rice is very soft and still
  moist. Place the hot rice in a blender and blend for a few minutes until
  it becomes very smooth. Scrape the sides of the blender and run the
  motor again for 1–2 minutes to make sure all the rice has been well
  blended. While the motor is running, gradually add the milk and the
  cream, if using. The consistency should be velvety. Put the mixture in the
  pan in which you cooked the rice and bring to the boil. Stir over
  medium-low heat for 30 seconds. Stir in the *miskee*, if using, and rose
  water, stir well and turn the heat off. Pour the rice pudding into a
  serving dish or glass bowl about 23 cm (9 in) in diameter. Leave to cool.
  As it cools spread the nuts over.

- Meanwhile, prepare the cornflour pudding. Dilute the cornflour with a
  few tablespoons of water and strain into a pan containing 600 ml
  (1 pint) water. Set the pan over the heat, and cook, stirring all the time,
  until the mixture thickens, about 3–4 minutes. As it thickens add the
  rose water. Turn the heat off and pour the pudding over the nuts and
  rice pudding. Leave to cool and set. Chill.

- Serve with syrup (see Lebanese Pain Perdu, page 275).

Salep Ice Cream
Bouza sahlab

SAHLAB (OR SALEP) is a starchy powder obtained by grinding the dried tubers of wild orchids. In Lebanon it is used to make a hot drink and an ice cream, both of which are very popular. In winter the drink is bought from street vendors by early risers on their way into town, and by travellers and hunters on their way to the Bekaa Valley or Syria. When Richard the Lionheart fell ill in St John Acre, Saladin sent him a sherbet made of ice from Mount Hermon and fruit juice. The Crusaders took the recipe back to their countries and the concoction became sorbet.

> 250 g (9 oz) sugar
> 2 tablespoons *sahlab* powder
> 1 litre (1¾ pints) milk
> 1 tablespoon orange flower water
> ½ tablespoon rose water
> ¼ teaspoon *miskee* pieces (see Glossary page 302) ground
>   with ½ teaspoon sugar (optional)

- In a pan over a low heat combine the sugar with the *sahlab*. Gradually add the milk, stirring so that the *sahlab* does not form any lumps. Keep stirring until the sugar has dissolved completely and the *sahlab* is well incorporated into the milk. Set the pan over medium heat and stir continuously until the mixture thickens. At this point add the orange flower and rose waters and the *miskee* if using. Mix thoroughly.

- If you have an ice-cream maker and follow the manufacturer's instructions. If not, place the mixture in a deep dish in the freezer. Remove several times before it freezes totally and mix with a whisk.

Semolina Cakes with Yoghurt
Smid bil laban (nammoura)

THESE CAKES ARE LOVELY to eat when you're in the mood for
something sweet. They can be an excellent standby and are a favourite
when family and friends gather at teatime or after a Sunday lunch.
They don't require a lot of work, and nor does they cost an arm or a leg,
so they are a good choice when you have a lot of people around. They're
also fun for children to make, so why not encourage them to help while
you're preparing them.

I tablespoon *tahini*
200 g (7 oz) semolina
90 g (3 oz) butter
I teaspoon baking powder
200 g (7 oz) yoghurt or 170 ml (6 fl oz) soured cream
½ tablespoon sugar
Almonds as necessary

For the syrup:
140 g (5 oz) sugar
I teaspoon lemon juice
½ teaspoon orange flower water
1½ teaspoons rose water

- Spread half the *tahini* in a 21 cm (8½ in) square oven baking tin and
place the semolina in a small mixing bowl. Melt half the butter and mix
it thoroughly with the semolina. Add the baking powder. Combine the
yoghurt well with the remaining *tahini* and the sugar or honey and add

to the semolina. Mix all the ingredients thoroughly and place the resulting dough in the baking tin. With moistened hands pat and spread it over the *tahini*. Leave for a little while to set, then melt the remaining butter and pour it all over the dough. Cut the dough into small squares and push one almond into each. Swirl the tin to ensure the butter spreads evenly. When the butter solidifies, cover the tin with clingfilm and place in the fridge. Leave for at least 2 hours.

- Preheat the oven to 180°C/350°F/Gas Mark 4. Prepare the syrup. In a pan combine the sugar with 120 ml (4 fl oz) water and set over medium heat. Stir until sugar is completely dissolved and water has come to the boil. Reduce the heat and simmer for about 6 minutes. Add the lemon juice and leave for 30 seconds. Add the orange flower and rose waters and turn the heat off. Leave to cool.

- Bake the cake for about 40 minutes or until the surface is nicely browned. Remove from the oven and drizzle with the cooled syrup. Return to the oven, leave for a minute or two, then turn the oven off but leave the tin in it for 30–40 minutes. Remove and allow to cool.

Coffee
Qahweh

Coffee is much appreciated by the Lebanese. It is enjoyed at all times, in homes, restaurants and cafés, and is served at all gatherings, including funerals. The best times are when you are among friends, one of whom can read the coffee grounds – many cafés in Beirut have their own *bassara* (fortune-teller). It is fun to meet up for a morning breakfast, and indulge in eating *kanafe*, a favourite dessert in Lebanon, sipping coffee and gossiping.

Whenever you order a coffee or are offered one, you are asked: 'How do you like it? *Helwé* [sweet] *'wasat* [half-sweet] or *sedah* [no sugar]?' For me the word *mazboutah*, meaning just right, neither sweet nor half-sweet nor bitter, used in Beirut before the war of 1975, describes what I prefer. It is said that coffee originated in the Levant and that the first coffee house was in Istanbul. There is a belief in Lebanon that if you spill coffee it brings you *al-hazz* (good luck).

I remember how impatiently we waited for my grandmother to make our morning cups of coffee. She used to stand by the door of the corridor that opened on to the sitting area, dressed as usual in a long, pale blue linen robe, her Egyptian white muslin veil partly covering her greyish braided hair. This dropped below her waist and outlined an expressive strong face that somewhat resembled ones found in Lucien Freud portraits. She held an ornate brass coffee mill under her left arm and used her right hand to grind the freshly toasted beans. When this operation was completed she would enter the kitchen to make the coffee in a wide-based, long-handled coffee pot. Water was poured into it and it was placed on the hob and fed coffee and sugar through its narrow neck. As the water boiled a golden brown froth appeared. My grandmother divided the coffee between tiny beautiful cups; one felt she was exercising her power. Before pouring the coffee she waited for a few seconds for the grounds to settle at the bottom of the pot and for the liquid to become clear.

Ready-ground beans for Lebanese coffee are available in Lebanese shops and some supermarkets. Some coffees are plain and others have cardamom added. Flavours vary from one brand to another and experimenting is the key to acquiring a proper coffee, which should be neither too strong nor too weak.

Another kind of Lebanese coffee is white coffee, which does not include any coffee beans and is very much enjoyed nowadays, especially by those who want to cut down on their caffeine intake. It's made by adding orange flower water to boiling water. Those who are lucky enough to have an orange tree can simply add water to some of its blossoms. White coffee is simple to make. Just put half a tablespoon of orange flower water (or more, according to taste) in a tea cup, pour over some boiling water and stir.

Serves 3–4
I teaspoon sugar
3 heaped teaspoons ground coffee with cardamom

• Pour 200 ml (7 fl oz) water into a traditional metal coffee pot or small pan and bring to the boil over medium heat. As it comes to the boil add the sugar and coffee. Be careful; the coffee will boil and froth, so you need to hold the handle and remove the pot or pan from the heat then return it to the heat to boil about three times. Taste and adjust the flavour. If it's too strong add a little water and if it's too weak add a touch of ground coffee. Wait 30 seconds for the grounds to settle and serve in small coffee cups.

Pickled Vegetables

Moukhallal

THE LEBANESE PANTRY is packed with jars filled with local produce. Pickling gives the vegetables an appetizing flavour and, most importantly, a long lifespan. The vinegar used in pickling stops the growth of bacteria, although some vegetables are preserved in brine alone. All sorts of vegetables are pickled in Lebanon – turnips, cucumbers, green beans, okra, onions and peppers, cauliflowers, and beetroot. They should be the finest and picked fresh.

Strict hygiene is required during the preparation. The glass jars should be washed with hot, soapy water and rinsed very well, then sterilized by placing them in a pan, covering them with warm water and boiling them over medium-low heat for about 10 minutes. The jars must be removed just before you need them, giving them time to drain, inverted over a clean cloth.

The ratio of vinegar to water varies from one household to another. I have found that for turnips 1 cup vinegar to 2 cups water is adequate. For cucumbers I use 1 cup vinegar to 1 cup water. Organic cider vinegar gives a fresh taste to the vegetables. For 1 kg (2 lb 2 oz) of vegetables, use 60 g (2 oz) sea salt, free of additives or the vegetables will spoil.

A quick method is to place a piece of bread in a jar with, for example, lightly steamed cauliflower and sliced cabbage. Add raw peeled beetroot, carrots and chillies, if desired. Cover with a mixture of water, vinegar, sea salt and another piece of bread. This will allow you to eat the pickles after four or five days. However, after adding the liquid and before closing the jar, make sure there aren't any bubbles. Drain the vegetables well before serving.

Pickles are offered at the start of a *mezzé* or to embellish a meal. Sliced cucumber and turnip pickles are often used in Lebanese sandwiches and add a subtle tangy flavour to chicken or meat.

Pickled Olives

IN EARLY AUTUMN olive picking is a feature of village life; it makes a charming spectacle but is hard work. Olive trees grow on coastal plains and hills, mostly up to a maximum height of 500 metres (1640 ft) above sea level. Olives are high in monounsaturated fatty acids, but they also have a high sodium content and calorific value. Below are some traditional ways of preparing green and black olives.

To make crushed green olives (*zaytoon akhdar marsous*), wash the olives and soak them for two days in several changes of water. Then crush them with a pebble or a pestle. Sprinkle them lavishly with sea salt and leave for four days to mature. Stir and mix them four times a day. After that, place the olives in a container; this may be of any material but earthenware preserves their flavour best. At this point the olives are ready to eat and should be consumed within a week.

If you have a freezer, crushed olives will last longer than a week. Soak the green olives in several changes of water for two days, drain and lightly crush with a clean pebble or wooden pestle (make sure not to break the stones). Place in a polythene freezer bag and freeze. When needed, remove the desired quantity, sprinkle with sea salt and leave for three to four days to mature, stirring the olives three or four times a day. Eat within two weeks. They will have an exceptional bitter, slightly salty taste as if they have just been freshly picked off the tree, and are delicious with *labneh* (concentrated yoghurt).

Al jarjir, also known as bitter olives, are most frequently used. They are picked already ripened and have wrinkled skins. To prepare, salt them lightly and place them with a little olive oil in a container. They can be used straight away. *Jarjir* are on sale at most Lebanese food stores.

Black olives need time to mature. They are rinsed in several changes of water, drained, lavishly sprinkled with sea salt and left in an earthenware container for 10 days. They are then packed in a jar half-full of boiled, cooled water, and topped up with extra virgin olive oil. Red chillies can be added if you wish.

Another interesting way of preparing black olives is to add vinegar or lemon juice. Follow the procedure for black olives, then combine about 100 ml (3½ fl oz) wine vinegar or lemon juice with 200 ml (7 fl oz) boiled, cooled water. Pour this over the black olives in the jar, then fill the jar with extra virgin olive oil. The olives are ready to eat after 21–28 days.

Olives can also be pickled in brine (one cup salt to six cups water).

> **900 g (2 lb) green olives**
> **I lemon, unpeeled, rinsed and cut into 4–6 pieces
>   (optional)**
> **2–3 green chillies (optional)**
> **I–2 sprigs of coriander, leaves and tender stems only,
>   or a handful of dill (optional)**
> **140 g (5 oz) coarse sea salt**
> **4 tablespoons extra virgin olive oil**

- Slit each olive longitudinally on the surface then soak the olives in several changes of water for 2 days to get rid of their bitterness. Drain and pack into a sterilized 1.17–2 litre (3–3½ pint) glass jar; if you are using the lemon pieces, chillies, coriander or dill, intersperse these among the olives. Bring 750 ml (1¼ pints) water to the boil, add the salt and stir until it dissolves completely. Leave to cool, then pour over the olives and other ingredients in the jar to cover fully. Top with the olive oil. Seal and leave in a kitchen cupboard. Eat after 1 month.

Pickled Cucumber
Moukhallal al-khiar

CUCUMBERS THAT GROW in Lebanon are small with very tasty flesh. They are picked young and preserved to lengthen their life. Pickled cucumbers are easy to prepare and good ingredients make for delicious results. These pickles are perfect to serve with a drink or to enliven sandwiches, especially roast meat and chicken.

500g (1lb 1oz) small cucumbers
1 tablespoon rock salt, free of any additives
200 ml (7fl oz) organic cider vinegar

- Barely trim both ends of the cucumbers and position them upright in a sterilized jar. Bring 250 ml (8 fl oz) water to the boil and add and completely dissolve the salt. Cool slightly and combine with the vinegar. Pour this liquid over the cucumbers to cover fully, then seal. Place the jar in a dark kitchen cupboard and leave to stand for 1 week before using.

Pickled Turnips
Moukhalal al-lift

TURNIP PICKLES are the ones most favoured by the Lebanese and
hardly a house is without them. Their preparation may vary from one
household to another; for instance, they can be sliced or left whole,
peeled or unpeeled. Beetroot is added to give colour; depending on the
quantity used, it may be ruby red or rosy pink. I prefer the latter. In
general, pickled turnips are served with *mezzé* and relished with *mjaddara*
(Cream of Lentils, see page 58). If you want to indulge in them as soon as
possible, place a piece of bread in the jar to cover the turnips. They
should be ready to consume within four to five days. Here I follow my
mother's method, which is to leave the turnips whole and unpeeled.

> **500 g (1 lb 1 oz) white-mauve turnips, unpeeled, both ends
>   trimmed**
> **20 g (¾ oz) beetroot, peeled and cut into 3 pieces**
> **1–2 chillies (optional)**
> **1½ tablespoons sea salt**
> **150 ml (¼ pint) organic cider vinegar**
> **Extra virgin olive oil, to cover the turnips (optional)**

• Make cuts along the length of turnips at 5 mm (¼ in) intervals but leave
  them whole. Pack the turnips, beetroot and chillies, if using, into a
  sterilized glass jar. Bring 400 ml (14 fl oz) water to the boil, add the salt
  and dissolve completely. Cool, stir in the vinegar, and pour over the
  vegetables in the jar to cover fully. If desired, add a thin film of olive oil
  to prevent them spoiling. Seal and keep in a dark kitchen cupboard. Eat
  after 10–14 days.

Pickled Cabbage Stuffed with Walnuts, Garlic and Chillies

Malfouf mkhalal

CABBAGE IS ONE of the oldest vegetables. In Lebanon they are whitish green with tender leaves and valued for their natural taste and freshness. The fresh leaves are used for salads and to eat with *tabbouleh*. Cabbages contain antioxidants that may help to lower the risk of colon cancer and are essential for a healthy balanced diet. Restaurants in Batroun, a coastal town outside Beirut, serve them with *mezzé*, washed down with *arak*. In this recipe the leaves enclose a most interesting and highly nutritious combination of walnuts, garlic and chillies. They are smothered with vinegar and a little olive oil and are ready to eat within five to six days. The large outside leaves are mainly used (the medium and smaller leaves are usually boiled so that they are pliable enough to be rolled). After steaming (instead of boiling) the leaves are sliced in two, stuffed and marinated. The only drawback is that they have to be consumed within two days or at the most three. This is why it is best to prepare only the quantity needed.

7 large cabbage leaves or 14 medium ones
150g (5 oz) shelled walnuts, coarsely crushed
2 large garlic cloves, pounded until creamy
A pinch of salt
¼–½ teaspoon cayenne pepper
1 small mild or hot red chilli, deseeded and finely chopped
**   (optional)**
Organic cider vinegar as necessary
1 tablespoon extra virgin olive oil, plus extra for drizzling

- Place the cabbage leaves in a steaming basket and set into a pan over 2.5 cm (1 in) of boiling water. Cover and steam for about 3–5 minutes or until soft and easily pliable.

- Meanwhile, in a bowl combine the walnuts, garlic, salt, cayenne and the chilli, if using. Take out 2–3 leaves that are close to the base of the basket. Place on a clean surface and trim the thick rib so that it is level with the leaf or flatten it down with your thumb. Spread about 1 tablespoon of the walnut mixture on the leaf end. Roll once, lightly tuck in the sides of the leaf and continue to roll enclosing filling completely and press down gently. Repeat until all the leaves have been filled.

- Arrange the leaves in a slightly deep dish, one next to the other. Cover with the vinegar and oil. Cover and leave to marinate for 5–6 days. The leaves can be stored in the fridge for 3 more days. Remove as many rolls of cabbage as you need, drizzle with a little more oil and serve.

Pickled Aubergines with Walnuts
Makdouss al-batinjan

THIS IS A MUCH-APPRECIATED delicacy as it contains a most interesting, delightful and nutritional filling. Walnuts, garlic and chillies are fully covered with extra virgin olive oil.

People of my mother's generation were fussy about the aubergines they used; they had to be tiny and of the baby, white variety that is supposedly seedless. Nowadays we make do with what is available, and the purple, medium-size ones are just as tasty. These pickles are simple to make and pleasant served with drinks. It is important that the aubergines drain well. Traditionally, after they have been stuffed the jar is turned upside down for at least 12 hours to get rid of excess moisture before they are covered with oil. When you take the aubergines you need out of the jar, make sure you add more oil, if necessary, to cover the remaining ones.

> 1¼ teaspoons sea salt
> 275 g (10 oz) baby aubergines, stems trimmed
> 100 g (3½ oz) walnuts, halved and crushed medium-fine
> 2–3 garlic cloves, crushed
> 1 red chilli, deseeded and finely chopped, or ½ teaspoon
>   cayenne pepper
> 2 whole red chillies
> Extra virgin olive oil, to cover the aubergines

- Bring 600 ml (1 pint) water to the boil in a large pan and add half the salt. Drop in the aubergines and return to the boil, then reduce the heat to medium and simmer for about 3–5 minutes or until the aubergines are half-cooked. Remove and drain well.

- Meanwhile, in a small bowl combine the walnuts, garlic, remaining salt and the chopped chilli or cayenne. Now use a pointed knife to make a slit lengthwise in one of the aubergines. Push about 1 teaspoon of the walnut mixture (depending on the size of the aubergine) into the slit. Gently press the aubergine to remove excess moisture and place in a sterilized jar. Repeat with the remaining aubergines. Partially cover the jar and turn it upside down for 8–12 hours over a small dish, or kitchen paper, to absorb the seeping liquid, if any. Then turn the jar the right way up and intersperse the whole chillies between the aubergines. Cover them completely with oil. Seal and keep in a dark kitchen cupboard. Use within 10–14 days.

Sauces

The following sauces are included in this book because they are peculiar to the Lebanese cuisine. They enhance the flavour of a dish without masking it.

❀ ❀ ❀

Tahini Sauce

AN ESSENTIAL SAUCE in Lebanese cuisine, *tahini* sauce accompanies dishes such as *shawarma*, *falafel* and baked fish. It is also thinned and used in cooking foods such as *arnabieh*, *tagen* and so on. It is easy to make, nutritious and flavourful. Turn a blind eye to the calories! A large handful of chopped parsley or boiled Swiss chard ribs can be added to this basic sauce. Coarsely diced olives are also a good addition.

½ **small garlic clove (optional)**
½ **teaspoon salt or to taste**
150 ml (¼ pint) *tahini*
6–7 tablespoons lemon, clementine or orange juice

- If using the garlic, pound it in a mixing bowl with the salt until smooth, then add the *tahini* and mix. Gradually add the lemon juice and 6–7 tablespoons water. Use a whisk to prevent any lumps forming. Keep whisking until the sauce has the consistency of double or single cream. Taste and adjust the lemon or salt.

Garlic Sauce
Salset al toum

Generally, this is served as an accompaniment to *chish taouk* or chicken kebab. It is made with garlic, lemon juice and olive oil, and its preparation, when slowly adding the oil, is not any different from making mayonnaise. The garlic is pounded until creamy, lemon juice is added and after that the oil. To cut down on the powerful taste of the garlic some people mix the sauce into a little mayonnaise. I prefer to add a little cooked or raw potato. Garlic sauce is very healthy, with a combination of nutrients that are said to keep viruses and illnesses at bay and helps to beautify the hair and skin.

> 90 g (3 oz) potato (optional)
> 170 g (6 oz) garlic cloves
> Good pinch of salt
> 70 ml (2½ fl oz) lemon juice
> 3–4 tablespoons extra virgin olive oil or as necessary
> ½ tablespoon fresh cream (optional)

- If using the potato place in a steaming basket and set into a pan over 2.5 cm (1 in) of boiling water. Cover and steam until tender (alternatively use raw in which case grate finely). Pound the potato with the garlic and salt until creamy. Add the lemon juice and gradually whisk in the oil; keep whisking until the sauce has a creamy consistency. Serve or keep in the refrigerator until needed. If this seems difficult use an electric blender, which is easier and may give a better result.

Glossary

Carob molasses (*dibs kharoub*): A thick syrup obtained from the pods
of leguminous (carob) trees that do not necessarily require watering.
Long ago carob molasses was used instead of sugar in certain sweets,
such as *maacaroun* (macaroons), and still is in some regions of
Lebanon. Mixed with *tahini*, it is a sweet delicacy to eat with bread.

Cassia (*kirfeh*): Comes from the laurel tree and was introduced into
Europe by the Phoenicians and inhabitants of the Arabian peninsula.
I use cassia bark or ground cassia in my recipes because of its strong
flavour. When unavailable, cinnamon can be used in its place.

Cream of sesame (*tahini*): A thick creamy liquid obtained from
sesame seeds. It has a delicious flavour and is widely used in dips,
savoury dishes, sauces and some sweets.

Kammouneh: A blend of spices used by the Shiite Muslims of south
Lebanon, and an important one for a meat dish known as *frakeh*,
which is made of goat's meat that is pounded on a marble slab until
very fine and then mixed with this very special spice. Also used in
vegetarian dishes such as *kibbet al-banadoura* and others. This spice
mixture is also known as *dakket al-kibbeh* and is made of dried and
fresh spices. The dried mixture is composed of marjoram, aniseeds,
basil, cumin seeds, *ward al-jouri* (rose petals), cayenne pepper and dried
mint. The fresh one comprises white and green onions, green chillies,
mint, basil and marjoram.

Kawarma: A delicacy made of lamb meat preserved in fat. The meat is
cut into small cubes (1 cm/$^1\!/_2$ in or less), seasoned with sea salt and a
touch of allspice and left for a day. Then it is fried in the lamb fat and

put in jars to be used instead of fresh meat, especially at a time when meat is scarce and expensive.

Kishk: A combination of *burghol* processed with milk and yoghurt; its preparation involves several stages. *Kishk* is a traditional staple food in mountain villages.

Mahlab: An aromatic spice obtained from the kernel of the black cherry. It is added to some sweets. To obtain the maximum flavour buy the kernels whole and grind them with a pestle and mortar.

Mastic (*miskee*): A resin obtained from a small evergreen tree, *Pistacia lentiscus*. It was originally used to enhance and add a distinctive characteristic taste to milk puddings, fig jam, ice cream, and meat and chicken marinades. I like to add it to rice dishes such as *markouk bil riz* (rice with *markouk* bread).

Mezzé: A traditional combination of appetizers, comprising several small dishes such as *tabbouleh* (cracked wheat salad), *hummous* (chick-pea dip), *fattouche* (bread salad), olives, *labneh* (concentrated yoghurt) etc.

Munee: Provisions consisting of different spices, dried vegetables, pickles, sacks of beans and legumes, oil, olives etc.

Pomegranate syrup (*dibs al-ruman*): Made from the juice extracted from the pomegranate. The juice is then boiled until it thickens and its colour changes from red to burgundy brown. Towards the end of cooking a tablespoon of lemon juice and a pinch of sea salt can be added to the syrup.

Sahlab: A starchy powder obtained from a variety of dried orchid tubers. It is used in the preparation of a hot drink, consumed traditionally in the early hours of the morning, and to make ice cream.

Sumac: Comes from the berries of a shrub that grows wild in Lebanon's mountains. The unripened berries are dried, then ground. *Sumac* provides a sour and lemony taste. In the past it was very useful as a substitute for lemons when they were out of season and expensive. *Sumac* is an essential part of *zaatar*.

Index

Acknowledgements

This book would not have been possible without the enthusiasm, encouragement and belief of Carey Smith. My sincere thanks to Sarah Lavelle for her patience and kindness throughout. My special thanks to my agent Deborah Rogers for her friendship and good advice at all times. I would like to express my gratitude and endless thanks to everyone at Ebury Publishing who worked on this book, especially to the editor Tessa Clark, to Tony Lyons for design and cover, and to Jonathan Baker for the typesetting.

I would like to extend my heartfelt thanks and offer my gratitude to everyone who has had an input in this book, I would like to mention in particular: Neila Obeid, Ilham Ahmad Ali, Raafat Bu-Chacra, Samira Sayegh and Farouk Mardam Bey. To Suzanne Walsh for typing some of my handwritten work.

To my husband Nabil for his patience and understanding during my work. Most importantly I would like to express my love to my daughter Nour who supported me all the way.